HUMANITIES

THEATRE OUTSIDE LONDON

THEATRE

Outside London , 1971.

JOHN ELSOM,

MACMILLAN

© John Elsom 1971

SBN boards: 333 11066 8

First published 1971 by
MACMILLAN LONDON LTD
London and Basingstoke
Associated companies in New York Toronto
Dublin Melbourne Johannesburg & Madras

Printed in Great Britain by
WESTERN PRINTING SERVICES LTD
Bristol

Contents

Contents

List of Illustrations

Acknowledgements

I WOULD like to express my thanks to E. A. Markham and Sally Mays for their help with the research and preparation of this book, to the actors and managers of repertory theatres who have given me so much of their time, to Victor Corti and John Olley for allowing me to use their plan for a community theatre, and to *London Magazine* and *Gambit*, who have allowed me to reprint extracts from previous articles.

JOHN ELSOM

Change and Prophecies

THOSE two masks, Comedy and Tragedy, the ancient shorthand for the theatre, still hang even today when tragedy is out of fashion – grinning and scowling in the new rep buildings, in an Equity organized, Arts Council subsidized profession. And, although the plays and productions we watch no longer suffer from so marked a division between gaiety and gloom, the image persists when we talk about the theatre, in our hopes and forebodings. Some directors echo the words of *Stage* that 'we are obviously on the brink of an exciting theatrical renaissance', while others argue that the theatre is on another brink altogether, hanging on to a thorn bush at the top of a crumbling cliff – one slight movement and the art and the profession together will be avalanched down.

Neither face is exactly dishonest. The fortunes of one section of the theatre have declined, while those of another (particularly the subsidized reps) have risen. The distortion comes with the melo-drama, the very theatrical tendency to over-project. This, too, would be no more than an error of taste, were it not that these cheerful or woebegone stances have the habit of growing inwards, from the mask to the face to the bone – so that while some prophesy revolu-tion and act accordingly, demanding an end to cupids and pro-scenium arches, nubile maids and tea ceremonies, others stand stolidly still, enquiring with John Counsell of the Theatre Royal, Windsor, where the new dramatists are coming from, the new 'Rattigans, Priestleys and Frys'. Some insist that the theatre is really a licensed play-area, where anti-social aggressions can be released and tolerated: others that it is a place for entertainment, mere entertainment, and to pretend otherwise is pretentious and economically disastrous. There seems to be a sort of incest taboo preventing these two faces, which share after all a common spine, from turning towards each other in a friendly fashion. What should be a dialogue sounds suspiciously like polemic, delivered unheard in opposite directions.

The problem is partly, I'm afraid, one of language and interpretation. Most rep directors would say, loudly and confidently, that 'the theatre should serve the community', but what is meant by *theatre, service* and *community*? Is the community that section of the public which acquired the habit, during the twenties and thirties, of going to the theatre – or should it refer to the public in general, to the students and factory workers, to both sides of the generation and class gap? And where does the value of the theatre lie – in the process or the performance? In the acting-out of an event in game form, or in the presentation of this game? Is the theatre the play, the profession, the building or the relationship between the actors and the audience? Is service a cant word useful to counter the still persistent puritanism towards the theatre – or is there some other meaning marginally more precise, creeping through the altruism? Does the theatre serve the public by amusing them when the day's work is over – or by presenting masterpieces of literature in elegant productions – or by confronting social problems directly, through local documentaries, theatre-in-education programmes and so forth? As these words are used, so one can select statistics, another form of language, to support the conclusions one wishes to draw – that the theatre is at a watershed, or a springboard, in decline or buoyant, or something like that.

If, for example, the word theatre is interpreted very broadly to mean the drama which can be – and is – watched by the public in general in any medium, then undoubtedly theatre is more important and popular today than it has ever been: more plays are watched by more people, more actors are better known, and, I suppose, drama has more influence. If, on the other hand, the word is limited to mean 'live theatre', the stage, but includes all the various facets of show business, from variety to straight plays, then the theatre has been on an erratic decline since the turn of the century. Seventy years ago, there were over five hundred music-halls, over fifty 'straight' theatres and many touring companies, some owning chains of part-time theatres, which were often little more than barns. By 1939, this number had slumped to between 200 and 300 theatres – of which not all were in full-time use – and, by 1970, to about 140. These figures are not easy to establish, as the Arts Council itself (whose facilities for checking are so much better than my own) has admitted. Not all the theatres were in use at one time: some were small local ventures, barely professional, whose work has sunk unrecorded. Much of the old music-hall trade has now gone to the clubs and pubs. Judged by the number of buildings devoted to the professional live theatre, there has been a general decline. Leicester used to have three theatres: now it has one. Between 1938 and 1958 no new theatres at all were built – although there were some conversions. It's not hard to find reasons for this decline – the impact of cinema and television, better travel and so on – but, interestingly enough, the number of buildings where 'straight plays' are performed has not noticeably declined. The numbers have fluctuated, but there has been no steady drift downwards: and indeed, since 1958, twenty new theatres have been built – of which fifteen are provincial reps – and many more are planned.

If, therefore, we define the word theatre fairly narrowly, to mean the live performance of straight plays or musicals, and we try to gauge the growth or otherwise of the theatre by the number of buildings devoted to that purpose, there are few signs of an over-all decline this century, and over the past twelve years in particular there has been a sort of resurgence, a revival of theatre. This is rather surprising, remembering the impact of television during the fifties. The theatre has held its own – not solidly like a strong-room door, but variably, like a revolving door in a hotel, throwing some managements out quickly, sucking others in. The most dramatic decline of all has been in the fate of touring commercial companies and of those theatres which depended on them for the product. These, according to the Arts Council Theatre Enquiry Report, 'have shrunk in numbers within the last 40 years, from 130 to about 30'. The Report proposes that the number of touring theatres should contract still further to provide a grid of between twelve and eighteen theatres, 'fed' by 'quality products' from the two national companies, several leading reps, opera and ballet companies, and some commercial companies. Partly to offset this decline in the number of provincial touring theatres – and the commercial companies which fed them – there has been a remarkable increase in the number of provincial reps, from about twelve in 1939 to about sixty in 1970. What has happened during the past few years has not been a growth or a decline in the theatre as such, but the rapid reorganization of the theatre as an industry, accelerated by the impact of television, assisted by the growth of the Arts Council and of local council support, and, above all, by a climate of opinion which has turned slowly and consistently towards the local product, to offset perhaps the growing pervasiveness of a national, televised and centralized culture.

This reorganization of the provincial theatre has happened – is continuing to happen – and the consequences cannot be brushed aside. It is now almost as difficult for a London management to turn its back on the provinces as it was once for a provincial management to ignore London. To take one small autobiographical example: in 1960, I joined the script department of Paramount Pictures, my job being to cover the theatre and to recommend to my script editor plays which might become suitable film-scripts. Sometimes, at the beginning, my editor would send me out of London, to Brighton or Windsor perhaps, to catch a production on a pre-London run. For the first five years, I went no further afield than Oxford or Brighton, and then it was only to forestall the West End opening, to steal a march on rivals. This is not to suggest that admirable work was not being achieved in Liverpool, Nottingham, Sheffield and elsewhere, but that it was safe for Paramount to assume that any good play or production would come to London and that to cover these places wasn't worth the added expense of travel. By the time I left Paramount, however, it was no longer safe to make these assumptions: in the last three years, I travelled all over the country – from Chichester to Bristol to Nottingham to Edinburgh. We could no longer accept as a fact of theatrical life that an admirable new play *would* come to London and that we would hear about it through the grapevine soon enough to buy. Many rep productions did come to London – but many more would be waiting in the pipeline for a suitable West End theatre. During these eight Paramount years, as well, there was a slow but noticeable change in the sort of theatres I was asked to visit. At the beginning, I visited the touring theatres, where various West End managements would try out new productions: at the end, if and when I reviewed outside London, I would probably be visiting the reps. In other words, during this period, the reps started to take over from the commercial managements as the major supplier of new drama.

This change has already had a considerable impact on the London theatre. Over the past year, 1969–70, the Nottingham Playhouse became the first rep company to offer two productions at the Old Vic (the temporary home of the National Theatre) – *The Alchemist* and *King Lear*: and the new ILEA Cockpit Theatre was opened by Peter Cheeseman's company from Stoke-on-Trent – in a documentary production, *The Burning Mountain*, which they had written and compiled themselves. *Hadrian VII*, which was first performed at the Birmingham Rep, is the longest running 'serious' play in London in the year of writing, still at the Haymarket: and one of the most successful boulevard comedies, *The Man Most Likely to . . .*, came originally from the Theatre Royal, Windsor. Among the revivals, Ian McKellen has scored a major personal triumph in two Prospect productions, *Edward II* and *Richard II* at the Piccadilly; another Nottingham production, Shaw's *Widowers' Houses*, was at the Royal Court; and Alastair Sim is starring in that magnificent Chichester production of Pinero's *The Magistrate* at the Cambridge. An interesting minor revival, Rodney Ackland's *The Old Ladies*, came from the Yvonne Arnaud Theatre, Guildford. Three productions from the Bristol Old Vic are currently running in London: *Conduct Unbecoming* at the Queen's; *It's a Two Foot Six Inches above the Ground World* at Wyndhams; and *Mandrake*, a musical, at the Criterion. Another musical, *'Erb*, at the Strand, came from the '69 Company in Manchester. And so on. . . . Not so long ago, *The Ruling Class* came from Nottingham, *The Narrow Road to the Deep North* received its first performance at Coventry, *Close the Coalhouse Door* from Newcastle, *The Blacks* from the Oxford Playhouse – without these plays and productions from the provincial reps, the theatre in the West End would have presented a very lean and impoverished face indeed over the past few years.

But to judge the success of the repertory movement solely by the number of transfers to the West End is to add to the folly of London superiority. A number of exciting new plays have not yet transferred and may not do so: W. J. Wetherby's *Breaking the Silence*, first produced at the Liverpool Playhouse, is an example. Nor have all the productions survived unscathed, though several have been greatly improved. A commercial management may buy up a well-balanced rep production, introduce a couple of stars and sometimes spoil the effect. Sometimes the ethos of a town adds to the success of a production, sometimes a permanent company playing on its home ground, sometimes the shape of the theatre for which the play was originally produced. London is notably short of new theatres, although, as I have said, twenty new theatres have been built in the provinces since 1958. The experiments in theatre design – thrust and arena stages, adaptable and environmental theatres – have taken place outside London. Nor has London yet felt the impact on a community which a successful rep can have – as an arts centre, through theatre-in-education programmes and studio productions. I found it almost disconcerting to enter a Nottingham coffee bar and overhear the students at the next table talking about Arrabal as if he were John Lennon. The head of the theatre-in-education programme at the Dundee Rep, Michael Barry, writing in a report for the Gulbenkian Foundation, mentions that theatre-in-education may be a way of lowering the crime rate in the town. Such ideas, in London, seem laughably naïve and optimistic: but in some provincial towns they are not only taken seriously – they also seem to have some facts to support them. I do not wish to convey the impression that Drury Lane will soon be part of the Number 2 Touring Circuit from Nottingham, but rather that the sun of the West End theatre no longer stands isolated and unrivalled by other stars in the sky. Or perhaps (to change the metaphor) London may still be the heart of British theatre, but this heart is fed with blood from several large and important veins from the repertory movement, which in turn, through their close contacts with different communities, are nurtured by the universities, amateur dramatic societies and student experimental theatres. These are the capillaries, and their importance as well should not be overlooked. *Zoo Zoo Widdershins Zoo* went to Nottingham from a student production: *Disabled* by Peter Ransley from an adult education group in London to the Stables Theatre, Manchester, and from there to television: *Rosencrantz and Guildenstern Are Dead* from an Oxford University production to the National Theatre. The modern repertory movement has become a vital link between local talent and national, has become involved in the life of the community in a way which was unthinkable fifty years ago, and in doing so has altered our conception as to what theatre is or can be. The comparative health of British theatre – which sometimes seems more enviable from across the Atlantic than from here, where we have got used to it – is very largely due to the growth of the repertory theatre movement particularly since the war, a growth which is more remarkable because of the decline in the other sections of the theatre.

This seesaw in the fortunes of different sections of the theatre is startling enough, and would be more so if there were not some good mechanical reasons governing the change. To say baldly that the number of touring theatres has declined from 130 to about 30 suggests that 100 theatres have closed. Not so. Some have certainly closed, but others have simply changed status. When, for example, the old Cheltenham Opera House closed in 1959, it opened again a few months later, this time as a repertory theatre, the Everyman, run by a non-profit-distributing limited company. Under this new status, the theatre could claim rate reductions, income-tax reductions, did not (later) have to pay Selective Employment Tax, and, of course, could apply for local and Arts Council grants. At first, the concessions were more important than the subsidies: and from the early fifties onwards the commercial theatre in the provinces found itself fighting a losing battle for trade against unfair odds. Commercial managements, by definition, are profit-distributing: they aim to make money. The non-profit-distributing companies were considered to offer a social service and therefore they received certain concessions. Even when the fortunes of a theatre were not desperate and no subsidies were expected – as at the De La Warr Pavilion, Bexhill, where the Penguin Players, although firmly established in the town, became a non-profit-distributing company in 1956 – the temptation to change status, to blow away a few clouds from a stormy and insecure living, was very strong. Only a few sturdily independent managements of commercial reps, such as John Counsell at Windsor or Charles Vance at Eastbourne, resisted – more, I would imagine, from conviction than economic logic. As the Arts Council funds increased, the subsidies to the non-profit-distributing theatres became more important, and the balance tilted still further against the commercial theatre in the provinces – either the reps, the touring companies or the productions on pre-London tours. These grants were given almost without *qualitative* restrictions. The Arts Council would try to assess the needs and potentialities of the theatres before awarding grants, but they wouldn't be cut on the basis of a bad season or because of uneven standards. In 1968, a major rep, the Belgrade Theatre, Coventry, with an annual Arts Council subsidy of £50,000, presented Frankie Howerd and Barbara Windsor in a spoof Western, *The Wind in the Sassafras Trees*, and what chance had the commercial theatre to survive against such competition? Very little. Many companies went out of business: others were forced to play in smaller towns without reps, in inadequate theatres. The commercial companies which did survive with some ease were the larger ones, who could afford, say, to present spectacular musicals on tour, *The Black and White Minstrel Show*, productions which were beyond the reach of reps to stage. But the risks with these spectacular productions were equally great, and the competition was keenest – and most ill-balanced – on a workaday level, in the small-cast, low-budget productions. The Arts Council has complained that West End managements do not release the rights of successful plays promptly, when the West End run is over, so that reps can stage them: but these managements are protecting their own interests. Low-budget 'winners' were hard enough to find, in any case: to release the rights to reps quickly would have made life in the provinces even more difficult for commercial managements. Indeed, to describe the reps as subsidized is slightly misleading: they receive subsidies, of course, but these subsidies do not condition their programmes, and most of their income still comes from the box office: seventy-five per cent, according to the Theatre Enquiry Report, but this average includes some heavily subsidized theatres, such as the Royal Shakespeare Company at Stratford and the Manchester '69 Company. Very few reps can afford to ignore the box office in the interests of Art. And so there has been direct competition between the assisted reps and the various commercial managements, and in this struggle the assisted reps have nearly all the advantages. Many commercial managements, faced by the choice of changing status or going out of business, preferred to throw themselves into the arms of the local authorities – if these were cautiously extended – to register as non-profit-distributing limited companies and hope for the best.

This situation could have arisen almost by accident. It could be argued that in a mixed economy the balance between private and public investment is never rigidly maintained but that there is always a drift from one direction to another. The Arts Council, I am sure, had no intention of depressing the commercial theatre, when, in the mid-fifties, it began to jack up the reps on small grants. On the contrary, it wanted to support the theatre in itself, and it saw no way of helping the commercial theatre on the money available and without contradicting the terms of its Charter. It even respected profit as a spur to Art. However, the commercial theatre in the provinces was depressed, and the assisted reps began to flourish: and in attempting to explain the behaviour of a society, as of an individual, it is never satisfactory to leave the word *accident* dangling, without further explanation. Why was the Arts Council formed?

Why was the theatre considered worthy of support? And why were the provincial reps so high on the list of priorities?

One answer to all these questions is that since the middle of the nineteenth century – and indeed before – the *idea* of non-commercial art, of art related more to social needs and concerns than to profit, has been expressed with increasing eloquence and urgency. In 1850 the first legislation was passed to establish public libraries, and gradually these libraries started to oust the private circulating libraries which still survive, of course, but in a very impoverished state. In 1879, Matthew Arnold wrote an article, 'The French Play in London', for the magazine, *The Nineteenth Century*: and in spite of the curiously uneven tone, the rhetoric which stumbles, the class distinctions which we would now prefer to express more euphemistically, his theme has a surprisingly modern ring, could be paired with speeches from Parliament today, with editorials from *Stage*, with prefaces from Arts Council reports:

We are at the end of a period, and have to deal with the facts and symptoms of a new period on which we are entering; and prominent among these fresh facts and symptoms is the irresistibility of the theatre. . . . The change is not due only to an increased liking in the upper class and in the working class for the theatre. Their liking for it has certainly increased, but this is not enough to account for the change. The attraction of the theatre begins to be felt again, after a long interval of insensibility, by the middle class also. . . . The human spirit has a vital need, as we say, for conduct and religion; but it has the need also for expansion, for intellect and knowledge, for beauty, for social life and manners. The revelation of these additional needs brings the middle class to the theatre. . . . The revelation was indispensable, the needs are real, the theatre is one of the mightiest means of satisfying them, and the theatre is therefore irresistible. That conclusion at any rate we may take for certain. But I see our community turning to the theatre with eagerness, and finding the English theatre without organization, or purpose, or dignity, and no modern English drama at all except a fantastical one.

And he concludes: 'The theatre is irresistible: organize the theatre.' Few nowadays would dismiss modern English drama so categorically, and many would say that the 'organization' has either taken place, or begun to take place. But the bones of the argument have remained the same – that there is a social need for the theatre, that the theatre is too important to be left drifting, prey to any hazard, and that the standards of the theatre must be raised, both in its product, in its organization and conditions, and in its availability and relevance to the public.

The modern repertory movement grew up in response to such calls, and indeed if we look at the complaints levelled against the organization of the theatre in the 1890s they too have a contemporary ring. Long runs and the star system were deplored: and unsteadiness of employment for the artists, no continuity of the company unit, insufficient tuition for the actor, the prohibitive cost of experimental and untried drama, and the debilitating control of London over the provinces. All these complaints still exist, although there is less cause for them. Spearbearers and Roman Citizens aren't picked up from the streets on the morning of the performance, as Booth hired James O'Neill, Eugene's father: nor can an actor buy up the rights of a play, and tour the country for years with it, as James O'Neill toured the States with *The Count of Monte Cristo*. Plays and productions aren't usually massacred to allow more light to shine on the star. One by one, these problems were almost met, but not quite: and the process was a gradual one. In 1864, for example, Marie Wilton-Bancroft joined forces with H. J. Byron to manage a little theatre in Tottenham Court Road, the Prince of Wales: and they tried to form a company of uniform excellence, where no member was allowed to hog the limelight. Marie Wilton (Mrs Bancroft) was a star actress: Dickens once wrote that 'I call her the cleverest girl I have ever seen on the stage in my time, and the most singularly original'. But she often played 'second' to Mrs Kendal, Ellen Terry or Mme Modjeska. In 1872, the critic of the *Athenaeum* wrote that 'no attempt is made by any one [member of the company] to eclipse his fellows, or to monopolize either the space on the boards, or the attention of the audience'.

Nor did this company follow the practice – popular then as now – of milking a winner to death. They would withdraw a play at the height of its popularity, so that its freshness could be maintained for a revival. This was a step towards the repertory system, which was defined by William Archer as the policy of having several productions ready at the same time, so that they could change from night to night. Nowadays, the word has become somewhat corrupted to mean the system whereby a company schedules a play for a short run, from a week to a month or longer, and then replaces it with another production. For convenience, I will distinguish in this book between *repertoire* and repertory: the first used to describe the system of having several productions ready at the same time, the second to describe the policy of short runs and those permanent or semi-permanent companies which aim to change their productions at regular intervals. One of the first repertory companies as such was F. R. Benson's, which toured the provinces for years and in 1886 established the Shakespeare Memorial Theatre at Stratford-upon-Avon. F. R. Benson was the grandfather of the modern repertory movement – the father was Sir Barry Jackson – and the slogans of his company might almost be borrowed by some contemporary repertory theatres. They were, according to Sir Sidney Lee, 'Shakespeare and the National Drama', 'Short runs', 'No stars', 'All round competence' and 'Unostentatious setting'.

The omission from this list of good resolutions was, of course, contemporary drama. And indeed F. R. Benson was much more concerned with exploring and presenting our National Heritage of Drama than with dabbling in anything new or experimental. His apprehensions were shared – then as now – by many other managements who might agree in abstract that new writers had to be found, that new seed should be sown, but at the same time found it more rewarding to mow an ancient lawn. In 1890 at the Haymarket, Beerbohm Tree set Monday nights aside for plays, mainly new, 'calculated to delight and charm the few'; and, with this modest advertisement, few indeed came.

And yet new plays had to be found. If Shaw had never lived, some other dramatist would have emerged, no doubt, to crystallize in one remarkable example that complicated Edwardian mixture of social concern and theatrical display. All the arguments and criticisms, all the vigorous discussion about theatre, ultimately homed on one ledge – that, if the theatre was to fulfil the role in society which Arnold had predicted and Archer proclaimed, new plays had to be written and produced. Writers had new models to follow – no longer Scribe but Ibsen, not Feydeau but Strindberg, Tolstoy and Maeterlinck. In 1891, John T. Grein established his Independent Theatre, which introduced to London the work of Maeterlinck and Tolstoy – and Shaw: in 1894, Miss Horniman backed a production of Shaw's *Arms and the Man*. Of the several managements who were prepared to tiptoe into daring, none was more successful or influential than the Barker–Vedrenne management of the Royal Court during the seasons 1904–7. In 1904, Granville Barker was asked to produce some Shakespeare plays at the Royal Court Theatre. He did so, and used the impetus from their success to plunge into the production of new plays – programmes in which the work of Shaw predominated. Of 908 performances given during these seasons, 701 were of Shaw plays: but Barker also produced works of his own – including the admirable *The Voysey Inheritance*, of Galsworthy, St John Hankin, Masefield, Maeterlinck and Ibsen. It was an extraordinary achievement, which fed the repertory theatres for years with intelligent plays – but, in a sense, Barker was rather lucky, in that he had found a stimulating new dramatist in Shaw, whose work did not veer too far from the technical 'norm'. Barker believed, with Irving, that the theatre should pay for itself – and to prove that profit was possible with new plays as well, if they were good enough, he could point to the example of Shaw. But this was perhaps a poor case on which to base an argument, for Shaw's plays, outwardly daring, were inwardly conventional. If one compares what passed for 'new' or 'experimental' drama in this country, with the experiments on the continent – with Expressionism, with Jarry and Pataphysics, with Wedekind, Toller and, later, Brecht – or, indeed, with Chekhov and Stanislavski – one receives the impression that the 1904–7 seasons at the Royal Court were more notable for good sense than daring, for gentle good-humoured charm than revolutionary insight. The attempt to combine profitability with serious new plays, an *avant-garde*, was the sort of English compromise which seemed to work when there were Shaws around, but in the long run may have retarded the development of a genuinely experimental theatre, and certainly delayed the realization that new drama has to be launched with the dedication and investment which would attend a new industrial product. This lesson should have been learnt more quickly. In 1910, Barker and Charles Frohman joined forces to start a new repertory theatre, the Duke of York's in London: and they hoped to repeat the success of the Royal Court. Charles Frohman stated their intentions quite clearly:

A repertory theatre should be the first home of the ambitious young dramatist. I advise him to learn the conventions of the stage, but chiefly that he may be able to disregard them. I have no preference for any particular kind of play. I want what is good of any kind. One sometimes hears it said, 'A good thing, but not a play'. This is one of the kinds I want.

The Duke of York's lost money and closed the following season.

From the beginning, the repertory movement needed money. Quite apart from the discovery and development of new forms of drama, the proposed reorganization of the theatre – short runs, all-round competence, availability to the public (which precluded high seat-prices) and so on – required capital to start with, and economic security to maintain. But, whereas books and libraries had the sort of reputation in the nineteenth century which encouraged philanthropy, the theatre did not. For one thing, the theatre was less blatantly uneconomic than literature – and the benefits to society still had to be proved. In an age without an Arts Council, private patrons had to be found with the wealth and foresight to start repertory theatres. It was a rich man's hobby. Shaw once said to Barry Jackson that he could run a steam yacht with the money he spent on the Birmingham Rep, and Barry Jackson replied, 'Ah, but a theatre is more fun.' But it was a rare man who wanted to afford that fun, which involved so much hard work, dedication and sometimes ridicule.

There were two 'angels' in particular during the early days of the provincial repertory movement: Miss A. E. F. Horniman and Sir Barry Jackson. Miss Horniman was wealthy, convinced of the social value of the theatre, but was neither a dramatist, director nor actress: her enthusiasm was singularly disinterested. 'At heart,' Basil Dean, the founder of the Liverpool Playhouse and one of her protégés, has recalled, 'she was not a lover of the theatre. She was a "do-gooder" who believed the theatre should educate and uplift the community in which it dwelt: a concept which she called "civilized theatre".' In 1903, she supported Yeats's plan for an Irish Repertory Theatre, converted the Mechanics' Institute Hall into the Abbey Theatre and gave it to the company of the Irish National Theatre, rent-free for six years. In 1907, she bought the Gaiety Theatre, Manchester, converted it and subsidized the company which opened there in 1908. The aims were that the Gaiety should be

a repertory theatre with a regular change of programme, not wedded to any one school of dramatists but thoroughly catholic, embracing the finest writing of the best authors of all ages and with an especially widely-open door to present-day British writers, who will not now need to sigh in vain for a hearing, provided that they have something to say worth listening to, and say it in an interesting and original manner.

These were admirable aims, which won imitators. In 1911, Basil Dean left Miss Horniman's company to start the Liverpool Playhouse, and in 1913 Barry Jackson, well aware of her example, opened his new repertory theatre in Birmingham. A new school of dramatists arose, the Manchester School, which included Brighouse, Houghton and McEvoy: she staged more than two hundred plays, over a hundred of which were new. She championed Shaw. In spite of these achievements, however, the Gaiety Theatre failed to make the local impact which she had hoped. Basil Dean has written that 'the general public regarded the Gaiety productions as lying outside the normal run of playgoing, a foreign body in the corpus of theatrical entertainment'. The Gaiety Theatre finally closed in 1921, and it is sad that a company which had contributed so much to the British theatre should have lacked that support in Manchester which would have enabled it to continue even without Miss Horniman's assistance.

But, in a sense, the closure of the Gaiety Theatre represented a wider problem: people were convinced, even those who worked at the Gaiety, that cultural leadership should come from elsewhere, from London, that the provinces were 'dead' areas, and that only the West End could bestow the accolade of success. A company which tried to generate its own light, and did not use the reflected glory of London, was fighting a hard battle for recognition. The Birmingham Rep only received recognition in Birmingham after Barry Jackson had taken over two theatres in London and could claim several West End hits. His own company shared all the London loftiness towards a Midlands industrial town. Felix Aylmer once called the Rep 'an oasis in a provincial desert', and you can't call a town the size of Birmingham a desert without offending someone. It's all very well being the yeast if someone else is prepared to be the dough. In spite of the many achievements of the Gaiety Theatre and the Birmingham Rep – and all the lofty aims, which may indeed have been pitched too high to compensate for this feeling of inferiority – the provincial repertory movement retained an aura of second-rateness. Within its social context, it may have been brave and valuable, but neither actors nor audiences were attracted to that context. For young actors, a spell in 'weekly' rep was 'good training', a preparation for better things: the weak alternative to 'resting' for the more experienced actor. In Northampton, for example, where the repertory company replaced a touring stock company in 1927, the change brought a definite improvement. The touring company tackled melodramas (*The Face at the Window*) and sentimental romances (*When the Angelus Is Ringing, Not Fit to Marry*), changing the programmes every other night and offering twice-nightly performances. The programmes at the repertory theatre for the first season included *A Midsummer Night's Dream, The School for Scandal, The Passing of the Third Floor Back, The Dover Road* and *His House in Order* – a marked change in tone and seriousness. But actors at that time preferred to tour, at least on the major circuits, and with managements who might bring the productions to London: and provincial managements still advertised – as many of them do now – new plays as West End successes and their casts as West End actors, even if their only experiences of the London theatre were as call-boys in a music-hall. For many actors, to settle down in a provincial town was a sign of failure, and yet what the provincial repertory movement needed was precisely this stability, this slow and sensible growth of good companies presenting reliable productions.

This is partly why the influence and example of the Birmingham Rep is so unavoidably important. The Birmingham Rep grew up from a small amateur company, the Pilgrim Players, which Barry Jackson ran before the First World War. He built an austere theatre, with a steeply raked auditorium and an undistracted view of the stage: he subsidized the rep for twenty years, losing about £100,000 in the process, and from its unpretentious beginnings as a rich man's folly its influence spread throughout the theatre in Britain, and indeed beyond. When Birmingham finally offered some financial help, the reputation of the Rep was unassailably firm. For forty years, the Birmingham Rep was the best training-ground for actors in the country, and a cast of the stars who graduated would bankrupt Hollywood, if this is still possible: Felix Aylmer, Stephen Murray, Ralph Richardson, Laurence Olivier, Stewart Grainger, Margaret Leighton, Greer Garson, Paul Scofield and Albert Finney. His Directors included H. K. Ayliff, Nigel Playfair and Peter Brook.

Emile Littler at one time helped him to manage the theatre. Barry Jackson's concern for the Birmingham Rep lasted until his death in 1961; he saw, in other words, the start of the post-war repertory revival. In 1932, he ran five repertory companies, all stemming from Birmingham – in the West End, Manchester, Malvern, Canada and on tour. With Miss Horniman, he destroyed the myth that provincial reps only put on cheap, local versions of West End hits. He imitated nobody when he first staged Shakespeare in modern dress. No other management would tackle *Back to Methuselah* or, a more subtle gamble, *The Farmer's Wife*. He started the Malvern Festival Theatre, as a tribute to Shaw, and revived Stratford after the war. The Birmingham Rep was the first provincial 'power-house' for the theatre, and it was, I'm afraid, the chauvinism of London, the provincialism of the metropolis, which prevented an earlier recognition of Barry Jackson's achievements. This had two results: firstly, his efforts at an early stage did not receive the publicity or serious criticism due to them, and, secondly, he was encouraged to diversify his resources perhaps unwisely to gain greater recognition.

The modern repertory movement owes no greater debt to anyone – not even to the pioneers of the Arts Council – than to Barry Jackson: not for his money or artistry, but for his persistence. A new theatre for the Birmingham Rep is now being built, a Palace of Culture in concrete and glass, seating nine hundred, with a modern and efficient stage, and excellent general 'facilities'. The old redbrick building with its Georgian façade, which Sir Barry Jackson built in 1913, now looks dowdy and neglected, primly withdrawn down Station Street, while the roads, shops and stalls with their smoky colours and eager noise thunder and whirl in the Bull Ring development near by. It is an ugly theatre. The foyer is dark and boxlike. The only bar is to the left of the stage, in a little basement annexe, hung with blow-ups of former productions. There's no apron stage, very little wing space, and the depth of the auditorium precludes close audience–actor contact. To move the Company from that dignified inadequacy to its gleaming new home is symbolic of a wider change – the end of one phase in the repertory movement and the start of another, where state patronage (and municipal) has started to replace private, where the provincial theatre need not feel always resentful of the greater glories of London and where even a certain optimism ought not to be considered unreasonable.

This change has arisen through no single factor: not the decline in commercial touring, nor the presence of the Arts Council, nor even the influence and effort of leaders like Miss Horniman and Sir Barry Jackson, Basil Dean and Herbert Prentice at Sheffield. All these elements, and many others, have contributed to a climate of opinion in favour of repertory theatres. It has been deeply felt for a long time by many people that the theatre – and all art – should not remain as the preserve of the wealthy and privileged, the sophisticated and lucky, but should relate to 'ordinary' people – whoever they may be – and their needs. Lord Goodman expressed this point clearly in his preface to the 1969 Arts Council Report:

> Within our society, there is now a widespread feeling that the provision of drama and music and painting and all culture in its broadest sense is no longer to be regarded as a privilege for the few but is the democratic right of the entire community. I think that any government – and happily there is no sign of any such government – that attempted to reverse this trend would find very rapidly how strong and deep it ran.

The prophecies of Matthew Arnold and the satisfaction of a chairman of the Arts Council shake hands.

But couldn't it be argued that this 'democratic right' can be met admirably – and more cheaply – through the mass media? Isn't the live theatre an anachronism? Do we really need these monuments of civic pride, which in a bad season, under a poor director, could so easily become useless and irrelevant? Isn't the theatre always less 'democratic' – if we want to use this doubtful word – than television? The Nottingham Playhouse may have the astonishing attendance-figures for each season of 85 per cent capacity, but this only means that about 4000 people visit the theatre every week. How many of the 300,000 Nottingham inhabitants watch television? There are two stock answers to these questions, but both of them have to be examined rather carefully because they are faiths and opinions. They are indeed the concealed themes to this book. One is that the value of the theatre is diminished if we receive the impact muffled, at second hand, and have no direct contact with those who manufacture the product. The sight of a pretty girl is better than a photograph of one: the relationship between actors and audience is a vital part of any performance, and it varies from place to place, from night to night. This argument in favour of local repertory theatres is also a concealed attack on mass media which have the effect, some would say, of dehumanizing drama, and indeed all culture. The second answer extends this opinion a little further. Culture isn't something which can be piped into a town like gas: it is a civilizing process in which we all take part. It is as important, say, for a child to act in a school production of *Macbeth* as to watch the Royal Shakespeare Company. The local repertory company acts as a focal point for theatrical activities of the community. It is one way in which a town can take part in all the social discussion, the therapy, the building of intense and exciting happenings which drama provides: it is a step towards communal self-expression and local independence: it is a means of asserting a natural pride.

One of the most characteristic features of the modern repertory movement is this search for a local relevance and an identity: it infuses the theatre-in-education programmes, the arts centre projects, the studio theatres and theatre clubs. 'The Theatre', one director told me, 'is a vital bridge between local interests and national ones. We must be a forum, a church, a platform and a football pitch.' But aren't all these aims rather different, and is all this commendable social concern really very useful? Does it work? Isn't it as naïve in its way as those early founders of the repertory movement who tried to bring 'culture' to the masses, to stage Shakespeare and Euripides in church halls and pubs? Is it ever possible for the theatre to fulfil the philanthropic ambitions of those who are reluctant to accept that drama is a game, an enjoyable one, but which may have no direct usefulness beyond passing the time satisfactorily, in an organized way?

2

To Which Roots Were You Referring?

ROGER CLISSOLD, formerly artistic director at the Derby Playhouse, started his career with the Salisbury Playhouse. 'What surprises me', he said, 'is not the difference between the audiences from these two towns, but the similarity.' They tend to be 'tidily dressed, tidily spoken', prepared to be shocked sometimes, but not bored. 'We could risk Pinter's *The Homecoming*, but not his double bill, *Landscape* and *Silence*.' In both places, class and age groups seem to respond when certain plays are angled towards them: *The Knack* for the young marrieds, *Boeing-Boeing* for the older ones, *Romeo and Juliet* for schools and parents, *The Prime of Miss Jean Brodie* for the nostalgic. Both reps therefore present mixed programmes, feeding each section of the community in turn, and only, like Jewish mothers, with wholesome food, a little drained of blood. The plays must be 'good of their kind' – that is, not low, ill-written and vulgar, and not too *avant-garde* either. A new version of *Lysistrata*, conceived as a flower-power hippy love-in, was staged in 1969. 'It was worth trying,' explained John Williams, the manager of the Derby Playhouse, a little cautiously. 'We didn't really have enough time,' said Roger Clissold.

But, if regional contrasts count at all in the theatre, the audiences from Derby and Salisbury *ought* to be different. The pubs and churches look different, even discounting (as good pollsters should) the wilder extremes, such as the cathedral. The shops look different, even the chain stores: different jobs are advertised in the Labour Exchange windows. Derby is in the industrial Midlands, with a population of over 128,000: Rolls-Royce is a local firm. Salisbury is in the heart of agricultural Wiltshire, with a population of 36,000: Southern Command is stationed near by. There is also an unfair contrast between them of theatrical wealth. The Playhouse at Salisbury has no immediate rivals. There are summer shows and a seasonal rep at Bournemouth, thirty miles away, and the little Watermill Theatre at Newbury. A radius of fifty miles centred on Salisbury would touch Bristol, Chichester and Guildford: but a Salisbury man who wanted to travel that distance to the theatre would probably choose to go to London – eighty-five miles away, but with a decent train service.

Within an hour's drive from Derby, however, there are at least a dozen good theatres. Sixteen miles east, across the M1, is the Nottingham Playhouse. Along the M1, travelling south, are the reps at Leicester, Coventry and Northampton: and, travelling north, at Chesterfield and Sheffield. Westwards, across the M6, there are the theatres at Crewe and Stoke-on-Trent. Northwards, along the M6, are the reps at Chester, Liverpool and Manchester, and, south-wards, at Birmingham and Stratford. These theatres are not only roughly within a fifty-mile radius: they can also helpfully be reached along motorways – and they include some of the best companies in the country. The Royal Shakespeare Company at Stratford is, of course, a second national theatre – some would say the first – with an Arts Council grant of about £200,000 and attendance figures topping ninety per cent. The theatre-in-education programmes at the Belgrade, Coventry, and at the Midlands Arts Centre, though very different in style and scope, are the most advanced in the country. Stephen Joseph chose the Victoria Theatre, Stoke-on-Trent, as the first permanent 'in-the-round' theatre in Britain – and Peter Cheeseman has developed this technique of production beyond the range of his imitators, sponsoring the plays of Peter Terson as well and pioneering local documentaries. The Nottingham Play-house was the first rep company to be invited to play at the National Theatre. In the Midlands, the repertory movement was born – with the Gaiety Theatre, the Liverpool Playhouse, the Birmingham Rep and the Sheffield Playhouse. Here regional drama gained an identity and an independence from London. Here, after the Second World War, the reps flourished, then waned under the impact of television, and were revived again, when the Belgrade Theatre, Coventry, was built as part of Coventry's ambitious redevelopment programme, which set an example to so many others.

And so, the Derby man, if he is prepared to travel, is faced by an embarrassment of riches. Only someone actually living in London has a wider (though not exactly comparable) range of choice. And in the Midlands, as John Williams pointed out, people do travel around: it is the centre of the car industry as well. Reps rival one another to snatch audiences from what is almost a common catchment area: and the competition, while it may have driven the weaker reps at Wolverhampton and Salford to the ground, seems generally to have raised the level of public interest and enthusiasm. Ambitious new theatres have been built at Coventry, Nottingham, Leicester and Birmingham, and others are planned at Birmingham, Sheffield, Derby, Stoke and Manchester. And the controversies they arouse aren't solely about money. An editorial in the *Sheffield Star and Telegraph* discussed the 'distinguished theatrical opposition to the stage and auditorium design of Sheffield Playhouse's replacement theatre'; Reginald Salberg, the manager at Salisbury, commented rather sadly that it's always easier to persuade a council to back a scheme for a new theatre if another town near by is planning to build one as well.

And yet (according to Roger Clissold) the audiences are not dissimilar. At the very least, one would have expected a greater theatrical perception in Derby. I thought I detected this keener perception, but only in nuances. In Salisbury, the audience received the première of William Douglas Home's play, *The Queen's Highland Servant*, very enthusiastically – laughing heartily at the undeferential treatment of Queen Victoria by her late husband's favourite ghillie, John Brown. They seemed to accept Home's assurances that all the rumours of royal laxness were unfounded. I didn't think that Derby audiences would be so kind to this bland gossip. Not an eyebrow was raised, or none perceptibly, at the Derby Playhouse when, during *Cat on a Hot Tin Roof*, Brick tells Maggie, his wife, to take a lover and stop bothering him. The line was received coolly and sensibly, as part of the tragedy. This slightly different response may – or may not – have been significant: the public attracted to a Victorian *cause célèbre* would probably not be the same as that lured by the deeply Freudian south. Audiences wouldn't walk out of *Cat on a Hot Tin Roof* in Salisbury: *The Queen's Highland Servant* wouldn't be booed off the stage in Derby. Judged solely by play selection – not, as we will see, a reliable criterion – the regional differences between reps are not significant. Some dramatists have strong regional followings: Bridie in Scotland, Waterhouse and Hall in the North-West, Plater in the North-East. But these are exceptional cases. CORT (the Council of Repertory Theatre Managements) sends around the affiliated reps a monthly analysis of box-office returns, from all over the country, which gives a quick guide to the popularity or otherwise of certain plays. Few managers are mechanically influenced by these figures, but fewer still ignore them altogether. When *You Can't Take It with You* played to eighty per cent houses at the Pitlochry Festival Theatre, Rae Hammond, the general manager of the Cheltenham Everyman, took notice and suggested to Michael Ashton, the artistic director, that they should fit it in somewhere during the coming season, 1969. *Boeing-Boeing* plays everywhere: *A Patriot for Me* nowhere. *The Homecoming* isn't, according to Peter Carpenter, the manager of the Marlowe Theatre, quite *Canterbury*. It isn't quite Colwyn Bay, Ayr or Billingham either. Throughout the country, new plays – 'world premières' as they are usually called, to convey the impression that managements in London, Paris and New York are eager to see what the Civic, Darlington, will do next – are slow starters, and usually finishers as well. On the other hand, classics – defined by Gordon Stratford, the manager of the Meadow Players, Oxford, as 'the plays which an unadventurous, middle-aged clergyman might have on his bookshelf' – usually do well. Some of the worst rep productions I have seen have been Shakespearian – and they were invariably the best attended.

I have mentioned, however, that one of the arguments in favour of local repertory theatres is that they provide a link between the culture of a smaller community and the national network of drama broadcast through the mass media, that they assist the development of regional identities and prides and that they can reflect the social problems within a town which may not exist elsewhere. But, if all towns want the same plays, if all audiences are similar, is this link really necessary? The question seems to knock the wind out of not only this argument, but of many other regional claims as well. Is Scottish culture really so different from the English one, as Hugh MacDiarmid would lead us to believe, when the same plays are popular in Pitlochry and Windsor? 'We would like to find', said Kenneth Ireland, the director of the Pitlochry Festival Theatre, 'some genuinely Scottish dramatists' – but, as he pointed out, his audiences weren't prepared to take much *avant-garde* stuff, and without an *avant-garde* it's hard to persuade talented dramatists to write. Writers circle where the risks are taken, and few provincial theatres have the economic security to take many risks. If the Playhouses at Derby and Salisbury present similar programmes, can reps claim any local identities at all?

The answer is that they can, but of the many environmental factors influencing a rep geography is only one – just as a public school in Yorkshire would probably differ more from a comprehensive near by than it would from another public school in Surrey. In spite of the fact that Salisbury and Derby are very different towns, the playhouses themselves are not dissimilar. They were both originally chapels, converted into proscenium-arch theatres at roughly the same time – during and just after the war. They have similar seating-capacities – about 400 – and similar grants from the Arts Council (Salisbury: £23,338; Derby: £19,879 in 1969). They are both situated within the towns, not in the suburbs, but not in the centres either. These physical facts, which may seem less important than they are, mould these two reps, condition the choice of plays, the size of the companies and even the audiences they are likely to attract.

Consider, for example, the date and nature of the conversions. The Salisbury Playhouse was built as a non-conformist chapel: before the war, it was converted into a cinema and then became a storehouse. It was taken over by ENSA during the war, who put on variety shows and plays for the troops. Edith Evans, Flora Robson and James Mason acted there. After the war, Salisbury was reluctant to lose its only live theatre, and CEMA (the Committee for the Encouragement of Music and the Arts, the forerunner of the Arts Council) organized a regional touring theatre, based on Salisbury. A permanent rep company was formed in 1951, the Arts Theatre Company, which received grants from the Arts Council, Salisbury City Council and neighbouring authorities. The Derby Playhouse grew from the Derby Little Theatre Club which, in 1952, converted an old school hall and an adjoining chapel into a theatre, which was gutted by fire in 1956 and rebuilt on the same site. The original conversion cost only £7000. Both theatres were therefore austerity conversions, undertaken at a time – with the war still echoing, before widespread television and with Sir Barry Jackson still alive – when the theatre was enjoying a minor vogue. Later on, in the sixties, there were drastic attempts to alter theatre designs – large Guthrie forestages, alterable proscenium arches, environmental and arena theatres. In the late forties and early fifties, there was really one shape for a theatre, a square or oblong room with a hole in one wall for a stage. The few experimental theatres at the time were deliberate archaisms – the Maddermarket Theatre, Norwich, for example. The playhouses at Derby and Salisbury weren't part of any major civic development schemes. They weren't converted as 'arts centres', but simply to present 'conventional' plays in a 'conventional' way – and to consider what these conventions were we must remember again the influence of Barry Jackson.

Sir Barry Jackson once said that few plays which he had presented at the Birmingham Rep wouldn't equally be worth producing in twenty years' time. He was a Matthew Arnold man, believing that time is a sieve, letting the poor stuff slip through and retaining the gold. 'We have the challenge of the mighty line,' wrote his friend, John Drinkwater, in his inimitable Victorian Tudor, 'God grant us grace to give the countersign.' The theatre was regarded as a place where masterpieces of literature could be presented, and when Barry Jackson designed the Birmingham Rep, for he was an architect as well as an actor, manager, director, designer, businessman and beneficiary of his father's will, he did so in such a way that the importance of the text was emphasized. He reacted against the cupids and fuss of the opulent Edwardian theatres. The auditorium with no pillars to obstruct the view sloped steeply down to a proscenium-arch stage. The merit of the proscenium-arch theatre is that, with a little care and by accepting the limitation of one acting-direction, from the stage out front to the audience, everything can be seen and heard by everyone, lines can be projected clearly, and facial gestures aren't buried behind someone's back. The raised stage and proscenium-arch perform the same function as a podium in a lecture hall. The lecturer may be cut off from his students, he may be raised in over-solemn isolation, unable to chat or answer informal questions, but he can put across his basic, verbal text with clarity.

In other words, Sir Barry Jackson was a sensible man – but a little stuffy perhaps and too saturated with the standards of Eng. Lit. He aimed to produce a mixture of plays, 'each good of their kind', a careful balance of ancient and modern, spiced with flavours from abroad, from the saucy French, the wise Greeks and the impassive Chinese. Looking back at the programmes of the Birmingham Rep, one is startled by the omissions. Sir Barry Jackson was a contemporary of Piscator and Brecht, of Jarry and Artaud, of the Dadaists, Surrealists and Expressionists, none of whom found a formal place in his theatre and had little influence on it either. His idea of an experimental play was *The Ascent of F.6* by Auden and Isherwood, that masterpiece of pretentiousness, with its mock Freudian ideology and its jumble of literary impersonations from Eliot to Kipling and Cole Porter to *King Lear*. No one said 'Shit' in his theatre, unless he was medieval, in which case it was all right. He showed, I would have thought, little concern for social or political issues, believing that Art rose above ephemeral considerations. With the slump on, he offered *Mr Pim Passes By* and Ashley Dukes' costume comedy, *The Man with a Load of Mischief*. At the time of Munich, the Birmingham Rep was playing *The Wooing of Anne Hathaway* by Grace Carlton. It's not inconsistent, I think, to acknowledge Sir Barry Jackson's achievements and be grateful for them, and to feel at the same time a little irritated that his influence excluded so much. The English theatre in the inter-war period badly needed someone else to balance his broad tastes and liberal-conservative approach with something more abrasive, egocentric and revolutionary. He made a respectable theatre more so – and steered it away from the uncomfortable turmoils abroad.

The Salisbury and Derby Playhouses grew up under his shadow. The theatres are, like the Birmingham Rep, austere, efficiently able to tackle most well-made, naturalistic plays, with simple sets, harsh on certain kinds of audience involvement, stern with opulence, poorly designed for visual effects. The seating capacities are too small – and so are the stages – to accommodate lavish spectaculars: the dimensions of both theatres are interestingly similar to those of the old Birmingham Rep, which seated 452. The plays most suitable for production at Derby and Salisbury are small-cast plays, with few set-changes or none, conceived in a literary way – that is, with a set text, no room for improvisation or directorial liberties, and preferably perhaps naturalistic. They were both founded as non-commercial theatres, and therefore were to be judged by certain standards of seriousness and social service, which did not exclude the boulevard comedy, but cut out the vulgar ones. The programmes at Salisbury during the 1959/60 season would have pleased Sir Barry; they included *A View from the Bridge*, *The Rivals*, *The Long, the Short and the Tall*, *As You Like It*, *Uncle Vanya*, *Five-Finger Exercise* and *Two for a Seesaw*. The autumn programme for the Derby Playhouse in 1969 included *Cat on a Hot Tin Roof* and *St Joan*. Both theatres reflect a certain middle-class tradition in drama, sensible and fruitful, though with some hidden inhibitions.

The word middle-class is too vague to be left without further definition. I mean: the desire to be well spoken and well thought of, a dislike of the provincial, a sceptical curiosity about what happens abroad, a care with dangerous subjects – notably politics and religion and sex – which have to be handled if at all in a certain tone of voice, flippantly gay or solemnly intent, a distrust of conceit, flamboyance and exhibitionism which are vices to be slapped down in children. The very position of these theatres in their different towns suggests a comfortable – not opulent, not poor – existence. They are not situated with the neon lights and office blocks, nor in some leisurely park outside the town, nor on a university campus – but on a corner down an urban side-street, a neighbourhood place.

With these associations, *middle-class* becomes an adjective to describe a state of mind, possibly but not necessarily linked with incomes and education. When Roger Clissold said that the audiences in Derby and Salisbury were similar, one assumed that the same income-groups were visiting the theatre – the professional and managerial classes perhaps, the 'better-educated' groups, whose jobs may not differ too much from town to town, and whose outlook in any case was influenced more by national than local issues. This may have been so – but there is another interpretation, that the public in both towns who visited the theatre might do so in a similar frame of mind, although elsewhere, at home or work, their preoccupations might have been totally different.

Ten years ago, in Cambridge, there were three theatres – the New (now closed), the A.D.C. and the Arts. The Arts Theatre (now the home of Prospect Productions) was for touring professional companies, mainly on a pre-London circuit, and for the best under-graduate productions by, say, the Marlowe Society. The A.D.C. Theatre was for the University, fairly well equipped and with a relaxed tolerant atmosphere, where we could experiment without losing too much money. The New Theatre showed at the time mainly touring variety shows, such as *Strip*, *Strip Hooray*, and the occasional play, *Good Time Girl* or *Wanton Lusts*. There was a strict class difference between these three theatres – although, naturally, we would visit them all. We simply dressed differently. For the Arts Theatre, I would wear a suit and a tie, my gown, and hope to take a pretty girl with me. For the A.D.C., I would wear a sweater and jeans, carry a gown across my arm and go with a crowd from the college. For the New Theatre, I would leave my gown behind. The place was filled with undergraduates, all pretending that the theatre was really part of the town. I would wear a raincoat, non-descript, collar turned up. At Billingham, the former artistic director, George Roman, told me that *The Killing of Sister George* was too sexually decadent a play for the Forum Theatre: the public was somewhat puritanical. But at the same time, of course, strip night at the club was always packed.

A 'middle-class' theatre, therefore, may not just appeal to the 'middle classes' – but to the middle-class strain in us all. Overt attempts to fit a theatre into a locality, to choose 'appropriate' plays, are often disastrous, because they sometimes conceal a loftiness towards the area which the potential public may well resent. It is no good putting on 'working-class' plays in a 'working-class' area where most of the inhabitants are trying to be 'middle class'. When Joan Littlewood was at the Theatre Royal, Stratford, East London, she produced a number of plays set in the working-class areas of Stepney, Salford and Liverpool, in pubs and prisons, admirable plays, many of them, and admirably directed, but better known in Sloane Square than Romford Road. I first visited the Theatre Royal at a time when Joan Littlewood's name was famous on Broadway, in the West End and in Paris: but the manager of a pub not half a mile away from the theatre had never heard of her, did not even know that the Company existed. It requires a certain attitude of mind, a certain readiness to accept praise and criticism, to want the theatre to comment on local and regional issues – a tolerant sophistication, in fact. Far from *expecting* a theatre to be Derby-minded in Derby, we should be surprised when this happens, for it reveals a self-assurance in the community, a sense of pride, an impatience with national follies and a willingness to commit local ones. The real difference between Derby and Salisbury is not that the programmes of the two 'middle-class' theatres should be markedly dissimilar, but that in Derby there is probably room for an experimental theatre as well, whereas in Salisbury there probably isn't.

And so the process of enquiry with which we began has to be partly reversed. We must define the theatres before the areas. We mustn't assume that the theatre is the *effect* caused by public opinion in the town, but rather that the audiences are the effect caused by the theatre. The question is why does this theatre have this impact in this town – and if we find that the pattern of theatre-going, judged not only by play selection but bearing many other factors in mind as well, changes significantly in different parts of the country – that certain kinds of theatre succeed here, but fail there – then and only then can we reach some regional conclusions. How, though, can we define the theatres? One way would be to describe the sources of income - another, the position in the neighbourhood – another, the size and nature of the companies – another still, the shape of the theatres, auditoriums and stages. And with all these environmental data discovered and put firmly into place, there still remains the element of chance – where did the enthusiasm come from, to build a theatre and keep it going? This random zeal, this arbitrary dedication, always raises some puzzling questions. Why, in Bolton of all places, should a new and fairly revolutionary theatre be built in *eighteen* months, at a time of a national squeeze, when Leeds had no rep, Preston no theatre at all and the rep at Southport near by closed down? Sometimes sheer ebullience will build a theatre when all the cooler estimates are against one.

3

Merit Marks

THERE is an unofficial Arts Council grading for repertory theatres, defined by grants and other nuances. Nine English reps, usually called in Arts Council reports 'the major reps', are entitled to print on their programmes and posters 'in association with the Arts Council', the theatrical equivalent of 'By appointment to . . .' on a bottle of jam. This distinguishes them from the National theatres, who are 'in *full* association with . . .', and from the lesser reps, which merely 'acknowledge the assistance of . . .', sometimes 'thankfully', sometimes not. Of the nine major reps, seven received in 1969 grants in the region of £50,000 from the Arts Council, and the other two received grants according to their needs. The Chichester Festival Theatre Company had a guarantee against loss of £12,500, of which they claimed £7500 during the 1968/9 season. Prospect Productions received £35,000 during the same year. There once was a suggestion that this unofficial table should be organized into a sort of league, along the lines of football. It was never seriously considered. The problems of promotion were hard enough, those of relegation quite impossible. To begin with, were all the reps playing the same game? Chichester, a summer seasonal theatre with fairly high seat-prices, presents elegant and well-spoken productions of *classics* or plays with *classic* potential – the *haute couture* of drama: whereas the programmes at the Belgrade Theatre, Coventry, are definitely *prêt-à-porter*. The seat prices are low, the plays varied, a standard range of material to suit most ages and tastes.

Jennie Lee, as Minister for the Arts, was once asked in the House of Commons 'what principles governed the giving of Arts Council grants to the repertory theatres in the East Midlands'. She replied that the principles were the same for all repertory theatres. The Arts Council, within the limits of the funds available, made grants after examination of estimates and took into account artistic standing and potential. This statement left many questions unanswered. To assess 'artistic standing' is hard enough, as a glance at theatre awards and prizes reveals: there is no accurate system of measurement. But 'potential'? How can one tell in advance that this theatre is likely to do good work next season and that rep won't? And yet comparisons have to be made. Nobody would suggest that the same size grant should be given to all theatres. Puzzling out the logic of Arts Council grants is a popular pastime with theatre managers, to rank with crosswords. Do the 'major reps' differ from the others in their standards of excellence? I would have thought not. The standards are high, and five of the major reps can boast of artistic directors whose reputations extend certainly to the West End and maybe beyond. But it would be rash and misleading to suggest that the standards of production at, say, the Liverpool or Sheffield Playhouses are superior to those at the Yvonne Arnaud Theatre, Guildford. Is the criterion then the *location*? Do reps in large cities receive more than those in smaller ones? Or those in the North more than those in the South, which can benefit from the pool of actors in London? Again no. Seven major reps have large cities in their catchment areas, if the theatre at Chichester can be said to serve Southampton and Portsmouth as well. But Oxford and Cambridge are not large cities, and they're close to London as well. Are the facilities at these major reps better? Not invariably. The Meadow Players at Oxford have to share a theatre with the University. What is then the mysterious class distinction which separates the U from the Non-U? Is the grading a historical accident, like accents and aristocracies? I asked one theatre manager for his explanation and he answered rather cautiously, 'Well, we send in our estimates and accounts every year . . . and explain to them what we need. They sometimes come down to see us . . . then there are committees, I suppose. . . .' Then he added, 'It's all Bingo really.'

There is a logic, however, which can be expressed in terms of a game: not Bingo – that's cynical – but one of those rambling, complicated family games, like *Monopoly* for Sunday afternoons. I am, of course, an outsider in this game: I can only guess at the rules. But there would seem to be, say, six suits of cards, and five cards in each suit, numbered one to five. Each player (the rep) receives one card from each suit, and he then adds together the numbers from each card. If the total exceeds twenty (out of a possible thirty), he is entitled to claim 'major rep' status, receiving a £50,000 bonus and advancing immediately to *Go*. He may not be able to do so, however, if he is sitting on a square marked *Chance*, which means that he has to pick up a chance card from a central pack. These *Chance* cards may read: *Economic Crisis: Immediate Cut-back on Public Expenditure: Arts First to Suffer* or *New Grants Delayed, Pending a Full-scale Review*. Most of the *Chance* cards are disastrous, but not all. One may read: *Old Vic Burnt Down. New National Theatre not yet Built. Your Theatre Has Been Chosen to House the National Company* – in which case the player can immediately claim thirty out of thirty, wins the game, is in *full* association with the Arts Council and can receive grants of up to a quarter of a million pounds per year.

The progress of the game is complicated, not to mention obscure. There are many home-made rules. The basic aim is to secure as many points as possible from a hand of six cards. Having secured a certain number of points, the player passes on to the next round with this aggregate intact. Only a disaster can force a player actually to lose points. His purpose each round is to exchange one of his low-ranking cards for a higher one, thus bringing up his total aggregate. Only rarely can more than one card be exchanged per round. Hence, in the suit marked *Length of Run*, he may wish to exchange *Fortnightly*, which counts as 1, for *Three-weekly*, which scores 2. But he can only do so if his box-office figures for *Fortnightly* rep exceed, say, 50 per cent, and audience loyalty really belongs to the *Location* suit. In other words, a high-scoring card in one suit may depend on a high-scoring card in another. You can only exchange *monthly* rep (3 points) for *repertoire* (5 points) if you possess a *Modern Theatre with Good Facilities* (4 points from the *Theatre Buildings* suit) and a *Large Permanent Company* (4 points from the *Company* suit). Readers will not be comforted to learn that there are exceptions to these rules, and that certain forms of cheating are permitted, but others aren't. A proper understanding of this supremely subtle game depends upon a thorough grasp of the scoring-system and the suits, about which many very boring volumes could be written. I shall limit myself to a brief summary, which will attempt to compensate for the boredom by sheer cursoriness.

The six suits would seem to be these: *Length of Run*, *Theatre Buildings*, *Company*, *Programmes and Services*, *Directors* and *Location*. There may be others. Some would assert that *Contacts* are also important, and *Trend* and *History*. I am inclined to place these cards with the *Chance* pack. The scoring-system is as follows:

1. LENGTH OF RUN

Weekly	0
Fortnightly	1
Three-weekly	2
Monthly	3
Repertoire	5

The Arts Council doesn't actually frown on weekly rep. It rarely frowns on anything. It does, however, purse its lips and walk past, humming a ruminative tune. The assumption is that the longer the run, the longer the rehearsal period – hence the better the production. Managements obviously can't keep a production on for longer than the public will allow, for most of the income comes from the box office, not from subsidies. And so the length of the run also roughly indicates the degree of public support which a management expects. *Repertoire*, the system whereby several productions are held in hand and offered either on different nights or sometimes for alternate weeks, has many advantages, but also many practical difficulties. Among the major reps, six play *Repertoire*, while the Bristol Old Vic is *Monthly*, the Belgrade, Coventry, varies from *Weekly* to *Monthly*, and the Liverpool Playhouse from *Fortnightly* to *Three-weekly*.

For a small company, *Repertoire* is usually an impractical system. The acting team should be large, well balanced and permanent. Outside stars can't be brought in for individual productions, which may only run for two nights a week. Since each production has to be kept together for two months or longer, actors can't drop out for a fortnight to take, say, a television engagement. In an ideal world, they would be paid more to compensate. Advertising has to be slick to prevent the public from mistaking the nights, from coming to see accidentally productions they don't want to see. Sets for each production have to be stored carefully – and few theatres have adequate storage space – they have to be quickly struck and erected. There has to be, therefore, good access to the stage from the workshops, and a well-drilled backstage team. Among the smaller reps, *Repertoire* is rare. Peter Cheeseman's Theatre-in-the-Round Company at the Victoria Theatre, Stoke-on-Trent, is one of the exceptions: but here the staging problems are simplified. He uses no built sets, only props.

For a major company, however, *Repertoire* offers great benefits.

An actor playing Hamlet for three to four weeks is under consider-able strain. The success of the production rests on his shoulders – together with all his own acting problems. *Repertoire* spreads the burden over a longer period. He can be properly rested. The alter-nation of plays prevents a company from becoming stale or too assured. Managements can also afford to be more adventurous. If an experimental play is tried out – and fails – it ought to be taken off fairly quickly. Under the normal system, a production has to play for its allotted span – and managements do not want to see the theatre nearly empty for three weeks. Therefore, they have to choose their plays cautiously. In *Repertoire*, an adventurous production can play with a 'safe' one, and if, after, say, ten performances, the risky play is still doing bad business, the safe one can be carefully scheduled for more nights. *Repertoire* uses a permanent company more efficiently. An actor not cast in one production under the normal system has to rest for three weeks. In *Repertoire*, if he isn't cast in one production, he'll appear in another.

For the major reps, there is a definite balance of artistic benefits over practical difficulties in the repertoire system. Even those which do not use this system now, would like to do so in the future. Warren Jenkins at Coventry would like to turn to *Repertoire*, but the scenery store at the Belgrade is too small. The development plans at the Theatre Royal, Bristol, include a large scenery-store and improved access to the stage – which is probably a step towards *Repertoire*. There are other less tangible benefits as well: improved team-spirit in the company. The Arts Council Theatre Enquiry Report pointed out that 'the merits of true repertoire are that it ensures a permanent company which attracts audiences who like to "follow" individual actors in a variety of performances'. One example of this following which an actor playing in *Repertoire* can attract is that of Ian McKellen, when he appeared as Richard II and Edward II in two Prospect productions.

2. THEATRE BUILDINGS

Large, ill-equipped, old-fashioned touring theatres	0
Converted halls and smaller touring theatres, suitable for conversion	1
A modernized touring theatre, adequately equipped	2
A pre-war repertory theatre, adequately equipped	3
A post-war repertory theatre, with good facilities	4

A post-war repertory theatre, with alterable staging, a
studio theatre and modern facilities   5

Theatre buildings and modernization programmes will be discussed
elsewhere. I want here to confine the subject solely to the way in
which the existing buildings raise or lower the statuses of repertory
theatres, and therefore their Arts Council subsidies. The financing of
development programmes is not usually included as part of the annual
grant. These are helped separately, either through the Arts Council
Housing the Arts programme, or through private subscription, or
through local subsidies – or (usually) through a combination of all three.

The Edwardian and Victorian touring theatres, many of them
fine buildings, present all sorts of problems today. The companies
on which they depended for product have largely dwindled away.
They are often not suitable for conversion into repertory theatres.
Many of them are too large: the Grand, Wolverhampton, seats 1410
and the Alexandra, Birmingham, 1562. Under such domes, audiences
of 500, a good house by normal repertory standards, seem sparsely
scattered, and their reaction is therefore muted and dispirited. The
stages, too, are large: the Grand, Wolverhampton, has a depth of
forty feet. To fill the stage, a production has to be elaborately
designed. The Alexandra is renowned for its pantomimes. Unfortunately, touring theatres rarely possess good stage workshops:
in the past, they didn't need them. Vans would bring the sets from
London workshops to the big double doors at the back and the
manager would sign for them. Many have fallen into a bad state of
disrepair, having now a gloomy Gothic appearance, boilers bursting
behind the crumbling plaster, loos leaking in the spring, dressing-
rooms with one tatty couch, a lamp without a shade and one faintly
dusty telegram pinned to the corner of a mirror. The Arts Council
Theatre Enquiry Report suggested that some 12–18 of them should
be bought and maintained by local authorities to provide the basis
of a touring-grid: but many local authorities are reluctant to venture
into such dubious investments, particularly because the commercial
managements who own them are well aware that the site values of
these theatres are worth far more than the theatres themselves. Not
all these theatres, of course, are in such straits. The Theatre Royal,
Brighton, is well maintained, very attractive, and has a good supply
of product, from managements bringing shows around the home
counties on pre-London tours.

Some of the smaller ones have been converted successfully into repertory theatres. At the Opera House, Harrogate, the area beneath the stage has been converted into a workshop. It is a bit inconvenient. The workshop ceiling is low, and sets have to be painted on stage. The smell of size from the wood-framed flats seeps through the boards of the stage, so that the cast acts in the fumes from a lake of glue. But the Opera House is an exceptionally pretty theatre, with a fine Pre-Raphaelite frieze in the foyer. The seating capacity is reasonable as well: 850. The Cheltenham Opera House (now the Everyman) has also been successfully transformed. But sometimes the very attractiveness of the old theatres enhances the problems: nobody wants to get rid of them, nor knows what to do with them either. And so they simply wait, like old music-hall stars, for some management to call. At Worthing, there is a fine Edwardian music-hall, now used as a workshop and scenery store for the Connaught Theatre: it is like meeting a once-famous comedian sitting in a cubby-hole beside the stage door.

The theatres built or converted for repertory purposes before and just after the Second World War have the virtues and defects of the Birmingham Rep, which we have already considered: smaller in general than the touring-theatres – the ideal size for a rep was considered to be between 500 and 800 seats – and efficiently able to cope with the demands of the naturalistic well-made play. Since the war, however, and particularly since the arrival of television, this type of drama, which still provides the stock for repertory programmes, has faced various criticisms: other forms of theatre have emerged – of the Absurd, of Sensation and Cruelty: Expressionism has at last made an impact. Since the early sixties, theatre design has been markedly more adventurous – the shapes of auditoriums, stages and equipment. And this is in a way surprising, for when these theatres were planned, some of them in the late fifties, the theatre in general was in a state of uncommon uncertainty. Nobody could guess what sort of audiences there would be for the live theatre in the late sixties and early seventies: most of the estimates were gloomy ones. When the Nottingham Playhouse was built in 1963, many said that it would prove to be disastrously large, quite uneconomic to run. The old Playhouse seated 350 and played season after season to 50 per cent capacity. The new Playhouse, however, seats 750 and plays to 85 per cent capacity. The old theatre club at Leatherhead seated 300, and, under cramped and difficult conditions, the company managed to arouse considerable local enthusiasm. When the new theatre, seating 530, was opened in 1969, the first few productions were sold out. This evidence suggests that where there is already keen local interest in the theatre new buildings stimulate a remarkable new growth in the size of audiences. In one sense, the Nottingham Playhouse is already too small. If the *average* attendance is 85 per cent capacity, what on earth happens when the company has a hit? Couldn't a larger theatre be run – let it be whispered – with a profit? The answer is probably not. Large theatres are not always more profitable to run – not simply because rates and maintenance bills are higher, but because they demand larger, and in some cases, more professional productions. At the old Leatherhead Theatre Club, audiences were prepared to accept the occasional amateurish performance. With the new theatre, they became more critical. The Arts Council, recognizing that a larger theatre, however modern, usually means disproportionately higher bills, usually raises the grant of a rep when a new theatre is built.

It is extremely hard to calculate the ideal seating-capacity for a repertory theatre: it varies from place to place. For every Leatherhead there is an East Grinstead, where a charming new theatre was built, the Adeline Genée, which was forced to close after a few months. The stage was perhaps unreasonably large for the size of the auditorium, and the theatre was difficult to find: but the real problem was perhaps that the new theatre was built before a local company had been formed which aroused support and enthusiasm. Two per cent of the population are supposed to be dedicated theatre-goers: but this is, of course, an average figure and therefore useless. Only in practice can the enthusiasm of a town be tested. On the most conservative estimate of audience potential, the Theatre Royal, Bristol, perhaps the most charming Georgian theatre in the country and certainly the best maintained, seems too small to house a major rep. The Theatre Royal seats 681, and when the new theatres at Birmingham and Sheffield are completed it will be the smallest theatre housing a major company in the country. But Bristol is a large city, the population is nearly half-a-million; and Cardiff and Swansea could also be included in the catchment area. Oxford, on the other hand, with a much smaller population – about 110,000 – seems overstocked with theatres: the New, which is included as part of the proposed touring-grid, seats over 1000; and the Playhouse, the home of the Meadow Players, a major rep, seats 700.

The size is only one uncertainty which dogs the building of a new theatre: the shape of the stage and the auditorium is another. Many directors are convinced that the close audience–actor contact which the thrust, open and arena stages provide is the theatre's answer to television: others that such defiance of well-established conventions merely complicates the problems. One solution is to build an adaptable theatre, with large movable forestages, adjustable proscenium arches and seats which can be taken out and replaced. This is an attractive compromise which, at Bolton, Exeter and other places, works very well. It fails, however, to take advantage of the technical possibilities which we know that theatres can – and probably will – have in the future. Some exciting experiments have taken place in recent years, along the lines of environmental theatre – where the audience is plunged into a whirlpool of sound and light effects, where the actors mingle with the audience and the public are asked to participate in what is really a *happening*. Oughtn't we perhaps to design a theatre which is a box for sensations?

Adaptable theatres reconcile well-known theatre traditions: they don't seek to widen the possibilities of the theatre. A truly *experimental* theatre – where, say, the walls of the auditorium are part of the set, where there is an electronic workshop for music and kinetic art effects, where stages and platforms can be raised at will – would be a far greater gamble. It is perhaps a gamble which should be taken, although few reps can afford to look beyond adaptable theatres. There is, however, one temporary solution. Some reps have acquired studio theatres – basically a large room, with movable seating, a lighting-grid covering the ceiling, loudspeakers in the wall and perhaps a projection room. Here experiments can be tried without too much cost which may eventually be fed into the main repertory programme. The Cockpit Theatre in London is one example. Here, in conditions of simple austerity, new plays can be tried out – and new theatre techniques: abstract plays, plays which may offend, participatory plays, and environmental theatre. The new Traverse Theatre, though not technically well-equipped, is also useful for this sort of experiment. And so are the Close Theatre, attached to the Glasgow Citizens' Theatre, the Vanguard Theatre at Sheffield, and the Theatre Upstairs at the Royal Court in London.

A studio theatre has other advantages as well. Students and young revolutionaries, who might be alienated by the bourgeois plays in the main theatre, can do their own thing in freedom. Theatres can sometimes, it is said, bring different sections of the community together, but these groups won't always come to the same plays. The youngsters who didn't go to *The Boy Friend* when it was staged at the Belgrade Theatre, Coventry, could go along to the studio theatre to see two new plays by Mrozek, transferring their loyalties to the main theatre when something more up to date appeared. In this way, the generation gap could be partly covered. The concerns of one group met the needs of another.

At Liverpool, for example, where there are two reps run by different managements in separate theatres, there seems to be a polarization of two age and – perhaps – class groups. The Playhouse, a major rep, has a reputation for safe, rather middle-aged productions, whereas the Everyman is for the young. This contrast may belittle the Playhouse. In 1969, they staged Edward Bond's *Saved* – which many managements still fear to tackle, and on Monday nights the company goes experimental, producing, say, *Oldenberg* and *Nathan and Tabileth* by Barry Bermange. There is also a large rehearsal room which is sometimes used as a studio theatre. During the intervals, however, Ronald Settle and Joan Ovens play selections from Percy Grainger and Ivor Novello, on two pianos – parlour entertainment, with trills like tassels. The programmes at the Everyman are more adventurous – not *Saved* by Edward Bond, but his later play, *Early Morning*. The very look of the two buildings – the Playhouse, with its sleek new foyer, fine offices, restaurant and elegant Empire auditorium, and the Everyman, with its tatty, casual, good-humoured atmosphere and battered cinema-seats – is a reproach to class distinction. The manager at my hotel in Liverpool had no doubt that the Playhouse was run by Tories and the Everyman by Labour. If these two theatres could be more closely integrated – and what a difficult transition that would be! – if, say, the Everyman were a studio theatre attached to the Playhouse, the social divisions would be less obviously opposed. The argument against having two reps, even in a city the size of Liverpool, is that a *community* theatre may not develop from either. The young will not transfer their loyalties away from the Everyman as they grow up. The very presence of two theatre buildings may sharpen rivalries, which a single one might help to subdue into friendship.

The nature of the theatre buildings alters therefore the sort of role which a rep can play in the community. Three of the major reps – Sheffield, Coventry and Bristol – have studio theatres, and

Birmingham will have one when the new theatre is completed in 1971. Three – Nottingham, Coventry and Chichester – have new theatres, although the facilities are not ideal in any of them. Two more, Birmingham and Sheffield, have theatres under construction. Two have modernized their existing theatres, or are in the process of doing so – Liverpool and Bristol. And two share university theatres, which provide the base for touring. Among the theatres in the second, £20,000-grant category, which includes fourteen reps, three companies have new theatres and there are plans for five more. In the second category, only two theatres have studios attached.

3. COMPANY

Occasional rep, occasional touring	0
Permanent managements, casting from a pool of actors in London	1
Permanent small companies	2
Permanent small companies, with guest stars	3
Permanent large companies	4
Permanent large companies, with guest stars	5

Many reps bring in outside companies for occasional seasons – during the summer, for example, when the actors are on holiday. This implies no loss of status, and they are not included in the first category. There are some theatres, however, particularly in seaside towns, where there is no consistent policy towards the theatre – where, say, a building is owned by a municipal authority and run by a manager whose duty is to supply entertainment, to make a profit if he can, if not, to minimize the loss. The manager then books what companies he can – choosing perhaps a small commercial repertory company for a short season – eight to ten weeks, some touring companies, a variety show and a pantomime. There is a marked shortage of small touring companies, and the larger commercial managements prefer to play in large theatres in major cities, such as Manchester and Leeds, rather than to tour the smaller centres. Companies similar to Sir Donald Wolfit's Shakespearian touring rep and groups masquerading as the *original* Aldwych farce team are rare, although the Civic Theatre, Darlington, in 1969 received Pomona Productions in *Rattle of a Simple Man* and Highlight Productions (Theatre) Ltd in *Who's Afraid of Virginia Woolf?* Both these plays have small casts, single sets and are therefore suitable for commercial companies working on little capital. The standards of these companies are variable, their survival always a matter for speculation, and those theatres which rely on them for product have been forced too often to go 'dark' or bring in variety. The Arts Council, it is said, is impressed by survival. The death rate among those theatres pursuing this policy is calculated to deter them.

The alternative for those theatres facing this unpredictable life and probable starvation is to manufacture the product themselves: this is another reason why some smaller touring theatres have changed status to become reps. At the Civic, Darlington, there is a Theatre Director, P. J. Hamilton-Moore, who runs the theatre and books various outside companies. At most reps, however, there are two men in charge, the general manager, who runs the theatre and administration, and the artistic director, who supervises the productions, either handling them himself or inviting outside directors. At the subsidized theatres, the managers and artistic directors are responsible to a governing board, who appoint them, who usually have to approve the estimates for each production and who, in the event of controversy, have the right to veto a production and sack the manager. The Theatre Enquiry Report has suggested that the ideal size of board should not number more than fifteen, and should be composed of up to five members selected from the 'founding fathers' of the theatre and their *natural successors* (my italics), up to five representatives of local authorities (assuming that a theatre receives local subsidies), not more than two representatives from audiences, and not more than three members from universities, arts associations and other local bodies. The Arts Council does not believe that they should be represented on these governing boards: 'the fact that theatre Boards enjoy complete and local self-government is the paramount expression of their democratic freedom'. This proposed composition of the Board carefully balances the 'founding fathers' - those who are supposed to have a particular interest in the survival of the theatre - with the council representatives, who may change for political reasons after local elections. The founding fathers are not usually hard to find - drawn from those local citizens who backed the theatre in the early days: their 'natural successors', however, are more difficult to determine. Sometimes this simply means a local angel, who has donated money to a development fund. The Theatre Enquiry Report states that 'between most of the present Artistic Directors and their Boards there is a relationship which can cope with inevitable differences of opinion in a rational and sympathetic way': and that 'it is only recently that instances have occurred in which their authority [that is, of the Board] has been questioned in disputes which received abundant publicity and provoked a good deal of controversy, such as the clash at Nottingham between the Board and its then Artistic Director [John Neville]'. This may, in general, be true, and it is certainly hard to think of a system which would work better: at the same time, this section of the Theatre Enquiry Report seems to me too sanguine, too bland. There are many controversies which receive no publicity, because it is in the interest of the artistic director and the manager to forget them, to tone them down. The Theatre Enquiry Report mentions that the artistic directors should have complete freedom in the choice of plays 'and all that is implied in the choice' – provided that he keeps within his budget and retains the confidence of the public. These qualifications however, can be interpreted in many different ways. Some boards believe – or seem to – that every production should cover or nearly cover costs: whereas, of course, an artistic director may want to balance a profitable low-cost production (such as *Boeing-Boeing*) against the losses to be expected from a 'daring' production (such as *Saved*) or from an ambitious and costly one (such as *Antony and Cleopatra*). Retaining the confidence of the public is another loose and awkward phrase – a director may try deliberately to bring a new potential public into the theatre, such as the students, even at the risk of alienating the stalwarts. This is another frequent contention. Some boards think of the theatre as being a preserve of the middle-aged and prosperous. Several bitter controversies during the 1969 season received little national publicity. When the Tories came to power at Watford the newly appointed Chairman of the Board of the Watford Civic Theatre, the late Alderman Gamble, stated that he had arrived with a mandate from the electorate to close the place down. The Watford Civic Theatre – the only rep in this suburban area to the North of London – had acquired an enviable reputation for the quality and ambitiousness of their productions. This was where, for example, Harold Pinter and Vivian Merchant appeared in a superb production of Pinter's *The Homecoming*. The artistic director at that time, Giles Havergal, left, and went to the Glasgow Citizens' Theatre, and the Board were then both slow and reluctant to appoint another artistic director. For a couple of months, the theatre was run by a young and efficient girl, Jane Davies, who had been on an Arts Council training course: the Watford Civic Theatre was her first appointment. The artistic director finally appointed was Kay Gardner, who had had much experience in theatre management but comparatively little as an artistic director. Giles Havergal, in the meantime, found an equally discouraging situation in Glasgow, at the Citizens' Theatre, a huge, unwieldy theatre in the Gorbals district, among slums which are being pulled down. The Citizens' Theatre Company – an important and famous rep in a city which needs one – wanted to be included in a new development scheme, affecting the centre of Glasgow: they were told plainly by the City Treasurer that beggars can't be choosers.

Unco-operative and unsympathetic theatre boards can cause great harm sometimes, and in a field of 'social service' where there has been considerable public investment. For this reason, I am inclined to question the wisdom of the Arts Council decision not to claim a seat on theatre boards: it may not be practicable – there may not be sufficient Arts Council representatives to go round; but this practical consideration is very different from the reason given by the Arts Council, that theatre boards should be autonomous, to preserve a certain democracy in the theatre.

Most of the reps around London do not have permanent acting companies. It is comparatively easy to cast from the pool of actors in London, and often with high-powered names. In January 1967, Sybil Thorndike and Max Adrian appeared in Laurier Lister's production of Marguerite Duras' fine play, *The Viaduct*: at the same theatre, the Yvonne Arnaud Theatre, Guildford, Flora Robson starred in Rodney Ackland's *The Old Ladies*. There are countless other examples. Some managements feel that this is an ideal situation: they can choose low-cast plays for the slack seasons of the year – July and August – and bring in a larger company for November and March. Each play can be cast separately: the right people can be found for various parts. A young acting A.S.M. doesn't have to dress up in a bald wig to play a doddering old man – it's always possible to find a doddering old star. But there are drawbacks. Directors with a *charisma* may be able to attract the stars down to play for three weeks on rep salaries: others cannot. Plays which require good teamwork – Brecht, Chekhov and Shakespeare wrote such plays – usually can't be tackled adequately under this system.

A company can't be formed during a three-week rehearsal-period to tackle adequately the nuances of an ensemble play. The plays which work best under this system are those which require fairly 'standard' performances from actors and routine productions. What also tends to happen is that the main parts are *over-cast* – that is, a star is brought in whose very presence overshadows the rest of the company – whereas the minor parts are *under-cast*. In a production of *Outward Bound* at the Intimate Theatre, Palmers Green, the director, Ernest Dudley, virtually rewrote the last act to give a bigger part to the star, the late Jimmy Hanley.

Some managements further away from London follow this policy as well – but with fewer advantages. Actors have to stay in the town. They can't commute from London. And many of them are reluctant to spend too much time away from the centre where all the jobs are supposed to be. They may, however, be tempted to join a permanent company, to sacrifice for a year their chances of a big film-contract for greater over-all security. Most managements outside the Home Counties prefer to have permanent or semi-permanent companies, meeting the slack and boom seasons by building the company up slowly from, say, six actors in the early autumn to about fifteen at Christmas. In this way, actors can be given short-term contracts and the company learns to act as a team.

In some theatres, actors are encouraged to stay for far longer periods, for a year or more, so that certain group projects can be tackled. Peter Cheeseman's Theatre-in-the-Round Company at Stoke-on-Trent uses a permanent company to develop the techniques of 'arena' acting, and to pioneer local documentaries. At the Theatre Royal, Lincoln, where there is a remarkably closely knit team, Philip Hedley, the director, follows directorial methods which few could imitate. He doesn't, for example, give 'moves' to his actors, or block out a production in advance. He prefers to let his actors discuss the play freely, to improvise certain scenes, and 'to allow the production to emerge' from the group. After one technical rehearsal of *Romeo and Juliet*, he was left with too little time for a full dress-rehearsal: and so he asked the company to *sing* through the play, trying to feel the atmosphere of each scene and the progress of the story, not through words and movement, but simply through the different vocal noises which they deliver. The Company has also tackled rather successfully their own form of *commedia dell' arte*. The productions at Lincoln are usually lively and stimulating, and without the hard over-disciplined gloss which some less ambitious, but perhaps more esteemed, companies manage to achieve.

Sometimes these small permanent companies can acquire the reputations which attract visiting stars and dramatists to work with them – hence, in a sense, getting the best of both worlds. The size of these companies is, however, the obstacle. By choosing a permanent company, the choice of plays is limited to those which this company can tackle. A play with more than ten parts is often excluded. And again, if the permanent company has a balance of six actors and four actresses, it can't play *Lysistrata* – except perhaps in drag – or Noël Coward's *Waiting in the Wings* if the cast are all in their twenties. The ideal solution is perhaps to have a large permanent company and a reputation which can attract stars, if they are wanted. Seven of the nine major reps have companies of more than fifteen actors. Frank Hauser, of the Meadow Players, prefers to cast each play separately from London, and Antony Tuckey at the Liverpool Playhouse has a permanent company of ten.

4. PROGRAMMES AND SERVICES:

Assorted popular	0
Prêt-à-porter	1
Prêt-à-porter and theatre-in-education	2
Prêt-à-porter, theatre-in-education, regional drama	3
Haute couture	4
Haute couture, theatre-in-education, arts centre and regional drama	5

By *popular*, I mean those programmes which are designed to attract mass audiences all the time – where minority interests are ignored. Some managements have an astonishing capacity for killing the goose which lays the golden eggs – Agatha Christie, sex farces. Unfortunately, the minorities may be lively ones potentially – the students, for example – and popular programmes have a habit of growing stale quickly. *Prêt-à-porter* is a phrase which I have borrowed from the rag trade to describe those programmes which are designed to suit most ages and sizes, to include a variety of styles and tastes: a Shakespeare, a Rattigan, a farce, a thriller, the occasional new play and so on. The difference between *popular* and *prêt-à-porter* resembles that between two supermarkets, one where you can buy instant coffee but not freshly ground and the other where you can buy both.

Prêt-à-porter is a good system for theatres without permanent companies, but it is difficult to maintain high standards with the same actors – asking them to play Shakespeare one run, and Noël Coward a fortnight later. It is sometimes argued that by swopping styles and periods, actors are kept alert and not bored. I rather doubt if this is so. It is a question of conviction. An actor who has just played Hamlet, really can't be expected to take the part of M. Bernard in *Boeing-Boeing* very seriously. His work perceptibly slackens, he relaxes and the production suffers. An actor must maintain a sense of purpose in his work, and sometimes this can be achieved not solely through the productions, but through his increasing sense of social responsibility – by visiting schools and universities, by playing one-night stands in pubs, by lecturing to Women's Institutes and so forth. Sometimes, then, the plays which he would be inclined to dismiss as trivial take on a social relevance. *The Winslow Boy* might well seem to an actor a very faded and outworn play, but if he becomes aware of the society around him in, say, a country town in the South, it might well carry more weight. Some directors believe that theatre-in-education programmes waste the energies of actors, and certainly it is hard to find time for one when playing fortnightly rep. My own opinion is that when actors become more aware of their audiences they usually become better actors. Regional drama – documentaries and so forth – has concentrated the attention on social problems in some reps recently.

Haute couture – another phrase stolen from the fashion world, because no theatre term exists – represents another view of the theatre and its role in the community – not socially orientated in the sense that productions are intended to comment on or reflect social problems, but designed instead to present the 'best' plays in the best possible setting. There are many who would argue that this is the only useful service which a theatre can offer the community – to remind the public that drama is an art form, and a high art form at that. These reps have to have fine facilities and a choice of excellent actors, able to star or to work with an acting team. Most major reps try to include at least one *haute-couture* production – a brilliant and 'authoritative' version of a classic play – in each season. The National theatres and Chichester are really attempting *haute-couture* productions the whole time – failing rather too often perhaps to reach the very high standards they set themselves. Failed *haute couture* not only leaves a sad feeling of futility among players and audiences alike – so much effort to so little effect – but it is also wasteful of resources. A director can rarely tackle more than two *major* productions a season, although he may be able to combine several experimental or less ambitious productions with one attempt at *haute couture*. At the Royal Shakespeare Theatre, Stratford, many excellent directors and actors have to wait for their turn to come – and smaller, less opulent and well-established companies glance enviously in their direction, watching an actor play spear-bearer who would star in their theatres. For this reason – to employ casts more fully and to prevent too great a concentration on authoritative productions – some major companies try to combine *haute couture* with elaborate arts-centre projects, theatre-in-education, touring companies and less-publicized productions of new, sometimes experimental, plays. The Royal Shakespeare Company has a Theatre-Go-Round project, a company touring schools, universities and arts centres. The National Theatre runs experimental seasons at the Jeannetta Cochrane Theatre in Holborn. The Meadow Players and Prospect Productions both tour. Five of the major reps attempt *haute couture*: two tour regularly, two intermittently and three consciously aim for regular transfers to the West End – say, two productions a year.

5. DIRECTORS

Young, untried	0
Troupers	1
Young, brilliant	2
Established, competent	3
Established, brilliant	4
Established, brilliant with *charisma*	5

Some would place this card with the *Chance* pack, arguing that artistic directors may come and go, but subsidies (one hopes) go on for ever. Certainly if a *young untried* took over from Warren Jenkins at the Belgrade, Coventry, the Arts Council grant would not automatically be cut, although they may well diplomatically oppose the choice. This is in accordance with one minor rule of the game, already mentioned, whereby aggregates are carried intact from round to round, except under unusual circumstances, such as the theatre closing down. It is also true to say that if an *established brilliant* took over a small, run-down rep, the Arts Council grant would not be automatically increased. There are theatres, however, where the basic facilities are very poor and only the presence of an inspirational director can keep them going, and equally there are theatres whose basic facilities are good but where the director is almost a liability. In the first case, the Arts Council would probably wait for a season or so to see whether the inspirational director was receiving a proper response from the neighbourhood: and in the second, the Arts Council grant would probably not be increased to meet the rise in the cost of living, until the director retired or was sacked.

Young untried directors, who count for nothing, have the comfort of knowing that one really good production will lift them into the third category, *young brilliant*. The difference between *troupers* and *established competent* may seem too subtle to merit a two-category separation: but *troupers* include those directors who stick unimaginatively to *assorted popular* programmes, whereas *established competent* can tackle the Shakespeares, Brechts and Chekhovs, when asked to do so, most of the material in a *prêt-à-porter* programme. The importance of *charisma* in the last category is that some directors can lure stars to work with them on ordinary rep salaries by their ability to generate an uncommon sense of excitement and purpose. John Neville at one time generated this intensity at Nottingham: Val May, Stuart Burge and Peter Dews – and perhaps Jonathan Miller – are also directors with *charisma*. It is, however, a quickly fading quality, rarely to be trusted. *Established brilliant* directors are usually reliable enough: one good transfer to the West End will produce an imitation of a *charisma*.

6 LOCATION

Small towns, low-density catchment areas, towns apathetic towards the theatre	0
Small towns, with tourists	1
Towns with universities, well-populated catchment areas	2
Well-populated catchment areas, with loyal theatre-going publics, within a hundred miles of London	3
Well-populated catchment areas, with loyal theatre-going publics, more than a hundred miles from London:	4
Meccas	5

When Miss Jennie Lee, as Minister for the Arts, was asked by Sir Geoffrey de Freitas what principles governed the giving of Arts Council grants to the repertory theatres in the East Midlands, the question implied that some areas of the country were favoured, others were not. Jennie Lee's answer did not perhaps retort with sufficient force to the implications, which are often expressed outside the House of Commons. I do not think that – with the possible exception of London – the Arts Council has *regional* preferences. The Arts Council, as we have said, is impressed by survival. Towns where the councils are generous towards the theatre, where the attendance figures at the box office are good and where there are other signs of private patronage – such as thriving theatre clubs and donations from different local sources – are always more likely to arouse interest and enthusiasm at the Arts Council. The Theatre Enquiry Report stresses the general inadequacy of local subsidies. 'It should be the prime responsibility of the Local Authority to provide and maintain a theatre at no charge whatever to the resident company.' Very few towns do this. At Nottingham, the theatre was built out of a fund established by the Council when gas was nationalized. However, the Company is repaying its debt to the tune of £27,000 per year. The local council offers as subsidy about £22,000 per year. Other theatres are in a similar situation – where rates, ground rents and repayment of initial loans far exceed the annual local subsidy. Some towns, such as Stratford, offer no subsidies at all – although the Royal Shakespeare Theatre must be a considerable economic asset to the town. A few councils, however, over-compensate. The Forum Theatre, Billingham, receives not only the building free from the Council, Teesside, but in 1969 a £60,000 subsidy as well. Some theatres, such as Chichester, Leatherhead and Guildford, have their supporters so well organized that public subsidies, either from local councils or the Arts Council, are not so urgently needed. Very generally, theatres which have large and densely populated catchment areas receive more than those with small or low-density catchment areas: but the nature of local enthusiasms and needs are taken into account. It is perhaps better to be in a medium-sized town with an appreciative public than in a larger town with an apathetic public: but there are too many exceptions for this to be a useful rule. The '69 Company in Manchester has a large subsidy, bearing in mind the short length of the season and the size of the University Theatre, which only seats

250–350. This is partly because Manchester is a large city without a major rep: the Library Theatre seats only 308, and the little Stables Theatre Club about 90. Manchester has the reputation of being a town financially quite generous to the Arts, but with small and apathetic audiences. The two major commercial theatres, the Opera House and the Palace, have both been in financial trouble in recent years. Clearly, the Arts Council and city council, not to mention the North West Arts Association, all feel that it is time for Manchester to have a really good permanent theatre company. The '69 Company has had several excellent transfers to the West End, has a powerful team – led by Michael Elliott and based on his '59 Company which ran an artistically successful, but financially disastrous, season at the Lyric Theatre, Hammersmith – and there are plans to house the '69 Company in a new theatre, seating 850. Hence, there is greater Arts Council generosity, although the City Council has yet to offer a subsidy. Manchester also has a university, which pays a certain amount to the '69 Company, owns the theatre and runs it. The close links between universities and theatres have become particularly important recently – not only in Manchester, Oxford or Cambridge – but in Sussex, Exeter, Kent, Southampton, Dundee and elsewhere.

It has been a general policy of the Arts Council to encourage the general growth of regional drama, not simply in the Midlands, but elsewhere. If the area is already well stocked with theatres – or within easy reach of the West End – then the encouragement may seem less needed. I have chosen a radius of a hundred miles as the rough dividing line, stopping just before Birmingham and Bristol: six major reps are outside this radius, and three within it, Chichester, Cambridge and Oxford. Chichester is, I would have thought, a *Mecca* theatre, defined not as a ballroom, but as a theatre attracting an international public. Nottingham may be another and the Royal Shakespeare Theatre certainly is. Malvern is definitely a *Mecca manqué*.

This is, I must stress, only a game – and a hypothetical game at that. I have never bugged an Arts Council Committee room to discover whether these really are the criteria governing the award of grants. The root problem is that in a mixed economy we are moving away from one form of patronage to another. In one sense, this change brings many benefits. Private patronage – either through the box office or through rich angels – is often very philistine, not because theatre-goers are a dull and stupid lot, but because they are simply not aware of alternatives. Public patronage is usually more enlightened, because those who administer Arts Council funds in this country are 'professionals' – they are generally alert to the theatre as an art form. Unfortunately, state subsidies are bedevilled by other uncertainties. To what extent is it possible to indulge personal preferences with public money? There are no absolute standards in the theatre against which subsidies can be gauged. As a private citizen, I may vastly prefer, say, the theatre at Watford to the one at Northampton – or, a more extreme contrast, the performances at the old Arts Laboratory in Drury Lane to those at the Theatre Royal, York: but if I were in a position to administer Arts Council funds would I be entitled to back up my opinion by offering a large subsidy to one, ignoring or belittling the other? I would say, 'Yes'. Eventually, I believe, state patronage has to work like private patronage, in that Arts Council administrators have to buy what they like, to encourage what they believe in: but I can well understand the caution of those who wish to pretend that state subsidies are above such subjective judgements. The Arts Council is the only patron in history which tries not to express preferences – which masks perfectly honourable and sensible tastes in some mock institutional formula. And it has to do so because at present the whole concept of state patronage is too new, too unfamiliar and indeed revolutionary, for us to relax into fruitful squabbles about tastes and values. The system of grants has to seem impartial and fair, above human fallibilities. In practice, this also means that the *status quo* is preferred, even when it seems to be in decline – and the new enthusiasms are regarded with an affectionate tolerance, which is rarely sublimated into positive support. The accepted canons of taste are adopted, are made sometimes to seem above criticism and beyond attack. The Arts Council has not yet become a reactionary institution – partly because of its valuable uncertainty about its own role – but it could so easily become one. The influence of the Arts Council is also partly offset by other forms of financing – box-office, private and local subsidies. There is, as we shall see, a patchwork quilt of theatre finance, lying crumpled and dishevelled across the country.

Even if, therefore, the criteria which I have suggested in the game are those adopted by the Arts Council the game would still be a game – it would be an attempt to impose a fictitious logic and order on various instincts, preferences and needs, and then to pretend that this system has some external validity. According to the suits and scoring envisaged above, the hands held by the nine major reps might rank as follows:

	Runs	Buildings	Company	Programme	Director	Location	Total
Birmingham Rep	5	2 (1969) 5 (1971)	4	3–4	5	4	23/4 (1969) 26/7 (1971)
Bristol Old Vic	3	3	4	3–4	5	4	22/3
Chichester Festival Theatre	5	4	5	4	5	5	28
Belgrade Theatre, Coventry	2	4	4	3	4	4	21
Liverpool Playhouse	2	3/4	3	3	3	4	18/19
Nottingham Playhouse	5	4	5	5	5	4/5	28/9
Oxford Playhouse (Meadow Players)	5	2	1	4	5	3	20
Prospect Productions	5	0	5	4	5	3	22
Sheffield Playhouse	5	3 (1969) 5 (1971)	4	3	4	4	23 (1969) 25 (1971)
Royal Shakespeare Company at Stratford (A National Theatre)	5	3	5	5	5	5	28

According to this assessment, the Liverpool Playhouse is lucky to be ranked as a major rep: its history and proud badge as the oldest rep in the country without awkward gaps in its tradition may tell in its favour. The Nottingham Playhouse and the Chichester Festival Theatre, on the other hand, may be unlucky not to be considered as National Theatres. The Nottingham Playhouse was, however, the first regional repertory theatre to be invited to play at the National Theatre in London, while the Chichester Festival Theatre housed the National Theatre Company from 1963–5. The ranking also underrates certain factors – the facilities of Prospect Productions cannot really be ranked under the *Buildings* suit, for their skill lies in touring.

If we compare these hands with those held by some companies

in less-favoured categories, the difference is marked. The size of the 1968/9 Arts Council subsidies are indicated:

	Runs	Buildings	Company	Programme	Director	Location	Total
Octagon Theatre, Bolton (£23,487)	2	4	2–3	3	2	4	17–18
Marlowe Theatre, Canterbury (£16,250)	1	2	3	1	3	2	12
Everyman, Cheltenham (£24,200)	1	2	3	1	3	1	11
Colchester Rep (£19,712)	2	2	1	1	3	2	11
Northcott Theatre, Exeter (£32,775)	3	4	3	3	2	2	17
Yvonne Arnaud Theatre, Guildford (£23,300)	2	4	1	1	4	3	15
Harrogate Theatre (£15,037)	1	2	2	2	3	2	12
Arts Theatre, Ipswich (£24,900)	2	2	2–3	3	2	3	14–15
Thorndike Theatre, Leatherhead (£19,913)	2	1 (1969) 4 (1969)	1–2	2	3	3	12–13 16–17
Phoenix Theatre, Leicester (£26,204)	2	4	3	2	3	2	16
Theatre Royal, Lincoln (£36,237)	1	2	2	3	4	4	16
Liverpool Everyman (£20,833)	2	0	2	3	4	4	15
Playhouse, Newcastle (£16,525)	2	1 (1969) 4 (1970)	2	3	3	2	13 (1969) 16 (1970)
Theatre Royal, Northampton (£18,750)	1	2–3	2–3	2	1	3	11–13
Playhouse, Salisbury (£23,395)	1	2	3	2	3	3	14
Victoria Theatre, Stoke-on-Trent (£24,395)	5	0	2	3	4	2	16
Civic Theatre, Watford (£14,638)	1	2	3	3	2	2	13
Theatre Royal, York	2?	2	2?	1–2	1	4	12–13

The question-marks against the scoring of the Theatre Royal, York, reflect my own bewilderment. Programmes didn't seem to be planned by the season, rather by the month. The theatre manager told me that there was no permanent company: the artistic director, Donald Bodley, that there was. The programmes seemed very mixed – ranging from *Stop It, Nurse* by Sam Cree to a rare production of Pirandello's late play, *When One Is Somebody* – from *assorted popular* nearly to *haute couture*. This example illustrates the difficulty of any precise grading. Different theatres define the terms in different ways. To one director, a theatre-in-education programme may simply mean that someone visits a school once a month to give a lecture on lighting. Or it can mean an elaborate dovetailing of community problems with improvisation sessions at schools and repertory programmes. This partly accounts for the variations in the grants given: that Lincoln, for example, with the same grading as the Phoenix Theatre, Leicester, should be given over £10,000 more. My assessments of the hands were originally made without reference to the actual Arts Council grants and it is interesting to see that the totals all fall within the 10–20 range, and that the grants vary from £14,638 to £36,237, loosely within the second category, defined by the Arts Council as the £20,000 group. There is a third £10,000 category: but if we move now to those theatres which did not receive Arts Council grants in the year 1968/9, there is again a marked difference in the scoring:

	Runs	Buildings	Company	Programme	Director	Location	Total
Civic Theatre, Ayr	0	1	1	0–1	1	1	4–5
Civic Theatre, Colwyn Bay	0	1	1	0–1	1	1	4–5
Civic Theatre, Darlington	1	2	0	0	0–1	0	3–4
Devonshire Park, Eastbourne	0	3	3–4	0–1	3	2	11–13
Theatre Royal, Windsor	0–1	2	1	1	1	3	8–9
Grand, Wolverhampton	0	0	0–1	0–1	1	0	1–3

The Eastbourne Repertory Theatre Company (playing at the Devonshire Park Theatre) and the Theatre Royal Company at Windsor are two of the rare commercial repertory companies, are therefore not registered as non-profit-distributing charities and not entitled to receive grants.

It is difficult for a theatre in a lower category to move into a higher. The most dramatic changes usually occur when a new theatre is built. The least dramatic – but most profitable perhaps – comes when there is a slow but steady improvement in attendance figures, which may well lead to the demand for a new theatre. At Colchester, for example, where the attendance figures have improved from 35 per cent in 1964 to 62 per cent in 1969 – due largely to the consistently admirable standards of production – there are plans for a new theatre and arts centre. Sometimes too, a player can pick up a favourable Chance Card – such as *University to be Built in Your Area* or *Council Changes Hands: More Money to be Spent on the Arts*. Having established a tradition of weekly rep, however, and found a small though constant audience, it is hard for a director to break with the past. A *young brilliant* can sometimes do so, although the task may wear him to the ground. The scores do not *necessarily* reflect the worth of a theatre. It is quite possible for a trouper staging a popular play to achieve a dramatic tension and interest which is really rather better than a failed, and possibly boring attempt at *haute couture*. Hence, there is an element of unfairness in the game, which is fortunately offset by some limited cheating. A theatre may pose as an arts centre simply by hanging some decadent water colours in the foyer, or by inviting a disc jockey to compère some folk music.

4

Drought and Irrigation

In the late fifties, the Profession cast Sir Jasper without difficulty: television, of course, the great snatcher of birthrights. The very jargon would twirl a moustache: TAM ratings, calculating audience reaction apparently in terms of the *mego-viewer*: 'a licence to print money'. This was not the first challenge to the living theatre by mass media, of course. In 1956, the Arts Council reported that 'with astonishing rapidity [sound] broadcasting is assuming the rôle of Universal Diffusor'. 'It would be no paradox to say that the man or woman with a relish for Shakespeare is more liable to have that appetite satisfied by a BBC production in the sightless theatre of the air than in a production by one of those eccentric men of the theatre who put the novelty of presentation before the delivery of Shakespeare's lines.' To a society conditioned by Sir Barry Jackson and others to think of good theatre in terms of fine poetry impeccably spoken, sound radio was the obvious answer. Fourteen years and many Peter Brook productions later, that phrase, 'the delivery of Shakespeare's lines', has in itself an eccentric ring. They must have been mad. Television effortlessly absorbed not only the 'better' plays but the bad ones as well, whose banality might have been exposed on the Third Programme. Who would want to go to see a 'tea-and-sympathy' play at the local rep, when they could sit at home and watch *Dixon of Dock Green* or – for that matter – *Tonight*? In the late fifties, the grey squirrels of broadcasting seemed certain eventually to oust the red: and the Arts Council was reduced to arguing a feeble case for the live theatre – that it provided good training for actors who would eventually be absorbed into television. In 1957, the last of three theatres in Leicester closed, and the Arts Council Annual Report made gloomy reading – 'the casualty rate is an alarming symptom of a malady which threatens to extinguish the provincial theatre'. The Annual Report for the following year was equally depressing: 'steadily and ominously throughout the year, more theatres have been closing their doors'.

These fears were not exaggerated, but, looking back at this time from the peaks of 1970, I am inclined to cast television, not as Sir Jasper, but as Lindquist in Strindberg's *Easter*, a threatening presence who scoured and purified the Heyst household before turning benevolent in the last Act. The temporary boom in English theatre after the war concealed weakness which became more apparent as austerity receded and television advanced. The actual buildings were old-fashioned – and usually inefficient and uncomfortable as well. Steeply rising costs were not offset by new forms of patronage: the total grant from the Government to the Arts Council, to cover opera, ballet, concerts and art exhibitions as well as the theatre, was no more than £250,000. The days of the private patron – the un-commercial 'angel' – were clearly numbered. Worse still, perhaps, the stock plays of the thirties seemed quite out of touch. The flippant farces with maids and butlers, the 'problem' plays about curable accents and bad manners, all the drama of sweet do-gooding and golden hearts seemed – and were – irrelevant in a world of cold wars and atom bombs. The disparity between our culture and the realities which we were always being forced to face was unavoidably marked. One could not begin to describe the other. Our most esteemed dramatist after the war was perhaps Christopher Fry – and Shaw, of course: names which could give comfort to nobody. Even in 1969 I saw Elizabeth Addyman's play *The Secret Tent* set 'in the present', in which the headmistress of an approved school stated, 'Ours is a special sort of school. Girls who are willing to work get a chance of something rather better than *domestic service*' – a line which caused no embarrassment at the Leas Pavilion, Folkestone, but would have done elsewhere. Confronted by plays like these, who could take the theatre seriously? The generation gap in the theatre became a vast abyss – harder to bridge than the gulf between income and expenditure.

New plays are always risky to stage, arriving with no banners from the past, unfamiliar and untried: but plays which are new in the sense that they seek fresh audiences and reflect modern dilemmas, in a culture accustomed to exclude them, require singular dedication and resources even to attempt. Theatre managers are not averse to change, but they have to be careful. Even Arthur Brough, at the Leas Pavilion, a likeable trouper, as upright and portly as any bank manager and with a smile quite as sweet, once tried out *A Taste of Honey* and *Roots* in the same season, 1961. As he left the theatre one evening, an elderly woman barred his way, trembling with indignation. 'Oh Mr Brough,' she said, 'why must you put on all these *terrible* plays? Don't you know that in Folkestone we're not used to this sort of thing?' Mr Brough raised his hat, 'And what will I do, madam, when you're dead?' The problem was – and is – that those who rejected the theatre in contempt wouldn't be lured back on the strength of one *progressive* production, but those old regulars who had visited the theatre for years might well feel not only shocked but betrayed. Without new plays, without change, the theatre was clearly going to die – but slowly. The way to kill it quickly, however, was to stage plays which were modern in outlook, without those resources to cover the time before all the modern people in the town realized that they had friends at the local rep. Sometimes a quick break with the past, an accident, a new management with a *charisma* from somewhere, covered this change smoothly. In Dundee, for example, the old theatre burnt down in 1953. The company had to move to a disused church hall, further from the city centre and nearer the University. The casual atmosphere, the efforts to make the new place work, the sense of starting afresh attracted the students, who in turn demanded a more ambitious play-policy. What happened to the old audiences? 'We killed them off,' Donald Sartain, the administrator, told me rather proudly – adding to take the cruelty away, 'Well, it was a little far for them to come.'

The emergence of television was the ham-fisted disguise which concealed many blessings. To begin with, the public became more sophisticated, more aware of alternatives. David Forder, the manager at Colchester Rep, pointed out to me that more people were coming to his theatre but less often: theatre-going was still a habit, but his audiences had become more selective in their choice of plays. His experience mirrored that of many other managers: and he rightly saw this change as an improvement. Television also absorbed chewing-gum drama, thus forcing the theatre to attempt, where possible, the more exciting. It also helped to create a new generation of 'stars', whose presence at the local rep would automatically guarantee an audience. The reps near London in particular benefited from this quick recognition of actors and casts.

Above all, however, it forced managers to realize that the theatre could drift no longer. No longer could a rep director pretend that next season would be better than the last – with a few more comedies, another leading actress, a slight *adjustment* to the seat prices. Throughout the country, theatres were closing. His might well be the next. In this situation, many directors either left the theatre altogether, or hung on, trying to discover escape routes into the B.B.C. A few fought on more determinedly, arguing that *particularly* in an age of mass media the living theatre was needed to humanize the social changes which were taking place, to bring drama more closely into contact with the lives people led, to link the neighbour- hood with the superstate. Some deep-set democratic instincts rose up to challenge the idea that the language of drama should be handed over to the men in the B.B.C. and I.T.V. who would use it for the good of us all.

To survive at all, the theatre had to offer what television could not, and therefore those plays which could easily transfer to tele- vision, which did not require the physical presence of an audience, fell into disfavour. They were still performed – and are – but many directors regarded them as routine, looking elsewhere for inspira- tion. The emphasis shifted. In the thirties, 'good' plays were those which had some 'perennial' quality, which had survived intact from society to society, from generation to generation. In the early sixties, however, plays which commented directly on social and political issues were also admired: in San Francisco, Jules Irving and Herbert Blau staged Arthur Miller's *The Crucible* at a time when Senator McCarthy was holding the televised trials of the supposed Com- munists in the State Department. This was a much-quoted example. In England, Joan Littlewood's company at the Theatre Royal, Stratford, and the Royal Court Company were both singularly alert to social change. This emphasis on the topical, on the immediate social problem, which did not exclude the wider significance but did not turn to the universal as its justification, characterized in a way the drama of the late fifties and early sixties: John Whiting was a victim of this change of fashion, which also led, in regional theatre, to the development of local documentaries. The key word in this mood was 'intimacy' – or perhaps 'involvement'. Audiences had to be 'involved'. Stages were thrust deep into the auditorium so that actors could *contact*. The concept of theatre changed, outside the building as well as in. The theatre had to play a new role in the community. Dramatists who had advocated new audience–actor relationships sidled into favour – Brecht, Artaud, and later, Grotowski and Julian Bec. Of these, perhaps only Brecht had a direct influence on repertory theatres, but they all contributed to a climate of opinion. Stephen Joseph, who pioneered theatre-in-the-round lovingly in the fifties, won more admirers, since in a way he reminded directors that drama could take place, if necessary, under the most austere conditions, in any square room with some lighting. Those who rejected such spartan surroundings looked firstly for new forms of patronage – no longer the single 'angel' such as Sir Barry Jackson, but the state and local councils – and secondly for cheaper ways of achieving necessary effects. The well-established theatres tried to develop their programmes along more ambitious lines.

The desperation in the profession, caused when the challenge of television met a lack-lustre theatre, resulted in a re-examination of the whole question of live drama. From this turmoil, 'the pile-driving operations' began, as the Arts Council later called them, 'on which a brighter prospect for tomorrow's theatre may . . . be confidently founded'.

It was, however, a long Dunkirk, a time when actors and directors muttered Arthur Hugh Clough to themselves while scanning the columns of *Stage*. But during these months, when the labour and the wounds seemed most vain, there were some signs of comfort and a few of hope. The comfort proved more illusory. Generally, the theatres in the South of England withstood the challenge of television better than those in the North. Some even seemed to be flourishing: the Theatre Royal, Windsor, the little theatre club at Leatherhead. Several factors were involved. The population in the South was wealthier: the habit of theatre-going was more deeply engrained. The reps around London did not have to carry permanent companies. West End managements, finding that provincial tours lost money, started to try out productions nearer to hand – at Windsor, Brighton or Canterbury. *Grab Me a Gondola*, the musical about films and film festivals, transferred to the West End from the Theatre Royal, Windsor, and became a medium 'smash hit'. Some coastal reps in the South also did well – the family companies at Bexhill and Folkestone. Here again local conditions were favourable. Businessmen retiring from combat and soldiers just retiring, tourists and widows, wanted some equivalent to the London theatre which they could no longer afford to visit. These theatres changed less under the impact of television, because they did not need to change. In 1967, I saw an appalling comedy, *Scotch on the Rocks*, at the

Theatre Royal, Windsor, and the house was full at a Thursday matinée.

These were the comforting reps, and some inferred from their example that the impact of television was superficial, that the craze would pass. Even the idea of subsidies was dismissed. John Counsell at Windsor is proud of the fact that his theatre has no grant. The new theatre at Guildford was built largely through the support of private patrons: £361,000 was the cost of the theatre, and seventy per cent of this money came from individual donations. The reps at Bexhill and Eastbourne have no grants, and only recently has Folkestone supported the Leas Pavilion. Even at Chichester, where the new National Theatre began, Robert Selbie, the production manager, while acknowledging the help of the Arts Council, insisted that in his opinion the theatre should be self-supporting. This, he claimed, was also the opinion of Sir John Clements. Because these theatres could rely on traditional audiences, they were not forced to seek out new ones. They experimented cautiously if at all.

Hence, the theatres which initially survived the impact of television without wavering were also those which failed to benefit from the subsequent revival of regional drama. The programmes at Windsor have changed little over the years. The sweet comfort turned somewhat sour in the sixties. The reps at Guildford, Leatherhead and later at Chichester managed to adjust successfully – with the aid of grants. But others – at Wimbledon, Richmond, Windsor and Folkestone – declined, in reputation, if not at the box office.

In the late fifties and early sixties, however, the signs of hope were not those of comfort. Dawn was not simply a question of surviving the night. In London, there emerged some forceful leadership – from two main sources, the Royal Court and the Theatre Royal, Stratford. During the thirties, Joan Littlewood had struggled vainly in Manchester to establish a 'committed' theatre, somewhat along the lines of Piscator, Brecht and the politically motivated drama in Germany. *Committed* is a harsh word, calling to mind mere propaganda and perhaps those anguished discussions about freedom, bad faith and defining oneself in action – post-war Existentialism in Paris, Colin Wilson here. Joan Littlewood's Theatre Workshop was firmly left-wing, with many predictable arguments and outlooks, but it was also lively, exciting and dedicated. In 1953, she took over the Theatre Royal in Stratford, East London, and gathered together a

devoted band of actors and writers, who worked together for subsistence wages. As a director, she had exceptional gifts – for creating
on stage miniature portraits of towns and societies, for expressing
social problems in human terms. Her actors – Barbara Ferris, Roy
Kinnear, Victor Spinetti, Stephen Lewis and many others – seemed
under her guidance extraordinarily responsive, particularly in projecting relationships. When, say, Barbara Ferris in *Sparrers Can't
Sing* (written by Stephen Lewis, a Workshop member) came on
stage, we knew at once that she was the daughter of so-and-so, the
girl friend of another, the sister, the granddaughter, the rival and
the tart. The productions may sometimes have seemed untidy, the
diction poor, the scripts in need of cutting: but they had a quality
about them which emanated from the group – of warmth, intelligence
and social concern, and also of a growing liveliness and assurance.
The cast could improvise without seeming lost or self-conscious.
Writers – Shelagh Delaney, Frank Norman, Alun Owen and others
– could work with her, fully aware that she would change their
scripts. Charles Chilton, who wrote *Oh What a Lovely War!*, told
me that when he thought he had finished the play Joan Littlewood
demanded more and more material: and when the rehearsals were
running close to opening night she suddenly decided to set the
whole script within a Pierrot Concert Party. From Joan Littlewood,
this kind of behaviour was acceptable: even endearing, in a
traumatic way.

Her ferocious determination was of the utmost importance at a
time when experiment was rare and leadership rarer still. The
repercussions of her work at Stratford are still to be felt, not indirectly through the Climate of Opinion, but directly through those
reps such as the Octagon Theatre, Bolton, and the Theatre Royal,
Lincoln, who consciously strive to imitate her example. The
brochure of the Octagon Theatre states that 'we are intending to
appoint a playwright and a musical director so that we can create
our own plays in much the same way as Joan Littlewood was doing
at Stratford East during the 1950s'. Other reps, less open in their
acknowledgement, also tried to secure that fruitful balance of actors,
writers, designers, musicians and directors, whose work was not
confined to mere imitation of West End hits, but who could attempt
original works, organized and inspired from within the group and
related to local issues and outlooks: Peter Cheeseman's company at
Stoke-on-Trent, the Sheffield Playhouse, the Newcastle Playhouse.

There was another beacon in the late 1950s. The Royal Court Theatre in Sloane Square, which in 1904 was the home of the Barker–Vedrenne management and the scene for one revival of British theatre, became in 1956 the home of the English Stage Company, under the directorship of the late George Devine. The English Stage Company stated their aims plainly: to encourage new writers, to try out new plays. They were, quite simply, successful. The dramatists they encouraged included John Osborne, Arnold Wesker, Edward Bond, Nigel Dennis and N. F. Simpson: they sponsored the revival of D. H. Lawrence's plays. The plays they discovered and first produced now fill our repertory programmes – and sometimes transferred under commercial managements to the West End. The Arts Council gave firm financial support to the Royal Court – in spite of many controversies – and their decision to do so was admirably far-sighted and well rewarded.

The two very different companies not only discovered the plays and the productions to offset the rather sterile 'stock' drama which threatened to swamp the repertory theatre with amiable irrelevance, but also spurred by their examples repertory managements to greater adventure. These two 'acts of faith', as they were later called, seemed in the fifties gestures of desperation: and so they would have been had there not been as well an attempt to reorganize the theatre – to discover new forms of patronage. Without the Arts Council, the English Stage Company could not have survived: but the Arts Council could not afford to support many English Stage Companies. Joan Littlewood was always being harassed not only by lack of money, but by the fact that the actors and writers whom she had discovered would be all too quickly lured away, to films, the West End, television and Broadway. The stable development of theatre companies throughout the country, still perhaps a hope for the future, was in the fifties an almost impossible dream. George Devine and Joan Littlewood, however, encouraged a sense of creative purpose in the theatre: and, with this stimulation, the long overdue reorganization of the theatre began to follow – not because a few thought it desirable, but because gradually it seemed to be needed.

Another decision in 1956 was of great practical and symbolic importance. The Corporation of Coventry announced that it would build a new theatre as part of the civic redevelopment scheme.

Coventry, gutted by fire and bombing during the war, was now the scene of an exemplary programme of urban renewal. This was where our hopes found brick. Here, we planned a cathedral, a traffic-free shopping-area, comprehensive schools, social centres – and a theatre. No new theatre had been built in Britain for twenty years. It was called the Belgrade – because Belgrade had sent a gift of wood to build the theatre at a time when wood in England was in short supply – and it opened in 1958. The name invoked a new era of international co-operation. The venture itself foreshadowed an age of municipal patronage of the arts. Today we may have doubts. The cathedral seems good only in parts, a rather uninspired collection of pleasant ideas. The concrete shops are stained. And the theatre is, according to Warren Jenkins, really a commercial one in disguise: if the box-office figures show a fall in attendance, then Warren Jenkins will schedule an Agatha Christie or a sex farce. Such qualms during the fifties would have seemed unpatriotic. Coventry would set an example to Britain: and so it did. Within six years, two new theatres were built near by, at Leicester and Nottingham, and several others were planned. In 1964, the Arts Council paid tribute to Coventry in its booklet *Policy into Practice*, and wrote a brightly encouraging chapter on provincial theatre: 'we haven't got a corpse on our hands any longer'.

Without the example at Coventry, without the leadership of George Devine and Joan Littlewood, this optimism would have had little tinder to burn with. Gradually, however, more branches were thrown on the fire. The Entertainments Tax was abolished on the living theatre. In 1958, Independent Television set up a central fund for Grants to Arts and Sciences, a gesture perhaps of enlightened self-interest, for as Warren Jenkins pointed out ten years later 'if you milk the provinces constantly, as they have been doing . . . you are not going to get any actors, because they never have the chance to learn'. This fund, whatever the motive, gave as direct aid a quarter of a million pounds to the theatre over the next six years, established a Chair of Drama at Bristol University, and offered a number of bursaries to young directors, so that they could study and work in repertory theatres. The Bridges Report, *Help for the Arts*, was published and influenced the Calouste Gulbenkian Foundation which gave £105,500 to the theatre from 1959 to 1964. The Arts Council set up an enquiry which resulted in the report, *Housing the Arts*, and gave a clear account of the inadequacy and dilapidation of theatres around Britain. No action, of course, was taken for three years, but in 1964 the Treasury set aside a quarter of a million pounds for a Capital Grants Fund, which was used for the renovation of old theatres and the building of new ones.

These sums, encouraging though they were, fell far short of the amount needed. In themselves, they would have been useless: or rather, they would only have subsidized a few productions, leaving the basic organization of the theatre untouched. Today £100,000 would probably only finance one West End musical, two or three straight plays. A commercial management in London would hope to recapture this money and make a profit. As basic investment money in the provincial theatre, however, with no immediate returns to be expected, the sums were clearly insufficient. But they were encouraging: they reflected a certain readiness to assist the theatre. And since the war skeletal systems of public patronage had been established which needed such encouragement to grow fatter. At first, the idea of public patronage was fiercely debated, and when this row subsided – partly because the sums involved were trivial – there was still considerable uncertainty – on national and local levels – as to the sort of grants which would be politically tolerable.

The Arts Council was established by Royal Charter in 1946, but by 1952 only a few repertory theatres received any grants at all. The most any theatre could expect was £500. In 1948, the Local Government Act was passed which allowed councils to spend up to the equivalent of a 6d rate on the Arts. Predictably, at first few councils wanted to patronize the Arts at all. Then some of them did so for the wrong reasons. Tourist towns sometimes felt that reps were an added attraction and were prepared to sponsor them under the auspices of the Entertainments Committee, which was in the hands of the Town Clerk and Borough Treasurer. In 1951, for example, Ayr Council took over a chapel outside the town centre, converted it into a pleasant theatre though with a small and inadequate stage, and leased it out to different rep companies, which did not at first receive any grants. Victor Graham's Company has been playing there for the past five years – weekly rep, no new plays, and a cast of eight including the stage manager. These were purely commercial ventures. Direct grants were rarely given. The usual system was that the rep company and the Council would split the box-office proceeds. The rep was relieved of the burden of theatre maintenance – rents, front-of-house staff, and so forth. The town

had another amenity to add to the list – and possibly some income
as well. The social and artistic value of the theatre was irrelevant.
If it made money, all was well. If it didn't – and wasn't much of a
tourist attraction either – the Entertainments Committee would
either sack the company or close the theatre down.

Other councils, however, were more enlightened. Before 1956,
Canterbury had committed itself to as much as a 4d rate to establish
the Marlowe Theatre, which became almost a regional theatre for
East Kent. The old Theatre Royal in Canterbury closed in 1926:
but in 1951 Peter Carpenter, the present General Manager, and
Christopher Hassall, the poet, persuaded the council to convert an
old cinema into a theatre – and then to underwrite any reasonable
losses on productions. Canterbury has a population of only 30,000.
It was a big undertaking for a small rural city, which had at the time
no university. But Canterbury is, of course, an exceptional place:
it has an identity, a history – which sometimes seems to be too
lovingly paraded – a certain pride. Towns with a sense of their own
dignity, with reputations to maintain, were more eager than others
to hang a genuine local theatre on their parlour walls: Salisbury and
Perth, St Andrews and Bristol, Oxford and York, Birmingham and
its neighbouring towns in the Midlands, Coventry, Nottingham and
Derby. I have asked somewhat rhetorically why Bolton should be
able to build a theatre – and to raise nearly £100,000 for it in six
months – while the rep at Southport near by was slowly dying and
Preston had no rep. The answer lies partly in the feel of the place –
the dignified town hall, the fountains and central shopping-square,
free from traffic, the sweep of stately civic buildings near the theatre
in Howell Croft South: clearly a town which looks after itself.
Manchester, it has been said, will give money to the Arts sometimes,
but won't participate: the Council has sponsored the Library
Theatre since 1952, but the attendance figures there are a little
disappointing for a city the size of Manchester. Liverpool, on the
other hand, will participate, but won't give money. Bolton obviously
has money, is prepared to spend it on the theatre and wants to
enjoy what it pays for.

Some of these collaborations between towns and their reps were
far-sighted, enlightened and practical – involving many aspects of
life, the Education and the Entertainments Committees, the universities and churches, social welfare, industry and the trade unions.
Rolls-Royce helped the Derby Playhouse: Charles Vance's old

company at Chelmsford visited Marconi's factory. At Billingham on Teesside, an area made rich by I.C.I., a new town centre has been built, which includes the Forum, a fun palace, where there are squash courts, an ice-skating rink, indoor tennis courts, a public gymnasium, swimming-pools, badminton, indoor cricket, a concert hall and a theatre, seating over 600. The stage and backstage facilities are first-class, and the auditorium is piled high with family boxes. The grant from the local council to the theatre in 1969 was lavish, £60,000, which encouraged the former director, George Roman, to try out a full-scale opera, *Don Pasquale*, in fortnightly rep – a very ambitious proposition.

Sometimes, indeed, councils became too enthusiastic, snatching up lofty plans, which were hardly likely to work – projecting, say, a 1500 seat theatre in a town of 35,000 inhabitants and brushing all criticism aside by pointing to the success of Stratford, Pitlochry and Chichester. To balance this misplaced *joie de vivre*, there were also depressing instances of philistinism, where thriving theatres were crippled or killed off to save a rate burden of perhaps £5000. This mixture of elation and defeatism was to be expected perhaps in the late fifties and early sixties, while councils were still learning how to patronize successfully. It is sad to find such immaturity still lounging around town halls.

A worse general problem, though, was the caution, itself the result of many uncertainties – would the public react badly to another burden on the rates, would political opponents make capital out of an unwise subsidy, did the theatre have any real value for the town and what was this value? Stratford, for example, gave no money at all to the Royal Shakespeare Company, not even to the theatre-in-education programme. Coventry and Nottingham, having helped to build the new theatres, then imposed repayment terms on the company which proved on occasions an almost crippling burden. Some councils in the fifties, taking over their theatres, tried out disastrously mixed programmes – a spell of rep, a few weeks of amateur productions, some touring companies, variety and panto-mime – designed apparently to please everybody, offend none, and, above all, to lose no money. This pattern still exists in some places – Darlington – and invariably achieves the worst of all worlds. The public starts to confuse amateur with professional productions, damning a rep for an amateur production of *Oklahoma*, expecting the amateurs to reach professional standards. A decent rep company has no chance to become established, but equally the town can't benefit from leading touring companies. Sometimes, too, obvious social opportunities seem to be ignored. At Ayr, for example, a seaside resort on the west coast of Scotland, the audiences for Victor Graham's Company are large and fairly loyal, but when I was there they didn't seem to include many tourists. The coffee bar in the interval was like a friendly club. During the autumn and winter, the rep closes down, together with all the other amenities in the town – the amusement park, the skating-rink, the variety show, the dance hall. A spell of pantomime, and that's all. Where can the residents go, if they want a night out? Only to Glasgow, fifty miles away. There is a similar situation in Folkestone, where the Leas Pavilion closes during the autumn and winter, although the bulk of the audiences seem to come from the residents. Arthur Brough told me that the theatre used to run throughout the year, but it started losing money in the winter and he couldn't afford to keep it open. Perhaps some slackening of attendances during the winter were to be expected: but a marked decline may be due to other factors. There are no theatre-in-education programmes at Ayr or Folkestone: the audiences seem to be elderly, disinclined to risk damp weather and wet leaves on the pavement: there seems to be little attempt to widen the social scope and range of the theatres. There seems to be a case for more vigorous council action to maintain these theatres during the winter – if only to prevent the season from becoming a long dreary Sunday.

For these reasons, some have argued that the 1948 Local Government Act, which was intended to encourage the growth of local patronage for the arts, was a mitigated disaster: mitigated because extra money was diverted into the theatre, though never a sixpenny rate, and some interesting local collaborations developed – but a disaster because it may have delayed the growth of an efficient and better-informed system of National Subsidies, left the reps prey to the vagaries of local politics and forced the reps to become parochially minded. In the fifties, municipal patronage was often too erratic and amateur either to use its own funds effectively or to meet the chronic instability in the theatre, particularly after the arrival of commercial television. The Arts Council gradually took more responsibility as it grew in size and scope.

The growth of local patronage, however, is of great importance and ranks with the development of the Arts Council itself. In 1956, the Arts Council and local authorities together only subsidized the arts to the tune of £1,000,000 – a figure which seemed unduly slender, not only in comparison with plumper subsidies abroad, particularly in Switzerland, Germany and Austria, but also with the amounts spent here in other directions (£13,300,000 on libraries and £3,000,000 on museums and art galleries). By 1970, however, over ten times this amount was being spent on 109 arts projects, mainly new theatres and arts centres. The Arts Council was contributing £2,250,000, and local authorities and private sources were giving about £8,250,000. These figures represent a dramatic, almost revolutionary, change in attitude and enthusiasm on the part of local authorities.

Nor am I convinced by the argument that the 1948 Local Government Act delayed the growth of the Arts Council. The original idea was to encourage local and voluntary patronage, supplemented on rare occasions from Arts Council funds. This was a sensible policy at a time when the whole idea of public patronage for the Arts was opposed from many quarters, was even regarded as subversively left-wing. A regional demand had to be proved before national action could be taken. It is said that the Arts Council is now always more inclined to help a town which is also prepared to help itself. This is so, I think, and for some good historical reasons. After the war, the Arts Council had to specify exactly what projects it wanted to help, *before* money could be given from the Treasury. It was only after these projects had been established that the Arts Council could plead on their behalf. And, therefore, far from *delaying* the growth of national patronage, the increasing interest and concern shown by local authorities accelerated it.

Nor have I found many examples of *artistic* arrogance among those councils supporting local reps, amateurs meddling and nagging at the work of professionals. Few rep directors complained that a council-dominated board has interfered with their choice of programme, except perhaps to veto a production on grounds of cost. There are some Mary Whitehouses around, but most boards take to heart the advice of the Arts Council that once an Artistic Director has been appointed to take charge of a theatre he should be left free to instigate his own programmes and productions, subject only to budgetary control. The more common problem is that a council may be amiably disposed towards the local rep but is uncertain as to its own role: it is a little deflating for a councillor interested in a theatre to have no say whatever in the programmes of that theatre, except perhaps in the appointment of an artistic director; at the same time, he realizes that directly to interfere would be tactless and ill-advised. For this reason, the various directives from the Arts Council as to the role of theatre boards are particularly valuable – protecting reps from undue interference where this seems likely to happen, and also giving some terms of reference to councils and theatre boards. These are only suggestions, of course: they aren't enforceable, although they do carry authoritative weight. In the Arts Council Theatre Enquiry Report, *The Theatre Today* (1970), it is advised that the council members on a theatre board of fifteen should number no more than five, thus partly protecting reps from political instabilities. It is also stated that the aim of a local council should be to provide a theatre at no cost whatever to the repertory company, and that the level of local subsidies *must* rise. However, the report also points out that 'the activity of local authorities in this field [that is, in the provision of theatres and the giving of subsidies] has been transformed within a decade'.

This is undoubtedly so, and not simply in these important practical matters: the level of sophistication seems to have risen as well. Under pressures from local councils – and the Arts Council – various regional associations have grown up, whose presence and vitality augur well for the future. The North West Arts Association has described its functions like this – to co-ordinate regional activity and to provide information, to promote major events and to give grant aid to events promoted by other bodies. It is financed partly by the Arts Council and the Gulbenkian Foundation, but also by local authorities, large and small, in the area, who contribute 1/32 of a penny rate. This very small over-all rate-burden nevertheless helps to lift the weight from particular councils and towns, and also helps to ensure a dispersal of events around the region – not only in Liverpool and Manchester, but in St Helens, Blackburn, Lancaster and Buxton. In 1969, the North West Arts Association promoted a most exciting and valuable series, *From Poland with Art*, which brought to the region the Polish Mime Theatre (which played at Manchester, Chester, Sheffield and St Helens), Grotowski and the Laboratory Theatre (Manchester, Liverpool and Lancaster), the Polish Radio Symphony Orchestra (Sheffield, Liverpool, Buxton and Blackburn), the Central Puppet Theatre, Polish films and contemporary paintings. The Southern Arts Association in its first year conducted a major survey into the cultural affairs of the region, ranging from the availability of grand pianos to the theatres and festivals, and to the popularity of certain musical programmes in the region. Precisely this information is needed, if councils are to plan properly for the future. The Arts Associations also sometimes act as fund-raisers: for the Polish series, the North West Arts Association raised money from many sources, notably Courtaulds, John Lewis Partnership, Provincial Insurance Company Ltd, and the Stone-Platt Industries Ltd. The Northern Arts Association in 1968/9 sponsored 1200 concerts, plays, exhibitions and festivals, gave over 300 grants to orchestras, theatres, art galleries and magazines, co-ordinated 150 events promoted by 30 local organizations, subsidized transport for 12,000 people and started a voucher booking-system, covering many events in the region.

The potential importance of the regional arts associations is hard to exaggerate. Already they are providing a much needed coherence and sense of purpose to locally sponsored activities. It would have been almost impossible for one authority to have sponsored the Polish series – or to have conducted the various surveys – or to analyse objectively the strengths and weaknesses in the cultural affairs of a region. But these are still early days: in 1963/4, the Arts Association received only £27,320 from the Arts Council – in 1970/1, they will receive £240,000, which is an indication of their very rapid growth. Many areas of the country, however, have no regional arts associations, and several have only recently been formed. The real value of the arts associations may well be in the future, to offset the centralized authority of the Arts Council, to provide alternative ideas and values in the problems of patronage. The Arts Council since the war has faced two sorts of difficulties, firstly that the tasks could never be adequately tackled by the funds and the facilities available to them, and secondly that the concept of state patronage of the arts has been constantly under attack. This has meant that the Council could not afford to associate with failure, which in turn has led to a somewhat conservative policy. The Arts Council has acquired considerable prestige and influence: 'Under Labour,' wrote Hugo Young in the *Sunday Times* (18 January 1970), 'fewer public authorities have done better than the Arts Council, and fewer still have shown more results for their money.' This is so – but there are signs that the prestige which this solid and useful work has brought may be limiting its powers of manœuvre: no respectable well-established tailor wants to be linked with the brash Carnaby Street con man up the road. In 1968, for example, the very lively Arts Laboratory in Drury Lane needed financial (and moral) support. Under Jim Haynes, the Arts Laboratory was in some respects a model arts-centre for students, presenting, say, Portable Theatre when nobody else was interested, a season of Andy Warhol films which no one else would show, holding discussions and meetings at which Wesker and Kops would speak. The Arts Laboratory was presenting regularly programmes which many arts festivals, receiving Arts Council support, could imitate and envy: electronic and aleatoric music, mixed-media shows, exhibitions of paintings. Many members of the Arts Council staff were Arts Laboratory enthusiasts – and yet the Arts Laboratory closed, lacking Arts Council support and £8000 to pay rates and rent. Why did it close? Because, I believe, the Arts Council was unwilling to lend its name to an organization, however dynamic, which seemed to be run by a bunch of long-haired students. The decision was taken, I understand, on the highest level: and with it the Arts Council placed itself firmly on the side of the parents in the generation war. The tone of the 1969 Arts Council report – *A Chairman's Introduction* – reveals a bemused, middle-aged benevolence.

We have tried at the Arts Council, to remain contemporary and 'with it'. We have enlisted youngsters to sit on our Panels. They have made an active and valuable contribution, but what we are now trying to do is to ascertain whether the considerable experi- mental activities in which many young people now engage, which deliberately discard the conventions and standards and methods of other generations can sensibly be helped or should be helped by us. For this purpose, we have established a committee. It has had its ups and downs. It has discovered that the major myth is the belief that it is employing a common language. It has to some extent, underrated the resentment arising from the very fact of its intrusion. It has also underrated the self-contained and palisaded character of the 'activities' and the fact that the occu- pants of the palisades regard themselves as a community develop- ing along their own lines and requiring nothing from the Arts Council, except possibly its premises and funds.

I find this paragraph almost embarrassing: it reveals all too clearly the problems of paternalism. There is no reason at all why the Arts Council should try to stay 'with it' if it doesn't like what it sees, nor is it under any obligation to uphold 'the conventions and standards and methods of other generations'. It need not take sides in the generation struggle. It should be concerned with artistic merit: and if it decides to give an annual grant of £20,000 to the Theatre Royal, York, to stage plays like Sam Cree's *Stop It, Nurse* and nothing to the Arts Laboratory, then this should be a decision based on artistic judgement. The last sentence quoted puzzles me: '. . . requiring nothing from the Arts Council, except possibly its premises and funds'. What else does the Arts Council expect that they should require? Good advice? It all sounds too much like the father who will increase his son's allowance, provided that he takes a solid job and wears a collar and tie. The son may feel that his 'work' is more important than his father's offer of a 'solid job': he may resent the interference. I doubt whether the Arts Council towards any rep offers 'good advice' with the grant, or would feel offended if the good advice were rejected. And again, one wonders how a former Arts Council would have tackled the *enfants terribles* of other generations – the Surrealists, the Impressionists, Beethoven – all of whom discarded the standards of their day. The Arts Council should avoid conveying the misleading impression that it is more reactionary than it is.

If the emergence of the arts associations in the regions brings diversity to the system of public patronage of the arts, then it would be a most welcome development. The great argument against state patronage is that it may prove to be monolithic, unsympathetic to change, experiment or deviation, the ample provider of Orthodox Thought. The chequered history of the Arts Council, the various battles for survival and public recognition, through which it fought so successfully, may have left a mark of premature self-satisfaction. The arts associations have little as yet to feel complacent about: they are in the process of discovering their priorities. Fortunately, with the Arts Council as well, the complacency has not yet become too stifling a blanket. There is still an acid of self-doubt. It is, however, an acid which could become watered away, if there is not an effective alternative system, if there is not a dialogue between different forms of patronage, and between the struggling emergent artists and those accepted by the Establishment. At a time when the Arts Council often seems out of touch with the new grass struggling through the blanket of old leaves, the arts associations are discovering, often with surprised delight, what regional activity exists, in schools, universities, music clubs and theatres. Without the crisis caused by television and other factors, without the increasing interest in the arts shown by local councils, this effective partnership might never have developed.

5

The Arts Council: Tone and Priorities

To carp at the tone of the Arts Council Theatre Enquiry Report, *The Theatre Today in England and Wales*, may seem unduly petty. Weren't many valuable changes proposed? A streamlined touring-system? A Theatre Investment Fund? A new Shakespeare Theatre? And yet, in a way, the style is the key to the Report – and, I would add, to the priorities which one has learnt to expect from the Arts Council. The language is bland but forthright, authoritative but colloquial, above the struggle but firmly in control. The Report could have been worded – and, who knows? perhaps was – in full accordance with the instructions laid down in a Do-It-Yourself-Bank-Manager kit. There are the jocular remarks to ease the strain of all that money: 'the investors [in the Theatre Investment fund] . . . would probably include many of the "angels" who already put money into plays, which prompts the fanciful notion that City men might nickname the Fund – Angels Amalgamated'. The Theatre Enquiry Committee was set up in 1967, and the Report was published in February 1970: in spite of this length of time, it was not a complete survey of the theatre in England and Wales. It was primarily concerned with a section of the theatre which seemed to be in trouble. The first chapter asks these questions: 'What are the causes of the dry-rot which afflicts the commercial theatre? Are they eradicable? What remedies or palliatives exist? Can the theatre continue as a mixed economy of private enterprise and public ownership? Is the subsidized theatre justifying the public money it receives? Should subsidies be also given to the ailing commercial sector? Is there a case for Government investment (rather than subsidy) in the theatre . . . ?' It analyses these problems and surfaces with three main solutions – that there should be a touring-grid of between 12–18 theatres fed by productions from the two national theatres, the leading reps, by some commercial companies and by leading opera and ballet companies – that there should be a Theatre Investment Fund, whose primary function is 'to encourage and assist reputable [commercial] managements to increase the production of new plays of interest, and revivals of quality, and to cause such productions to tour as widely as possible in the provinces' – and that there should be a new Shakespeare Theatre Company centred on London, but touring the provinces for three months of the year.

The main problem, therefore, on which the Enquiry chose to concentrate was the decline of the commercial theatre and, in particular, of touring: and this decision itself revealed a tendency in the Arts Council to be concerned with preserving a *status quo* which seems to be crumbling, rather than with possible new developments. The Report has nothing to say about the role of the theatre in a society where more people will have more leisure, where the need is for mass daytime activities rather than economically restricted evening entertainment: it has little to say about the growth of the theatre as the cultural centre for the community, nothing about the way in which schools and adult education can be related to the theatre – nothing to say about the changing patterns of drama, of regional documentaries, theatre-in-the-round, environmental theatre and so forth. The Report can be criticized, I think, in two ways: firstly, that the terms of reference chosen by the Committee exclude too much, that the very title, *The Theatre Today*, is therefore a misnomer; and, secondly, that the proposals themselves sound sensible, but in detail raise all sorts of problems.

In the touring-grid proposals, for example, there is no proper distinction between pre- and post-West End touring. Many commercial companies visit the Theatre Royal, Brighton, say, and the New Theatre, Oxford, as a way of playing a production in, before it has to face the London critics. These two theatres are part of the proposed touring-grid. They're both close enough to London to avoid some of the heavy incidental expenses connected with touring. Actors can rehearse for a television date during the day, and commute to Oxford for an evening performance. The public in these two towns are guinea-pigs for managements. Sometimes – fairly often – the public are lucky: at others are conned into watching disasters. Post-London touring, particularly in the North, is expensive for managements, disliked by actors who have nothing to anticipate except more digs and a settled salary: the public, however, benefits from seeing a tried and settled, if slightly stale, product.

If I were a commercial management, I would need little persuasion to undertake a short pre-London tour, be very reluctant to tackle a post-London one. To try to encourage touring without making such a distinction could lead to complications – particularly when touring in general is made one of the criteria by which a management and a production is deemed worthy to receive investment sums from the Theatre Investment Fund.

That is one detail. Here is another. One of the theatres proposed as part of the touring-grid is the New Theatre, Oxford, a large old-fashioned building around the corner from the smaller Oxford Playhouse, which houses a major rep, the Meadow Players. The Oxford Playhouse is owned by the University: the Meadow Players have to share the building, with an amateur organization. The Meadow Players are virtually forced to tour, simply because the theatre is occupied for about six weeks in every university term by undergraduate companies. The public, I am told, is sometimes confused as to whether a production is professional or amateur. Together, the Oxford Playhouse and the New Theatre seat just over 2000 people, and the population of Oxford is about 100,000. Therefore, 2 per cent of the population of Oxford would have to visit the theatres *every* night to secure full houses – 14 per cent for a weekly run, 28 per cent for fortnightly runs – which is absurd. This situation would be less silly if the two theatres were showing different sorts of drama. But the Meadow Players already belong to DALTA, the collection of touring reps and commercial companies, which in an expanded form is proposed to supply the product for the touring-theatres. It is theoretically possible, therefore, for the Meadow Players simply to nip around the corner to the New Theatre to tour under the new system. The present situation at the Playhouse is full of difficulties. The Meadow Players will soon be the only major rep without a sensible home. The obvious solution would seem to be that the Meadow Players should move to the New Theatre, which is then maintained as the only professional theatre in Oxford. This solution is positively discouraged in the Report, by the suggestion that the New Theatre should become part of a grid of major touring-theatres. But why is the New Theatre favoured, whereas say, the Alhambra, Bradford, is not? Partly because the New Theatre is so useful for pre-London touring. This at any rate is my guess. But the purpose of touring is to bring theatre to the theatre-less areas of the country, not to assist managements to play their productions in. And, therefore, while the New Theatre may seem a convenient theatre to retain as part of the touring-grid – simply because managements want to go there – it doesn't really forward the cause and aims of touring.

But there are wider objections to the touring-grid proposals, which lie in the very nature of these aged and imposing buildings, the old touring-theatres, the objects of preservation. The new theatres, such as Chichester or Bolton, or the new Sheffield Playhouse, set new standards for intimacy, sight lines and acoustics. The Chichester Festival Theatre seats 1365, but, with its thrust stage, no member of the audience sits further than sixty-five feet from the stage. I rather doubt whether an audience which has ever become accustomed to these new theatres will ever willingly revert to a huge auditorium with a proscenium opening which from the back of the circle seems little bigger than a television screen and has to be watched in less comfort. I do not see how these touring-theatres can be converted into what we would now regard as a modern theatre. The main stage at the new National Theatre will be basically open-end, though with a large curving forestage, so productions moving (as is proposed in the Report) from the National Theatre to these touring-theatres will have to be redesigned for a proscenium-arch stage. Those plays which transfer from Chichester to London – such as the recent *The Magistrate* – come from a thrust stage which has been converted for the production into a proscenium-arch stage, partly to ease the transfer. Some theatres in the proposed touring-grid ought to be retained simply because they're beautiful and historic buildings, for instance, the Theatre Royal, Brighton: but in future they will surely require productions designed for them. Hence, they would seem to be particularly unsuitable for widespread touring. Most new theatres aim at adaptability – movable proscenium arches, movable forestages and so on. These touring-theatres, however, are singularly rigid: the presence of circles and balconies, for example, limits the use of the forestage. Are they worth the cost of patching them up? The Grand, Wolverhampton, the New, Oxford, the Alexandra, Birmingham? I rather doubt it. The life-span of these theatres would seem to me to be for only as long as the public remains unaware of alternatives – say, ten years.

The Theatre Investment Fund also sounds a more sensible scheme than on reflection it is. The Report envisages a pool of money – about £250,000 – which can be used to back commercial productions,

up to 50 per cent of the costs of the production. It is suggested that
the money be raised, firstly, from the Arts Council, who should
supply £100,000 in 'new' money – that is, not deducted from other
moneys spent on the theatre – and, secondly, from an issue of shares
and long-term stock. The shares and stock should raise £150,000 –
and the Report indicates that this money should come from 'angels'
who now invest in the theatre. This £150,000, therefore, cannot be
regarded as 'new' money – it is merely money redirected into a
central pool and *possibly* used in a more efficient way. Therefore,
of the total funds, only £100,000 can be regarded as new money.
Charlie Girl, it is said, cost £100,000 on the pre-London tour and
production costs. The new money would therefore finance about
two new musicals – bearing in mind that half the production costs
has to be carried by the promoting management – or three to four
straight plays. This amount of money is therefore useful, but it
isn't likely to produce a revolution in the commercial theatre –
except perhaps indirectly. Among the various clauses concerning
the investment of money from the T.I.F. are some ideas which
raise qualms. The money is to be given on 'qualitative' considerations, and 'in exercising its qualitative judgement of a proposed
production, the Fund would take into account not only the nature
of the play but also the credentials of the management and the
records (financial and otherwise) of its recent productions'.

In giving subsidies to ordinary repertory theatres – or even to the
Royal Court – the Arts Council has up till now tried to avoid making
general qualitative judgements. The grant to a rep isn't cut on the
basis of a couple of unsuccessful productions, and this has led to
the strange anomaly of some really bad repertory companies receiving far more money than some really good ones. In this case,
however, the T.I.F. – which is to be run independently of the Arts
Council – is apparently planning to make qualitative judgements not
only about the production it may help to finance, but about the
status of the management which is promoting it. The new money
which the T.I.F. will invest in productions is less than that given,
say, in annual grants to two major reps, but it is tied by more
strings. In practice, I suppose, a management will have to demonstrate the value of its coming production, before any money can be
invested in it. It's hard to say what new plays are likely to be
interesting, particularly before a board which may not share one's
instincts. It's easier to justify a revival. Among the newer plays, I

would imagine that Shaffer's *The Battle of Shrivings* would be quickly accepted, but Edward Bond's *Saved* or *Early Morning* would not. In practice again, I would imagine that this clause about qualitative judgements would lead to a spate of commercially sponsored revivals – *Caesar and Cleopatra*, *Lady Windermere's Fan* – and some rather dull, middlebrow, 'serious' plays.

There are some other disconcerting features. I doubt whether the funds offered to a management would properly offset the cost of post-London touring – touring in general is one of the conditions of investment – but a management might well wish to agree to post-London touring in order to take advantage of the Fund, knowing that he can always hire a second-rate company to tour. Hence, the benefits of touring to the public might well be considerably reduced. Furthermore, if a management has received money from the T.I.F. and lost it on a production, it is required to offer all its future productions to the Fund for investment 'until the position [is] reached in which the Fund [has] not lost by its association with the management'. In this way it is hoped that the T.I.F. will become a self-perpetuating pool of money: it is not proposed that the £100,000 grant from the Arts Council should be an annual event. But will it have this effect? Commercial managements – and indeed most managements are commercial in the sense that they rely more on the box-office than on subsidies – often run 'pot-boilers' to offset the losses on 'better' plays and more elaborate productions. Will the T.I.F. rely on these pot-boilers too? – in which case it seems unlikely that the T.I.F. will raise the standards of the commercial theatre. Or will it wait for the commercially successful 'quality' production to come along? – in which case the funds of the T.I.F. seem likely to run out fairly quickly.

(Some of these problems with the T.I.F. were recognized shortly after the Report appeared. At the end of April 1970, a Working Group of the Theatres' Advisory Council met and issued two immediate comments – urging that the funds of the T.I.F. raised from the Government should total not less than £250,000 and be supplemented by funds from other sources, such as I.T.V., and also submitting recommendations as to how members should be appointed to the Advisory Board of the T.I.F., a point which the Report neglected to mention.)

I am not sure that I should even begin to comment on the last main proposal, for a new Shakespeare Theatre and Company based in London. My views are so totally opposed to those of the Committee and I've expressed them already (in *London Magazine*, October 1969). The Committee feels that audiences in London and the Provinces need 'the long-lost experience of discovering the work of the world's greatest dramatist', whereas I feel that too much Shakespeare is still being played. The Committee mourns the loss of the old Shakespearian touring companies, such as Sir Donald Wolfit's. I remember all too vividly a school party to Sir Donald Wolfit's *Macbeth* at the old Cheltenham Opera House – and emerging from the theatre quietly convinced that they were all mad, the actors, this man Shakespeare, my teachers, the lot. Where is this Shakespeare starvation? Both the national companies in London include one or two Shakespearian productions in each seasonal repertoire. They may not belt through the entire corpus in three to five years, but anyone who wants to submit to this endurance test can surely drive up the M1 to Stratford. Reps usually give annual productions of Shakespeare plays: and only four of the towns in the proposed touring-grid are not supplied by – or in close contact with – a rep. Indeed, these rep productions fill the gap left by the touring Shakespeare companies. The standards of production may vary, but they're often outstandingly good – Nottingham's *King Lear*, Birmingham Rep's *Hamlet*, the Prospect productions (which do tour), Lincoln's *Romeo and Juliet* and many others. The best Shakespeare productions at Stratford, *Troilus and Cressida* for example, usually transfer to the Aldwych. The cost of a new Shakespeare company in London would be extremely high, rivalling that of Stratford, and really I cannot see why the priorities should lie in this direction. There is surely a better case for a 'shop-window' theatre in London for the best rep productions – or perhaps for a theatre which would form one link in a chain of world theatres, to be visited in turn by leading international companies.

There are some more convincing sections of the Report – on censorship and vertical monopoly – but as a whole it is an unsatisfactory document, a poor result of two years' work, even *within* its chosen terms of reference. But the main criticism is that the Committee didn't cast its net widely enough – either in assessing how this present situation has arisen or in looking to the future. The Committee was supposed to be independent of the Arts Council (though appointed by them), and yet it contains no really balanced assessment as to how Arts Council subsidies have affected the theatre in general, and the survival of the commercial theatre in particular. I stress 'really balanced', because the Report is full of praise for the Arts Council: it notes the firm establishment of the reps receiving subsidies and that the commercial theatre outside London is on its last legs – but isn't really disposed to relate these two facts. By giving grants to reps without specifying the nature and type of productions for which this money should be used, by giving patronage without making qualitative decisions, the Arts Council itself has tilted the balance against the commercial theatre. The side references in the Report to those commercial managements who fail to move with the times, to prepare for the future when they could afford to do so, have therefore a cruel ring. I am in favour of State patronage. I believe that it is more important that the reps should survive in a healthy form than that we should have many financially insecure private companies, with varying standards and facilities and no built-in responsibilities to society other than to make money. We have tried this system: it produces, on the whole, bad theatre. At the same time, it is hypocrisy for the Theatre Enquiry Committee to turn round to commercial managements, who have suffered under this necessary and valuable reorganization process, and to imply that their waning fortunes are somehow due to their own faults.

The opening sentence of the chapter on 'The Subsidized Theatre in London' reveals this tendency to whitewash the Arts Council very clearly: 'the present quality and fertility of the subsidized theatre in London is mainly due to the irrigation system of public patronage through the Arts Council'. On one level, this sentence is almost tautological, on another, self-congratulatory. One can readily admit that the *presence* of subsidized theatres is due to Arts Council subsidies. Local council subsidies (except in the case of the Mermaid Theatre) still count for little in London. But is the *quality* and *fertility* of the subsidized theatre due to the Arts Council? To prove this point, one would have to believe that there is something singularly holy and inspirational about Arts Council money. Was George Devine, who received Arts Council funds, consequently a more inspired director than Joan Littlewood, who did not? Joan Littlewood's name seems to be neglected in Arts Council reports about the growth of the British theatre since 1956. In the section on Youth Theatre, no mention is made of the Arts Laboratory, Drury Lane, which closed lacking Arts Council support.

This sort of bias smacks of a rewriting of history – an unnecessary process, I would have thought, because there is no need nowadays for the Arts Council to be defended at all costs: its value has been demonstrated. The past is, alas, not the only space of time which can be rewritten. The future can also be re-estimated, replanned. One theme which has dominated discussion about the theatre in recent years has been the role which it should play during the seventies and eighties, in an age presumably of increased leisure. M.P.s have called for a Ministry of Leisure: the electricians in New York have demanded (and received) a three-and-a-half-day working week: Chairs of Leisure are offered at some universities. It is not a new topic. The Theatre Enquiry Report has nothing to say about the subject: there is no attempt to provide either leadership – or guide-lines for leadership. This is, in itself, a serious omission: but it reflects other aspects of Arts Council policy – its priorities and failings. Indeed, the significance of the Theatre Enquiry Report is not that it is particularly good or bad – but that it is typical of the Arts Council. The Arts Council has never been willing to speculate: it has supported the theatres which seemed to be functioning effectively and often propped up those which seemed to be waning – but it has rarely taken the initiative, and, indeed, during the early days in particular, has rarely had the capacity to do so. It had to choose its priorities carefully – both to safeguard against the criticism which might hamper its growth and to invest wisely. Most of these priorities were sensible ones and they have responded to concerned treatment. But we now have reached the stage when this good sense is not enough. In spite of the English Stage Company, the I.C.A. and the New Activities Committee, the Arts Council now seems like an institution all too ready to support and maintain the existing state of affairs, somewhat short-sighted and a little resentful of change – or, at least, of all the new demands upon its resources and attention which its success has helped to produce. The consequences of this cautious growth are now reflected in the repertory movement – both in its achievements and in its failings: and, in future, no doubt, the development of the theatre, particularly in response to the challenges of a more affluent age, will rest on the leadership from the Arts Council. This is why the 'holding' operations which the Arts Council has so successfully used in the past may be of less value now. This is also why the development of the Arts Council through its formative years is of particular interest.

The Arts Council was granted a Royal Charter on 9 August 1946. It had developed from the Committee for the Encouragement of Music and the Arts, which had been established in 1939. During its first year, 1945–6, it received from the Exchequer £235,000, a sum which in ten years rose to £820,000 (1955–6). This money was to be spent not solely on the theatre – not even primarily – but on orchestras, festivals, ballet and opera companies, and art exhibitions as well. It was clearly insufficient. By 1964, the total expenditure of the Arts Council had risen to £2,689,700 and the amount spent on the theatre (excluding opera and ballet) was about £600,000. Even with this increase, the funds of the Arts Council could not meet all the demands which were being made – not the lunatic ones, the serious needs – particularly from the provinces. Priorities had to be established: and one was a thriving London theatre. Of this £600,000 spent on the theatre, London-based theatres received about £227,000. During the following years, the total amount spent on the theatre rose steeply – £1,000,000 in 1965/6, nearly £2,000,000 in 1967/8 – but the proportion spent in London dropped slightly. In 1967/8, just over £500,000 was spent in London – about a quarter of the total amount – whereas over a third had been spent there in 1964/5. Three companies benefited in particular – the National Theatre with a 1967/8 grant of £340,000, the English Stage Company with £94,000 and the Mermaid Theatre Trust with £35,000. The Royal Shakespeare Company, dividing its resources between Stratford and the Aldwych Theatre in London, received £200,000.

Many rep directors in the provinces resented the fact that so much money should be spent in London and on the two *prestige* theatres, the National and the Royal Shakespeare Company. They weren't comforted by the argument that the proportions were changing. London, it was felt, was lucky enough already, with a catchment area of 12,000,000 people, with a comparatively high average income, and a fit, if not booming, commercial theatre. The Arts Council retorted that London was the major tourist centre of Britain, perhaps of Europe – and who would believe in a buoyant provincial theatre, if the goods in the shop window were shoddy?

This answer left some dissatisfaction. Why should the Arts Council undertake a public-relations job for Britain? At the Victoria Theatre, Stoke-on-Trent, during the summer of 1969, there was a demonstration programme on local documentaries, *Potters and Rebels*, followed by a discussion. Ron Daniels, from the Victoria

Theatre Company, was asked by a member of the audience why they should even attempt to keep a permanent regional company together. Wasn't it inevitable that the really good actors would be lured away to films and television where the big money was – or to the West End? The tone of his reply was reasonable – the feelings expressed were bitter. London had robbed the provinces of talent for years. They were trying to fight back. The West End provided a decadent, expense-account theatre – all sex-comedies – corrupting the talent it stole. The Arts Council was a conspirator – a centralized body, doling out grants like mere charity to provincial theatres, but carefully preserving the pre-eminence of London. The people of Stoke-on-Trent, who paid taxes like everyone else, deserved to have the theatre they paid for. Their rights were being neglected in the interests of Southerners.

This answer was, of course, unfair – in argument, if not in spirit. The West End is not as decadent as all that, and very few theatres in London receive Arts Council grants. On simple arithmetic, too, if the Arts Council gives half-a-million to London, with a population of 12,000,000, it should only give about £10,000 to Stoke-on-Trent which has 276,000 inhabitants. The Victoria Theatre received a 1967/8 grant of £15,714. Of course, the *needs* of Stoke may be greater – but to ask for preferential treatment is somewhat different than to call for parity in an injured tone. And yet, the sense of grievance may not have been entirely misplaced: for the dominance of London – one of the nineteenth-century complaints – has in some respects increased since the war, partly due to the attraction of television for actors. If the Arts Council had wanted to stop the drift, it should have acted perhaps with greater vigour and consistency.

The Arts Council policy towards regional drama has been pragmatic: full of good ideas which didn't always work and had to be abandoned at the expense of some bad faith and broken promises. This sounds harsh, and left as a bald statement would be so, for the Arts Council's policy was intolerably restricted from the beginning. 'The Council each year presents the Chancellor with an itemized account of the subsidies which it believes necessary for maintaining the many organizations it supports' (*The First Ten Years*, Arts Council Pamphlet, 1956). There was, therefore, no block grant. Even the small funds which the Arts Council had at its disposal had to be approved by the Treasury.

Some of the dissidents who would like to see the so-called doctrine of 'fair shares' applied in the Council's allocations to London and the Provinces appear to assume that if the Arts Council decided no longer to subsidize, say, Covent Garden, its present grant (£270,000) to that theatre would be automatically available for distribution elsewhere. Not at all. The sum of £270,000 in the estimates is earmarked for the specific object named; if the Council withdrew its grant from Covent Garden it would not receive that sum from the Treasury.

And so, annually the Arts Council had to make out a case for each individual grant given. No forward planning was possible – certainly not the complicated planning required to redress the balance between London and the Provinces. In the early days of the Arts Council, it was a delicate and difficult matter to persuade the Treasury to take any but the most obvious financial initiative. The Arts Council had to try to steer the ship of culture – while eking out a hand-to-mouth existence – and flying blind at the same time: a task to contort an acrobat or a diplomat.

Although these beggar-pilots had long-term objectives of which strong regional theatre was one, they weren't able to pursue these aims consistently. When the Arts Council took over from CEMA (the Council for the Encouragement of Music and the Arts) it tried at once to decentralize by setting up eleven regional councils. But the funds were too small to sustain all these bodies or to be wasted on duplicate offices. And so by 1955 all the regional offices were closed, leaving only London, Edinburgh and Cardiff. The Arts Council insisted at the time that this was only an administrative change. There wasn't any *policy* of centralization. And they had probably expected more rapid development from the 1948 Local Government Act – so that their role would be similar to that which the arts associations are now playing, to co-ordinate regional activity rather than to be patron. But their expectations were not fulfilled, and the closing of regional offices was a decision open to misinterpretation. Councils which had learnt to rely on the regional Arts Council had their trust shaken at a time when faith was most needed. CEMA used to promote concert tours and theatres, such as the one at Salisbury. The Arts Council decided to assist independent managements in the regions rather than to promote: hence, a grant would be given to the Salisbury Playhouse, but the theatre wouldn't be *run* by the Arts Council. This was intended to give greater autonomy to regional theatres – but there were some who argued that the Arts Council was trying to unload its responsibility. The poor can never be right.

There were other abandoned plans as well. Originally, the Arts Council sought to stimulate regional drama by encouraging a policy of touring repertory. An established company would take a production on tour playing in theatreless towns, setting up in church and town halls or wherever there was a stage and a room. The advantage was that – apart from visiting many otherwise deprived towns – a production could be held together for several weeks, thus affording longer rehearsal time. Salisbury was one of these reps, and the Company used to visit Southampton, Basingstoke, Newbury, Winchester, Dorchester, Weymouth and Yeovil – a tiring tour for the actors, and one which also required a large company to sustain. This policy proved inconvenient and expensive: the halls were awkwardly different, the stages variable in size, the acoustics presented problems. Nor were the plays chosen by Salisbury always suitable – *The Cocktail Party, See How They Run* and *Mr Bolfry* – simple, stock plays apparently, but ones which required naturalistic sets, hard to transfer from stage to stage. 'Touring', the Arts Council later concluded, 'is best left in the hands of experts' – and in the sixties, expert touring repertory companies emerged – the Meadow Players and Prospect, Theatre-Go-Round, the Century Theatre and, later, the Northcott Company, Exeter. Theatre-Go-Round, the touring branch of the Royal Shakespeare Company, took a sloping circular stage with them: the Century Theatre had a mobile theatre, constructed from several lorries. In agricultural areas, thinly populated but with small market towns, these touring companies have been highly successful: but at the beginning, before the problems were understood – let alone surmounted – touring was an easy way to lose money. Even when attendances were as high as ninety per cent of capacity, a £300 weekly loss was sustained as an average by each touring company. 'Touring', the Arts Council decided, could never be anything more than 'a token service'. A better system was to subsidize transport to bring audiences to the theatre from outlying towns: and by this means the Northampton Theatre Royal Company used a subsidy of £400 in a year to bring 8500 people to the theatre and £1600 to the box office.

This made better economic sense – and better theatrical sense as well, perhaps, for at least the conditions in a proper repertory theatre were better than those which could be improvised from a church hall. This sensible change left feelings of resentment, however, among those towns which had grown accustomed to the regular visits of Arts Council subsidized theatre companies. There is a subtle psychological difference between Star Personal Appearances and cheap bus-rides. This change also presupposed strong regional theatre centres – but the whole of Wales had no such centre, nor had the North-East, nor Devon and Cornwall, nor Scotland above the Glasgow–Edinburgh line. 'The Arts Council believes that the first claim on its attention and assistance is that of maintaining in London and the larger cities effective power-houses of opera, music and drama; for unless these quality institutions can be maintained, the arts are bound to decline into mediocrity' (from *The First Ten Years*). But how big is a 'larger city'? Leeds had no rep, nor, discounting the Library Theatre, which only seats 308, had Manchester. Nor had Southampton, Plymouth, Preston or Durham. The way in which the Arts Council interpreted this priority, when they could afford to do so, was to try to establish seven or eight regional theatres in England (three in Scotland), which would act as mini-National Theatres – touchstones of excellence within the region and a focal point for other theatres. This was really the outlook behind the division of grants in 1965/6, which has already been described, when the Arts Council selected seven major theatres to receive £50,000 grants in England, fourteen smaller ones to receive £20,000 each, and thirteen others who would receive £10,000 each. These grants were to maintain companies, not to finance rebuilding programmes – but, before they were given, other considerations had to be borne in mind. The Arts Council had to be convinced that they weren't financing white elephants, that there was genuine interest and support for a theatre in a particular town, that the theatre company itself had demonstrated its capability to realize some of the standards required and that there was no other way of effectively financing the theatre.

There were, of course, objections to this scheme as well – more in practice than in theory. Five of the seven chosen theatres were in the Midlands or North Midlands. Nottingham, Coventry and Birmingham were barely forty miles apart. The only exceptions were Bristol in the South and Oxford in the West Midlands. There were good reasons for this apparently poor distribution. The

Midlands is a densely populated region, with a good theatre tradition: the South of England has more private wealth, and therefore needed heavily subsidized theatres less. Unfortunately the theory of regional centres depends on having these centres in different regions. Another problem was that the differentials in grants did not cover all the additional services that the regional theatre centres were at first expected to provide. To fulfil all the expectations, a regional rep should have, say, a company of thirty, one theatre seating between 700 and a thousand, and a smaller studio theatre. The actors should be first-class, and the salaries sufficient to lure them away from television and the West End. The Arts Council recommended that the artistic director of one of these major rep companies should be paid £60 a week – not a generous bait. The regional reps were also encouraged to undertake touring: they were expected to provide theatre-in-education teams. All these hopes were invested in the seven regional reps, and the grant differential between the first and second categories, £30,000, didn't begin to cover them all. One of the stated reasons why John Neville originally resigned from the Nottingham Playhouse was that the Arts Council hadn't increased the grant. He wasn't just taking umbrage, or defending *his* theatre: he was trying to protect a certain policy towards regional drama.

But was the policy worth defending? I would have thought not. The strength of the Arts Council – and perhaps its main weakness as well – has always been its benevolent pragmatism, a willingness to give help where help seemed both deserved and needed. Few of the *policy* ideas have taken into account the complexity of all the problems. Regional theatre centres sound sensible enough, and would be, if the population were evenly spread around the country, and equally friendly towards the theatre – and state-subsidized theatre at that. But in the South, as we have seen, the idea of private patronage dies hard: in the North-East, where theatres are few and far between, the Forum Theatre, Billingham, an ambitious venture, fell into difficulties during the second year. Touring works in some areas, with proper conditions and an awareness of the problems – but fails in others. Had the Arts Council at the start become lured into dangerously expensive, though perfectly logical, ventures, the opposition to public patronage might have grown. Even the restrictions placed on the Arts Council in the early days had some value, because a demand had to be *proved* before money from the Treasury

1   *Sir Barry Jackson in the 1930s*

2   *The interior of the Birmingham Repertory Theatre*

3   *The entrance to the theatre in 1931. The man on the right in the doorway is Emile Littler, then General Manager*

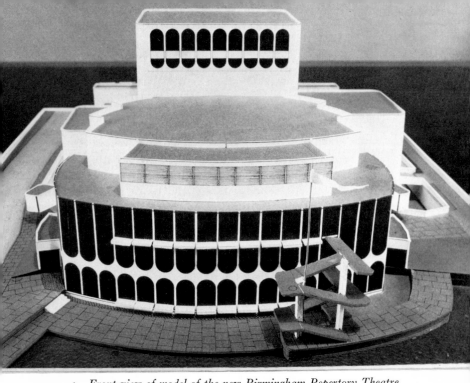

4   *Front view of model of the new Birmingham Repertory Theatre*

5   *The Georgian Theatre, Richmond, Yorkshire*

6   *The Theatre Royal, Bury St Edmunds*

7   *The Theatre Royal, Bristol*

8 *Festival Theatre, Chichester (1962). Powell and Moya with Christopher Stephens*

9 *Nottingham Playhouse (1963). Peter Moro and Partners*

10   *Octagon, Bolton (1967). Geoffrey Brooks, ARIBA*

11   *Northcott, Exeter (1968). Sir William Holford and Partners*

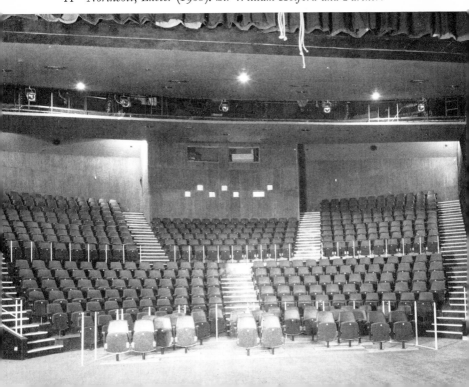

12 *Arts Centre, University of Sussex (1969). Sir Basil Spence, Bonnington and Collins*

13 *Thorndike Theatre, Leatherhead (1969). Roderick Ham, ARIBA*

14   *Mermaid, London (1959). Elidir Davies, FRIBA*

15   *Cockpit, Marylebone*

16 *Victoria, Stoke-on-Trent (1962). Conversion of a cinema. The figure standing in the centre with his*

was given. And so, when the Ministry for the Arts was finally established, the Arts Council had learnt through sheer and often bitter experience how its funds could be best used. The Labour administration has provided three times more money for the Arts than the previous Conservative government, and yet this increase has attracted comparatively little controversy. However resentful some rep managers may still feel that the Arts Council has not been more generous towards the regions, that so much money is spent in London and on the two prestige companies, the fact remains that the money spent on regional theatre has increased steadily year by year and this growth hasn't been disturbed by violent political opposition.

The real problems with the Arts Council are somewhat different – nothing to do with regional bias, lack of consistency or tact. It is simply unimaginative. The Arts Council is a kindly uncle, benevolent but careful with money, free with advice, unwilling to let people down. It is shy with qualitative judgements, preferring to help everyone a little. I once asked a representative of the Arts Council what would happen if, say, a rep receiving a £20,000 grant turned out disappointing programmes year after year. The question was not entirely hypothetical. I was told that the grant wouldn't be cut, but it wouldn't be raised either. What would happen if an established and talented director working in a £10,000 subsidized theatre were offering an especially exciting and ambitious plan for the following season? Would the grant to the theatre be raised? It is unlikely. There are grants sometimes for new plays – or to pay perhaps for an extension to the theatre-in-education programme – or (rarely) to pay for a dramatist to work with the company. But few grants are given simply on merit – and then that merit has to be so well established that the Arts Council cannot be accused of giving preferential treatment. If grants are increased, they're usually increased all round, following a larger allocation of funds from the Treasury. The Arts Council fear that every increase in grant is a further step up an endless ladder, that each year every rep director will come to them with bright new schemes requiring more money and that having once said 'Yes' it will be hard to say 'No'. Hence, increased grants and new ones are given carefully, not for something as intangible as sheer merit, but for productivity.

Unfortunately, cultural patronage is not always something which can be conducted on the lines of union negotiations. Directors and theatre companies cannot usually strike. Increases in grants are nearly always seen as a reward for merit, even though this is not so, simply because there are no physical levers by which a theatre can extract more money from the State. The only companies which are in a prestige position to demand higher grants are perhaps the National Theatre Company and the Royal Shakespeare. Patronage which is given automatically, which is not a gesture of appreciation and a reward of merit, dies from the heart down – both for the patron and the patronized. A rep director knows that the grant to his theatre will not be raised, however hard or imaginatively he works – nor will it be cut if the results are poor. Similarly, someone working in the Arts Council may feel frustrated if he cannot secure what he regards as a deserved financial support for a theatre he believes in. The danger of this subsidy system which irons out both the enthusiasm of the giver and hope of the receiver is that it leads to an establishment lack of commitment: 'Yes, we will give money to this theatre because we always have – not because we like the programmes.' The blandness of the Arts Council, which has seen it through so many crises and has given the repertory movement a stability when it needed it most, could easily solidify into a Forsyte paternalism.

Those who work at the Arts Council are well aware of this problem, but it is hard to avoid the odd lurch towards bureaucracy. One telling phrase in the Theatre Enquiry Report refers to 'contemporary plays' occupying 'the same field' – which is the sort of philistinism normally associated with the B.B.C. There was no consideration at all in the report of Victor Corti's interesting suggestion for low-cost theatres and arts centres, which could be erected on almost any stretch of under-used land, such as disused coal-bunkering sites near railway stations. Touring was discussed in some detail, but without any reference to those travelling bands of actors, Portable Theatre and Freehold, whose productions, without scenery, have given so much pleasure in London and around the country. If we want good 'church-hall' drama, this is where we will find it. The Report dismissed categorically the idea for a travelling tent-theatre in Wales – without mentioning the ingenious system currently used by the Century Theatre or the various tent theatres in the United States. There was little consideration of the ways in which existing reps have integrated into various communities: nothing about the value of the theatre in an age of leisure. I asked an Arts Council representative what he thought of regional documentaries, and other plays of a purely local and topical interest. He replied, 'Not much' – although he added that they might have some use as social therapy. This seemed a casual response to me. 'Social therapy' – if we mean by this 'helping a town to become aware of its problems' and 'illustrating various ways of coping with them' – is a very valuable function of theatre, historically anointed moreover by the Greeks. The technical development of regional documentaries – from rather slipshod affairs into more sophisticated ones – has been a significant feature of the repertory movement recently, steadily growing from its roots perhaps in Joan Littlewood's company at Stratford into the bole and branches of Peter Cheeseman's company at Stoke-on-Trent and flowering in Exeter, Newcastle, Ipswich, Bolton and Lincoln. The representative also felt that the learning-through-drama side of educational theatre was outside the province of the Arts Council, who were only concerned really with teaching about theatre.

The Arts Council is a diffuse body. It is hard to say whether the Theatre Enquiry Report or the representative I met properly reflect the climate of opinion at that large sedate building, 105 Piccadilly. If they do, then it would seem that the Arts Council is neglecting – not from lack of money or other unavoidable reasons – precisely those opportunities which the growth of the repertory movement has helped to discover. The Arts Council still seems primarily concerned with preserving that sort of theatre which we have known for the past fifty years – Shakespeare in London, Grand Touring – with large commercial and subsidized companies visiting the New, Oxford, and the Grand, Wolverhampton, lectures about Shakespeare to schools and so forth. The Arts Council, it is true, offers grants for the production of new plays and rare or unusually interesting revivals, and sometimes bursaries for dramatists to work with reps. The sums involved are, however, significantly small, and resident dramatists partly supported by Arts Council funds are harder to find than new theatres. Matthew Arnold deplored the fact that there was no drama in his day for the intelligently alert, theatrically interested middle classes. Now we are in danger of having nothing else but 'bourgeois' drama – solid, easily digested, rather unadventurous stuff, backward-looking where it looks in any direction at all. By playing safe, by supporting the known and the tried, by sidestepping those experiments which sound sensible but may not work, the Arts Council runs the risk of being a dependable institution – but not an exciting one: worse, it does not seem to be looking towards a time when, with more money and leisure, art and the theatre in particular is seen as the vital part of every community, however small, as invaluable as the library or indeed the hospital, a necessary 'play area' where ideas can be tried out, examined and transformed perhaps into something pleasing, aesthetically pleasing as well as providing other enjoyments.

I have implied that the reps are more adventurous than the Arts Council, more alert to their opportunities, and that the Council could become a reactionary organization, pulling them back, instead of spurring them on. But is this generally so? There may be some exceptional companies, but do the reps in general reveal this forward-looking approach? Do they offer 'daring' plays – and 'daring' in what sense? And should the Arts Council be a dynamic force, instead of a paternalistic one? Does not the strength of the Arts Council precisely lie in the fact that it reflects a prevailing mood in the theatre – even to its open-minded though slightly limp response to experiment? Should the Arts Council risk its hard-won prestige on dangerous living? Should the reps do so? Where will – or should – the pressure for change come?

6

Living Dangerously

THE main danger to repertory theatres is not of lawsuits or the police, but of insolvency, still the strictest censor we have. The poorest ones, who hope to struggle on to the end of the season, sometimes face this danger quite cheerfully, like hippies who tour the continent on £5 10s. The most brilliant and successful ones, whose books at the end of the season may balance quite as badly, can sometimes afford to ignore the prospect of bankruptcy, confident as old lords that their friends will bail them out. But the not too prosperous, middle-brow and -class reps, pillars of the theatrical community, have to take this threat very seriously; and the word 'living', under such conditions, is a sort of euphemism. These reps live like suburban wives, not dogmatically faithful to their husbands, the audiences, who seem on the whole a dreary lot. They are quite prepared to be tempted, but they have to be careful. If they read a 'daring' new script, they write back to the author praising his 'honesty' and 'his handling of the contemporary idiom'. If they see some marvellous production at the Aldwych, they wonder at once how it would seem, behind their proscenium arch, with their company of ten. Faced with an actual proposal, however, which seems a bit risky, they hesitate and say, 'Perhaps . . .' or 'Soon maybe . . .': and an agent, unless he's careful, gets trapped in the time-wasting snare of most seductions, trying to transform a tentative agreement on principle into an actual assignation, with dates, places and so forth. 'If I were running an ordinary rep,' Robert Selby, the production manager at Chichester told me, 'I would choose nine plays out of ten to suit the tastes of the audience. But the tenth play would have to be different. It would have to break new ground. . . .' 'The Canterbury audiences', said Peter Carpenter, who runs the Marlowe Theatre, 'are far from averse to the experimental or the *avant-garde*. But they need to become attuned gradually – say, in three stages, instead of one.' Unfortunately, the tenth play rarely comes and the stages of attunement can be indefinitely prolonged: and so when the exciting new advance finally happens it is as familiar as *French without Tears*.

To an outsider these flirtations with the *avant-garde* which so rarely lead to bed may seem unduly timid – particularly because the *avant-garde* in this context, the repertory movement in 1970, usually means Pinter and Joe Orton – not Arrabal or even Genet. Why (he may well ask) should the Liverpool Everyman with its church-hall stage and an Arts Council grant specifically for theatre-in-education, be able to offer *Early Morning* and *The Homecoming* for the autumn seasons in 1969 and 1970, while Laurier Lister down at Guildford with a sizeable grant and all the resources of the Yvonne Arnaud Theatre feels a bit apprehensive about *Loot*? Are the audiences in Liverpool so much more responsive, and, if so, why does the Liverpool Playhouse stand shivering on the brink for so long, dipping its toe in on Monday nights with *Waiting for Godot* and withdrawing it quickly on Tuesdays? And he may answer in the terms of personalities – the personalities which must be kept out of all serious discussions because they have a habit of becoming too personal – that Peter James who runs the Everyman is simply more dynamic than Laurier Lister or Antony Tuckey at the Playhouse.

I don't want to underrate the influence of the director, for he is the man who steers the car, but there are many factors involved: and often a bright young director can take over a grey rep, and turn (it would seem) middle-aged overnight. One went to a Midlands theatre with a brilliant reputation and some ambitious plans for productions which included Brecht and local documentaries. He tried to put some of these plans into action and the theatre lost money. He got into trouble with his board, and tried to recoup his losses by presenting a 'popular' programme. But he had already damaged the image of the theatre with the traditional audiences, who didn't come back, and the new audiences, particularly the students, whom he was trying to win, felt betrayed. The box-office receipts fell by £7000 in one season and no director could stay after that. The director of a fairly well-established middle-class rep often has less real room to manœuvre than someone like Peter James or Peter Cheeseman (at the Victoria Theatre, Stoke) – both of whom took over disused cinemas with a few friends and had to find some sort of audience from a large city. Obviously, the size of the catchment area is important. A twenty-mile radius centred on Liverpool would net a million and a half potential patrons: a similar radius centred on Guildford would catch about a third of that number. The nature of the community is equally important. Guildford belongs to the gin-and-tonic belt of London, and unlike Liverpool quite a large proportion of the population do go to the theatre, not regularly perhaps, but as part of their social education. Laurier Lister has to provide the convenient local equivalent to a night out in the West End: and his patrons know what they want, boulevard drama generally, with some well-dressed star-spangled revivals. The Yvonne Arnaud Theatre boasts an excellent restaurant, a fine view of the river, and a chandelier. It would be difficult for Laurier Lister in these circumstances to try out, say, a local documentary, or plays with a left-wing bias – right-wing plays are accepted without question – or any play which verges on the *avant-garde*. 'If I put on an experimental play,' Laurier Lister told me, 'I would never find an audience.' His public would simply choose what they want from the West End. There are no untapped student audiences and his chances of reaching the factory workers of Guildford are equally remote. He can only stretch the ropes a little – by offering, say, the British première of Duras' tantalizing and difficult play, *The Viaduct*, with Sybil Thorndike as the draw, or by trying out *Loot* and advertising it carefully as Not For Children.

The moral of this example is that one cannot decide by external criteria alone whether a rep is living dangerously. Ionesco's *The Chairs* would seem old hat at the Traverse, Edinburgh, hopelessly obscure at the Grand, Wolverhampton. It all depends on what the community is like, and from which sections the audiences are drawn. All reps should, in my opinion, dare more than their accountants would advise, but this is not to suggest that they should all play Arrabal. If we apply the same standards of ambition to every rep in the country, using the same authors and plays as examples, we are in fact suggesting that these theatres can – and should – uproot themselves from their communities, which would be, I think, a retrograde step. This is one of the arguments against 'free theatre', which usually means nationally subsidized theatres. If a rep depended on national subsidies alone – and not on box-office receipts or local subsidies – the fear is sometimes expressed that rep directors would want to sprint ahead too quickly, leaving their audiences to drop away, exhausted and bored. This fear may have little justification, but I do think that if a rep director had in the last resort to acquire the good will only of the Arts Council he might neglect the slower process of seeking out new audiences, trying to extend the appreciate range of the old ones, and, above all, attempting to bring together different sections of the community under one roof. It is on this level that the risks are most rewarding, for if a rep director caters merely to the middle-aged or the students he is not only sharpening the divisions within society – he is also potentially impoverishing the theatre. I have already mentioned the three theatres in Cambridge during the fifties – the Arts (respectable), the A.D.C. (for students) and the New (variety, striptease and sex plays): if these three theatres had been placed in one building, there would have been the chance of a greater *rapprochement* not just between the dons, the students and the town – but also between the different aspects of someone like myself who could happily watch strip at the New, yet twist with sexual embarrassment at the Arts if an actress had an accident with her bra. Only a brave and far-sighted director would have attempted to cross these barriers – which were more social than sexual – and yet they were there to be crossed. It was what both the community and the theatres needed. The plays at the Arts were too polished, too well dressed and spoken: those at the A.D.C. were rougher, more improvisatory, and, in spite of the intense solemnity of the many experiments, were more gaily in contact with the student atmosphere; those at the New Theatre lumbered along the trail to some sexual wild west, a direction which the other two theatres primly tended to ignore. But men are both Apollonian and Dionysian, old and young at the same time, hopelessly rich and irretrievably poor; and for a theatre to ignore this confusion of opposites is to reduce the game to mere grind.

Many rep directors have tried, particularly in the past ten years, to chip away at the barriers which loomed so formidably at Cambridge. It is always a risky process. It is much easier to fall right down the generation gap than to bridge it. The gains have to be made slowly, if they are to be made at all. At Salisbury – and at the Liverpool Playhouse – Monday nights are set aside for students, with reduced seat-prices and more adventurous scripts. The Sheffield Playhouse has started an experimental offshoot to the main company, where actors not involved in the current production can work with the students in the little Vanguard Theatre. I saw a gay, little sketch there, fairly bawdy, about computerized sex; and the room was packed, and had an off-off-Broadway atmosphere – smoke, pretty girls with beads, and friendliness. In the studio annexe at the Gateway Theatre, Chester, there are some lively productions without décor – of plays by Lorca and Arrabal, Ionesco and Pinter. At Ipswich, Nicholas Barter runs a drama studio connected to the main theatre, which acts as a try-out theatre, a youth club and a drama school. At the Midlands Arts Centre, Cannon Hill, Birmingham, the professional repertory team work side by side with amateurs: the amateur workshop is next to the professional one, the studio theatre (originally intended for amateur and try-out productions) is being used also by the professional company until the Cygnet Theatre is built; the centre is primarily for youth theatre – up to the age of twenty-five – but parents can come (suitably accompanied by children) to watch either the puppet productions in the Hexagon Theatre or the main productions such as Henry Livings' *Eh?* in the Studio Theatre. The significance of all these ventures is that there has been an attempt to break down the image of the theatre as a stuffy, middle-aged activity – while at the same time retaining the support of the traditional audiences. Sometimes, of course, this image is broken unintentionally – and without retaining this support. At the Grand, Wolverhampton, in 1969, when it was still pursuing a policy of weekly rep and 'subsistence' plays in an effort to stave off bankruptcy, they tried out Ann Jellicoe's *The Knack*, and were dismayed to find that the stalls were empty on the second night. Later on in the week, however, they noticed that the balcony and upper circle were fuller than usual and that the audience was younger.

The general effect of these attempts to cross over generation and class barriers has been that more people come to the theatre less often. This trend has been noticed by many rep directors, who on the whole regard it favourably – as a sign that the public are becoming more selective in their choice of plays. They're pleased, that is, when the over-all box-office attendance-figures are rising, as they are at Colchester, for example. But equally, when the box-office figures are falling, the temptation to retrench, to hold the loyalists and neglect the rest, is very great. At the Everyman Theatre, Cheltenham, where the box-office figures hold respectably steady at 55 per cent capacity, there was an audience survey conducted by the very active Young Everyman group, over 900 strong, which revealed that 27·1 per cent of the audience came to every production, 38·9 per cent came to be 'entertained' and 59·9 per cent came to be 'informed and entertained'. The majority of those who wanted only to be 'entertained' came from the older age-groups: the younger groups seemed to want a more 'serious' approach. Rae Hammond, the manager, was surprised that only about a quarter of the audience were 'regulars' and also that age-groups were balanced like this: 61·1 per cent were over 25, 13·2 per cent between 20 and 25, and 25·7 per cent under 20. This revealed in his opinion that there was a swing away from the 'traditional' audiences, and that the policy of more adventurous programmes was starting to pay off. *Salad Days* might still ensure a good audience at the Everyman, but *The Knack* also did well. On the other hand, Edward Albee's *Zoo Story* raised a furore, and *Who's Afraid of Virginia Woolf?* also did badly, perhaps because a good production coincided with a spell of exceptionally sunny weather. He would be reluctant to try Pinter's *The Homecoming* or Joe Orton's *What the Butler Saw*.

The real taboos, therefore, which a rep director has to face are therefore these complicated social ones – the generation gap, the class barriers: and sexual attitudes, which loom so large in our discussions about formal censorship, are deeply entwined with these wider questions. The very man who visits a strip club in Billingham would be shocked if the Forum Theatre staged *The Killing of Sister George* or, to take a wilder extreme, *Oh, Calcutta!* David Forder, who runs the Colchester Rep, and Brian Howard, who manages Harrogate, both pointed out to me that there were no protests at all over *Boeing-Boeing*, whereas *The Knack* aroused some very indignant comments. 'It is all a question of idiom,' David Forder said, a bit too suavely perhaps to one indignant customer. 'What you call idiom,' retorted the patron, 'I call *filth*!' *Boeing-Boeing* and *The Knack* are both comedies about seducers and seductions. The girls are prettier in *Boeing-Boeing* and wear less. The tone in *Boeing-Boeing* is more cynical and the girls are handed from man to man more freely. By any *conscious* standards, *Boeing-Boeing* is the more 'immoral' play – but, of course, the real problem is not on this level. To begin with, *Boeing-Boeing* is set in a luxury Paris flat, and the girls are air-hostesses. Thus, an unreal glamour hangs over the proceedings. *The Knack*, however, is set in a dingy bed-sitter and the girl is on her way to the Y.W.C.A. The closer a sexual fantasy comes to reality, the harder it is to avoid the implications. Behind the silken doors of *Boeing-Boeing* would copulation actually take place? I can only imagine the air-hostesses, as in some bra advertisement, leaping in slow motion over a tasselled pouffe, while M. Bernard flexes his muscles in front of a gilded mirror. In *The Knack*, however, there's a real bed, one that collapses. The rich, moreover, as one trade unionist stated on television, are more immoral than the rest of us. It's all right for them – they can pay for abortions and bastards, divorces and alimony. Or – to put the same idea another way – what's the point in having money if you can't be 'immoral'? 'You can put anything on,' said David Forder, 'if there's a chandelier.' Or else, as Brian Shelton, the former artistic director of Pitlochry, pointed out, 'You can be far more daring in a costume drama.' Wealth and history soften the blow of a nerve-tightening image. Edward Bond, in Robert Selby's opinion, would be 'far too savage' for Chichester: and yet, in *Antony and Cleopatra*, which was playing there when I spoke to him, Antony slashes his guts with a sword and fails to die. In the South of England, in particular, at Windsor, Guildford, Brighton, Leatherhead, Folkestone, Bexhill and Worthing, audiences react less indignantly to infidelities and cruelties which take place in opulent settings – luxury hotels, apartments and drawing-rooms. 'I go to the theatre to enjoy myself,' wrote a correspondent to the *Daily Telegraph* who lived in Sunbury, 'not to see all this "kitchen-sink" rubbish.' In the North, though not at Harrogate, and in the industrial Midlands, the reaction is slightly different, although still, if one chooses a sexually daring play, one should also have an opulent set. The difference is a subtle one. Audiences laugh more at the drawing-room surroundings – handing round afternoon tea would probably seem funny in Liverpool, deadly serious in Windsor. The fantasy element, too, seems stronger. The set of the Chester *Boeing-Boeing* was like something from a James Bond film – all aluminium and inflatable cushions. M. Bernard looked like Omar Sharif, and his friend from the country like George Formby. Nor is there the same dislike of kitchen-sink drama; Keith Waterhouse and Willis Hall are, after all, regional dramatists.

In themselves, these sexual double-standards, one for the rich, another for the poor, do not seem to me very shocking. On the contrary, I would have thought that the audiences were bravely recognizing a sad fact – that it is easier and less messy for the rich to have mistresses and lovers than the poor. To protest against this state of affairs is to protest generally against inequalities of income. Nor, of course, do audiences follow up this recognition by suggesting that 'immoral books should only be printed in expensive editions'

– or that the frustrations of the poor should be curbed, those of the rich indulged. What disturbs me more is the alienation from experience which ostentatious wealth, historical costumes and so forth usually provide – and that these experiences, sexual or otherwise, can only apparently be accepted by the audience through a filter. Wealth and history are not the only filters: things can be said and done in comedies which would not be tolerated in dramas. There are no regional differences here. In London, not so long ago, in 1966, *A Patriot for Me*, John Osborne's finest play perhaps, had to be staged in a club theatre (the Royal Court, legally transformed for the occasion) because of the homosexual scenes, the drag ball, and the bitter quarrels. At the same time, *The Killing of Sister George* with its various scenes of Lesbianism, was shown publicly. Legally, of course, the situation has changed – but the atmosphere remains the same. *The Killing of Sister George* plays everywhere, except Colwyn Bay or Billingham: *A Patriot for Me* scarcely anywhere. Both plays tackle sexual perversions, but in one we are forced to feel the situation through to its limits – and in the other the sexual material has been predigested for us and spat out in epigrams. A classic feature of all comedy technique is to give the audience knowledge about the situation, which is denied the characters on stage. Hence, we can watch them twitching like puppets, blindly unaware of the strings which we can see. In comedies, sexual perversions become kinks which other people can't control. The audience is encouraged to take a lofty attitude. Psychologically, I would have thought, to have so great a concentration on this attitude is disastrous, coarsening our sympathies, encouraging us to be patronizing, and, in the last resort, forcing us to be more inhibited and defensive. Among the reps 'comedies' about sex generally raise few problems – although Joe Orton is always being accused of 'bad taste'. 'Dramas', however, are rare and inhibited. It is as if, for all our greater 'permissiveness', we still don't want to take sex seriously. And when a rep tries to put on a play where eroticism *is* taken seriously, as in *Antony and Cleopatra*, the effect is often embarrassing, a combination of back-seat pawing and cocktail-party frigidity. This situation will probably not improve until we admit erotic pleasure more freely into the theatre. We still prefer to keep our sex spectacles in the night clubs, rather like a man who thinks so highly of marriage that he has to keep a mistress to avoid sullying his wife.

The question, therefore, which confronts rep directors who want to live dangerously is not simply 'Is this topic or treatment taboo?' but rather 'In what *context* is this topic taboo?' And I am using the word 'context', like elastic, to include social attitudes and surroundings, and also 'frames of mind' – fantasy or reality, detachment or involvement. No rep director can afford to affront his public – however morally desirable he may feel this shock to be: the censorship of economics is too tough. In 1969, there were two instances where reps introduced physical nakedness on the stage: in the Northcott Theatre's *Abelard and Héloïse* and the Connaught Theatre's *Romeo and Juliet*. The historical setting for both productions helped to subdue the impact: and both plays were so tastefully presented that the nakedness could have been mistaken, in the elegant shadows, for some less floppy medieval costume. Eroticism was out of the question. Some student theatres have been more adventurous – the Brighton Combination, the Traverse, Edinburgh – using not only *visible* nakedness, but moments and scenes which were intended to shock. The Traverse, Edinburgh, originally took over a converted brothel, and promptly ran into trouble with the authorities who thought they were using the building for immoral purposes. Their first production in January 1963 was Arrabal's *Orison*, which was followed a few weeks later by Jarry's *Ubu Roi*, which starts with the word 'Shit'. It was the first time, one Edinburgh citizen told me, that he had heard the word publicly spoken in Edinburgh, and he trembled (as Yeats had done sixty years before in Paris) at the impact such vulgarities could have on Culture. The record of these student theatres is a proud one – not only in challenging orthodox attitudes, but in discovering some genuinely exciting new dramatists – Stanley Eveling and Cecil Taylor: and to some extent they have become incorporated into the repertory movement through the studio theatres. However, it is sad to remember that there has been no complete repertory production of Wedekind's admirable and sensible play about adolescent love, *Spring Awakening*, which was written in 1891 and only produced in this country at the Royal Court in 1963, and even then with drastic cuts ordered by the Lord Chamberlain.

Through the student theatres in particular, a limited daring has entered the repertory movement, and not only on sexual matters. The real daring, I suppose, has been in the way in which the shock physical and psychological effects of Artaud and the Living Theatre, the masks and the mime, have been cautiously fed into the main-stream from these small experimental springs. Repertory theatres themselves are far more cautious than the students – but still Warren Jenkins bravely staged the première of Bond's *Narrow Road to the Deep North*, although he only risked a week. The Liverpool Everyman is an adventurous theatre: but in the main the repertory movement handles the *avant-garde*, any sort of *avant-garde*, with a caution amounting almost to neglect.

There is one other noticeable area of taboo, which has not really attracted an *avant-garde*. Many rep directors agree with Peter Carpenter that the stage should not become 'a platform for opinions'. Now, superficially, this idea sounds just silly, for how can a writer avoid having opinions or prevent these opinions from affecting his choice of subject matter? And haven't some of the finest dramatists this century been the most opinionated – Shaw, Brecht and Sartre? Wasn't even Shakespeare a feudal propagandist? The underlying attitude, however, is more complex and the key word is not 'opinions' but 'platform'. Rep directors dislike – and tend to underrate as a theatrical effect – the direct didactic assault on the audience, the sort of preaching to be found in Peter Brook's *US*. And the reason for this dislike is fundamental to the policy of most repertory theatres, who are trying to bring in different sections of the public to the theatre, to alienate none of them, to woo audiences and invite their co-operation. Sometimes this attitude leaves the impression of a certain weak-kneed liberalism, a good-humoured acceptance of everything that comes along. Few rep directors will describe their choice of programmes as anything other than 'broadly based', 'mixed', 'catholic'. Fewer still will commit themselves as firmly as Peter Cheeseman has done at Stoke to plays on local subjects, staged in the round. They are, in other words, sacrificing a more dogmatic and strident cultural leadership to provide something more subtle – a club atmosphere where no one is blackballed, or insulted, or left out.

From London, this gentle, long-term process can sometimes seem timid, and we only admire the end-product – the theatrical richness of a town like Nottingham where nearly everyone is aware of the fervour of the Playhouse. But long before the Playhouse was built or John Neville or Stuart Burge went there Val May was patiently experimenting with his small permanent company, encouraging authors to write for his actors and developing a regional repertoire of plays. We don't see from London the gradual development of taste, and interest and excitement which is where the real challenges of the repertory theatre lie. Every rep director, it seems, tours around the Women's Institutes to lecture: and visits schools and factories. Many are trying, as Arnold Wesker tried to do more spectacularly, to work with unions, and in factories. The ordinary tolerance displayed by local reps of social differences within their towns, of students and their parents, of all class levels, can be in its way adventurous, daring even, for it implies a reluctance to accept the hidden social patterns. By encouraging this tolerance in others, particularly through theatre-in-education programmes, rep directors are not only laying the foundations for more adventurous drama in the future – a drama which can hold together many different social themes and technical effects, many problems concerning the community which would otherwise have no expressive outlet – but they are also gradually changing the role in the community which the theatre can play. Too great an initial daring could damage this wider cause. We may perhaps be watching the growth of a genuine People's theatre, an ideal which has haunted us for rather too long and from which other revolutions may stem.

But even if the repertory theatres are aiming at this rather subtle revolution, achieved through tolerance and reconciliation, rather than shock, are they more reactionary than London and the West End? Obviously not. This is why there are so many transfers from various reps to the West End. There aren't many provincial attitudes among the reps which can't also be observed on Shaftesbury Avenue. The reps are generally a few years behind the Royal Court, the Open Space or the Aldwych, but so is the commercial theatre: and the record of student theatres like the Traverse is not noticeably less adventurous than the Open Space. But, if, as I have suggested, the real aim is not to stage *avant-garde* plays but to become an open-minded forum for the community – and that to achieve this end reps *are* prepared to take risks, then this sort of comparison is unfair: not to the reps, but to London. No London theatre has yet attempted to be a community theatre in this sense: perhaps in a huge cauldron like London, with students, tourists, commuters and residents all boiled up together, it may be impossible to have community theatres. The Arts Council has often praised the idea of community theatre. Are they spurring the reps on to greater achievements in this direction? Are the reps falling behind the expectations of the Arts Council? Might they be reactionary in this sense? Again, I would have thought not. Hugh Jenkins M.P. may talk about the reps being the 'churches of the future' from his position on the Arts Council: but in practical terms the Arts Council often seems to take a somewhat reactionary stance. Even disregarding the Theatre Enquiry Report, which as we have seen is primarily concerned with preserving the waning commercial theatre in its present form and with encouraging touring, we can notice other symptoms of a slightly arthritic response to the aims which so many reps have in common. At a time, for example, when the reps were desperately trying to extend their public support into the less well-paid classes, not only the students but factory workers, the Arts Council urged them most forcibly to look for further revenue, not from state or local grants, but from increased seat-prices. The top price at Nottingham is currently 12s 6d, having recently been raised from 10s. Nottingham was urged to look towards Chichester, where the *average* seat price is currently just over a pound. If the Chichester Festival Theatre charges so much for a seat, why (it was asked) can't Nottingham? The answer is, of course, that the Nottingham Playhouse can – but to do so would immediately restrict the audience to those who could afford to come. Hence, the whole idea of a community theatre would be threatened.

Compared to the commercial theatre nowadays, the repertory theatres are adventurous, and commercial managements would add that they can, with subsidies, afford to be. Compared to various *avant-garde* theatre-movements – Grotowski and Julian Bec, Artaud and Arrabal – they seem a conservative bunch. Within the context of British theatre as a whole – and in our prevailing cultural climate – the reps are in a vanguard of sorts, not in the discovery of new forms of drama, but in the attempt to find a new role for the theatre. From this role, I believe that new theatrical forms have come – regional documentaries – and will continue to come in the future.

7

Teaching and Learning

Approximately two-thirds of the repertory theatres in this country carry theatre-in-education programmes: but these programmes vary greatly in scope, style and ambition. Some rep directors view them cynically, arguing that at best they're a cheap form of publicity, and at worst a time-wasting extra chore. 'If you visit schools too often,' Joan Knight, the artistic director at Perth, told me, 'you become a teacher.' These directors will sometimes offer cheap prices to students – or school matinées perhaps – a little nibble from the House of Gingerbread to lure them into the cage of theatre-going: but nothing more. 'It is not our job', one theatre manager told me, 'to compensate for the deficiencies of the educational system.' At other theatres, however, the relationship with schools – and adult education institutes – is taken very seriously indeed. Teams of actor/teachers are employed to tour around the schools, not simply to advertise the theatre, but to encourage the idea that the theatre is the place where the problems of the community can be argued out, ritualized into a coherent shape and examined freely and intelligently. Some companies prefer to visit schools, to co-operate with the teachers: others prefer to ignore the school system altogether, trying instead to attract the children into the actual theatre building – by offering, say, open rehearsal sessions or improvisation groups on Saturday mornings. The Midlands Arts Centre in Birmingham, specially designed for youth activities, refuses either to visit schools or to present the 'set text' plays: they want to present drama which is of interest to children – but not school-ridden or exam-bound. Sometimes, the school programmes are directly related to the plays offered in the adult theatre: sometimes, theatre-in-education teams deliberately divorce themselves from the main repertory programmes, believing that it is only through such a separation that the interests of the children can be raised above the crude struggle for audiences and good box-office figures at the end of the season.

Probably every rep manager – and nearly every actor/teacher – would interpret the idea of theatre-in-education slightly differently: and yet from this confusion certain patterns emerge – models, rather than principles, shared experiences perhaps, rather than models. One distinction to be made is between 'teaching about theatre' and 'learning through drama'. The aim of one is to tell children about the theatre as an art form, interpreting the theatre as a body of dramatic literature which is staged in a certain way towards certain ends: the purpose of the other is to encourage children to act out situations, to improvise and invent – to take part in the activity of drama as a means of self-expression. One is basically *inflow* teaching – that is, where the children are supposed to be in a passive role, watching and listening to the actors, or a lecture about Shakespeare: whereas the other is *outflow*, where the children are the ones who act, while the actors encourage them and suggest ideas, but, when the play begins, drift to the sidelines and watch. Here the role of the actor/teacher is firstly to give the children sufficient confidence and freedom to act, and secondly to ask those questions which will stimulate the children to direct their attention towards particular facts and emotional situations, rather than to allow the activity to wander into vagueness, and eventually boredom. Gavin Bolton, from the Durham University Institute of Education, expressed this point clearly at the 1969 Clifton College conference. It is, he argued, the 'teacher's judicious questioning' that translates 'the frivolous into something worth pursuing': and he gave the example of a group of young children who were dealing insensitively with the theme of a plague. The teacher added the order that all cats and dogs were to be killed – and thus, by particularizing the feelings of the children, they had 'another, more demanding situation to deal with'.

Very high claims have been made for learning through drama. Michael Barry of the Dundee Rep prepared a report for the Gulbenkian Foundation on the theatre-in-education scheme operating in Dundee, and in it he accepts as a premise that 'the best education and greater academic achievement come when "inflow" and "outflow" are properly balanced'. The team concentrated on *outflow* methods, perhaps to compensate for the basically *inflow* forms of teaching current in Dundee schools at this time, January 1969. He reported some remarkable results. 'With one class in Dundee very noticeable effects were observed during one term only: the teacher said that her class of C stream children's weekly I.Q. tests had shown a general increase in the I.Q.s of 25 per cent over the term and she could only put it down to our weekly drama class.' Michael Barry goes on to suggest that with an extension of these learning-through-drama programmes the crime rate in Dundee will be lowered, that children will grow up into adults with a more positive sense of purpose, happier and more able to use their leisure constructively. The trouble with such a report is that it sounds too good to be true. It makes theatre-in-education sound like a new health food. And indeed educationists are well aware of this rather naïve ring: Gordon Chambers pointed out in the Bristol University *New Theatre Magazine* that a conference on theatre-in-education has in previous years merely provided an excuse for self-indulgence. 'The ultimate aim of drama', he quoted ironically, 'is to train human beings to be human beings.' Nowadays, he states that the prevailing attitude is more like this: 'it is presumptuous to assert that if there were no drama, people would not mature – but it can be said that one matures more quickly if one has encountered drama'.

This is still, however, a high enough claim, and some have said that any form of education which arouses the commitment of the teachers shows spectacular results. If the claims for learning-through-drama are at all valid, they cast an unhappy light on I.Q. tests, and indeed on the whole educational system which can ignore, if only in some areas, so valuable a form of teaching. Shouldn't we train teachers to take acting classes, rather than actors to teach? And, indeed, those educationists who believe in learning through drama would argue that both approaches are valuable. If these claims are not valid, however, mightn't a rep company be lured into wasting energy on a doubtful form of social service? 'Actors are not equipped', said John Williams, manager of the Derby Playhouse, 'to be social workers.' The Derby Playhouse has a 'teaching-about-theatre' programme, but not a 'learning-through-drama' one. The Company toured around the local schools with a production of Ionesco's *Exit the King*, but there was no student participation, except in the subsequent discussions.

This distinction then between *inflow* and *outflow* theatre-in-education programmes is an important one, for it implies more than a different teaching method – rather a different place for the theatre within the community. In one, the rep provides drama as an art form for the community to watch: in the other, the rep is a focal point for community self-expression. As a rough guide, the more sedate managements (although these include the Royal Shakespeare Company and the Victoria Theatre, Stoke-on-Trent, two highly adventurous companies) prefer teaching-about-theatre. On a simple level, this may mean that the director or actors go around the schools, telling the children about the Life of an Actor, the Problems of Lighting and Make-up, the current programme at the Rep, and so on. Derek Salberg who manages what used to be a family theatre, the Alexandra, Birmingham, has given an unpaid weekly lecture to schools for years, believing rightly that it is an easy and useful form of publicity. The Victoria Theatre, Stoke-on-Trent, runs an advisory service for schools, so that teachers and children who need help with the annual production can go to them for assistance. Most reps are very well aware of the set-text plays in the G.C.E. and C.S.E. syllabuses, and probably they'll try to stage them, always an easy way to gain an audience. If not, they may try to send actors around the schools to act various scenes from the set text, to discuss the dramatic possibilities with the classes, and generally to try to bring life and vitality into what otherwise might seem a dull exam routine. At Cheltenham, in 1969, where *Romeo and Juliet* was the set text for many schools, Michael Ashton staged a production for three weeks in November. He also went out to schools to direct children in scenes from the play, and sometimes took a team of actors to illustrate. The cost of these excursions was borne by the schools, and were £10 for a visit from Michael Ashton, £20 for a Shakespeare Anthology programme, performed by a team of five actors: bargains, I would have thought. The Connaught Theatre, Worthing, took around a modern version of *Richard III* – rewritten by Christopher Denys, the artistic director, and set in a power-game world of big business. The script may have been a useful introduction to Shakespeare, but the dialogue seemed a bit impoverished in places

> *Richard:* Did you send that memo to Catesby about the press
> releases concerning my brother George?
> *Miss Simpson (a secretary):* I was just about to, sir, when. . . .
> *Richard:* Well, get on with it. Move, girl, move.

One Worthing citizen saw the whole venture as a concealed Communist plot. 'It was not even about a hunchback,' he wrote in the local paper, 'and it actually had a black man, singing calypsos to a guitar accompaniment!' The most elaborate teaching-about-theatre programme is probably *Theatre-Go-Round*, run by the Royal Shakespeare Company – where the actors present extracts from different styles and periods of drama, on a portable stage – an excellent introduction to the theatre, which fails only in that it is an anthology, a kaleidoscopic experience, rather than a single, unified sweep of an idea.

The value to schools of such excursions is obvious, although some headmasters resent the interruption to routine. The value to the theatre lies partly in the publicity it brings, and partly in that actors are brought into contact – through discussions and questions – with the children whose attitudes often reflect with depressing accuracy those of their parents. Most managements, however, would not think in these bartering terms. They would say that this is a service to the community – helping children to become aware of an art form – and most education authorities recognize this service in tangible, financial ways – by offering grants to the theatre, or by offsetting the price of seat reductions. Often, however, this financial aid isn't enough to compensate the theatre. At Colchester the student concessions cost the theatre £1300 and the grant from the Essex Education Authority amounted to only £750. And sometimes schools and education authorities assume all too readily that reps are prepared to go to this extra effort, simply for publicity, simply to attract the Audience of the Future. When this happens, actors and directors feel that they are being exploited and grow resentful. I visited one school with an acting team, and watched them amuse and inform three hundred children for a whole afternoon: the team of five was paid twenty-five pounds. The headmaster complained to me that he didn't look forward to these visits: 'You can hear the children laughing, you know, down the corridor.' I felt that the actors were being underpaid and underappreciated. Where educational authorities fail to realize the value of these visits – and don't pay for them, or only inadequately – then actors are inclined to feel that theatre-in-education is another distracting chore, to be relegated into the odd, unnecessary corners of the day or to compensate for having a small part in the current production. There are also a number of small itinerant and very badly paid theatre-in-education companies, performing perhaps four times a day, and travelling from school to school in old buses driven by one of the actors.

Some rep directors, too, are wary of linking their theatres too much with the Establishment in schools, believing that this may make the theatre seem an unnecessarily dull place. A poor Shakespearian production can do much to blunt the keenness for drama. On one level, a child is told that a Shakespeare play represents the Summit of Drama. But when he visits the theatre, he hears language which is hard to follow, delivered in a sing-song voice, accompanied by rather ridiculous gestures. The less intelligent will simply give up; the brighter ones may reject the feudal and nationalistic ideas expressed; and the submissive ones – who accept what they are told – come to believe that the theatre has to be high-flown, concerned with the deaths of kings, and indecisive, over-romantic love affairs – that, in other words, drama has little relevance to the lives they lead, but is a stately social ritual, like school assembly or Corps on Thursdays. Some may even enjoy the experience on this level. Most will fidget. To exorcise the ghost of Eng. Lit., some rep directors prefer to bring children to an open rehearsal session before seeing the performance, so that they can learn about the aims of the production, what each actor has to do and why. This is a good way of forestalling boredom, for the children start to learn that the actors are human too, and that even the stateliness has some roots in human experience. Other companies tackle this problem differently, by incorporating children into crowd scenes. The Nottingham Playhouse sent around a team of actors with the school set text, *Julius Caesar*, and the students were asked to be Roman citizens. In 1969, Stuart Burge followed up this experiment by producing David Caute's play, *The Demonstration*, which was about a student revolution. It transferred to the main Nottingham Playhouse, still with students in the production.

These teaching-about-theatre programmes and the learning-through-drama ones have in some towns generated an extraordinarily keen and knowledgeable interest in the theatre among students. At the Octagon Theatre, Bolton, when I was there, schoolchildren drifted purposefully around the building, sometimes watching quietly and intently a rehearsal for *Oedipus Rex*, then moving away to the coffee bar. When the seating has to be changed – a laborious business to alter the shape of the stage – the children help. John Wackett, the former theatre manager, told me that this conversion used to take a day and a half, but has now been cut to half-a-day because the children are so well drilled. Some teenagers at Lincoln were painting the Theatre Royal – legally. 'It keeps them off the streets,' one mother said to me. 'No, really it's good for them. I wish I'd had a theatre to play in.'

Many rep directors – probably most – would dislike this youth club atmosphere, regarding hordes of youth in the foyers and corridors as a heavy price to pay for the wall occasionally painted, the stalls manned, the litter swept up and distributed elsewhere. Lincoln and Bolton have other compensations, however – a young involved and alert public, the best guarantee of a theatre's future. At Billingham, there were perhaps two basic mistakes during the first years of the Forum Theatre's existence: one was that the theatre was shut away from the flow of activities elsewhere in the building, the ice-skating and swimming, by a heavy brick wall – and the other was no theatre-in-education programme. At Lincoln and Bolton, the aim is not to teach children about theatre but to encourage them to use drama for their own purposes. The syllabus for the Octagon Theatre's Education Programme states specifically that children cannot be allowed in as audience. They must take part. Sometimes, the children are invited back to the theatre to watch a production, but this is after the first visits to schools have taken place. There is a team of five actors – part of the main company – who offered during the Autumn Term 1969 four separate programmes: *Hocus Pocus* for six- or seven-year-olds, *Road Up* for one class of less able lower juniors, *People of Atago* for one class of second- or third-form secondary-school pupils, and *Suburbia* for a group of 'not more than thirty-five fifth- or sixth-form pupils'.

Hocus Pocus is really a development from the primary-school work of Brian Way, an authority on child drama. Brian Way runs Theatre Centre Ltd in London, and from here he sends out seven school companies. He has also written a number of plays for children, including *The Tramp and the Signpost* which the Dundee Rep used in their education programme. The actors tell a story to the children, which they then act out with the actors. The children take part in crowd scenes, chases, mountain-climbing expeditions and so forth. In *Hocus Pocus*, the actors try not to impose a story on the children, but to use whatever suggestions come to hand from the initial discussion. In *Road Up*, the basic story concerned two Gas Board workers who dig a hole under the ground to repair a gas leak. One of the men mysteriously disappears, and the children are needed to solve the clues and 'to make a dangerous journey'. In *People of Atago*, the theme was of an ancient race, whose culture was jeopardized by the arrival of a stranger whose presence has a disruptive influence on the community. 'Within the framework presented by the Company,' the syllabus stated, 'there will be short periods when groups of pupils will be responsible for creating the next stage of the story. Ideas will be interpreted through improvisation, creative writing and movement, so that after the initial stimulus, pupils will participate throughout.' *Suburbia* for the older pupils starts with improvised presentation of social problems, offered by different groups of pupils. The students then offer solutions to these problems: and in the second stage act out the various tasks and steps involved in building a community centre.

Bolton's learning-through-drama programme is typical of many others – at Chester, Coventry, Dundee, Edinburgh, Exeter, Glasgow, Ipswich, Lancaster, Lincoln, Liverpool, Manchester, Newcastle, Sheffield, Watford, Worthing and York. Sometimes these programmes are more extensive than Bolton's – sometimes less so. *The Blue Blanket*, a programme devised by the Edinburgh theatre-in-education team (attached to the Royal Lyceum), concerned the evolution of the City Council during the fifteenth century in Edinburgh. One class of children acted as merchants, another were craftsmen, and from their bargaining the concept of councils and business ethics emerged. The Library Theatre, Manchester, presented a similar programme about the Peterloo Massacre. Sometimes the learning-through-drama programmes are linked with the main repertory programme. At the Belgrade Theatre, Coventry, before the Company's production of John Arden's play, *Live like Pigs*, Warren Jenkins sent his team of actor/teachers around the schools, encouraging the children to improvise stories, firstly about strangers invading the family circle, then about war refugees arriving in a town, and lastly, about the immigrant families living in England. *Live like Pigs* is a play about a gipsy family coming to live in a genteel suburban neighbourhood: John Arden balances the arguments rather carefully between those of the casual, dirty, free gipsies and those of the more conventional neighbours. The children could compare their versions of immigrant problems with that expressed by John Arden and the repertory company. It was in many respects a noble experiment, tackling directly – perhaps too directly – the problems of immigration in an area which is, after all, not far from Wolverhampton geographically. But there are a number of objections which could be raised. One is that to link West Indians and Pakistanis even indirectly, by implication, with the gipsies in *Live like Pigs* is perhaps to insult them, or, worse, to perpetuate a crude stereotype. This is perhaps an example of the well-intentioned meddling with complex problems which John Williams at Derby most fears. Another objection was that *Live like Pigs* was bad box-office. Why? The play itself is perhaps not a commercially attractive one. Possibly it was chosen for other reasons. Did the public come to associate the production with an effort to smooth racial integration? Or did they stay away from apathy, disapproval, or from the feeling that somehow the theatre was stepping out of line? The idea dies hard that the theatre is a purveyor of entertainment only, and that entertainment itself has no other usefulness.

To integrate learning-through-drama programmes with the plays at the local rep is a step towards a different over-all idea of *theatre*. The audience is not asked to sit passively at the end of a day's work and be amused: but to relate what they themselves have already expressed – and the manner of the expression – with what the professionals say and do. It is an attempt to balance *inflow* and *outflow* in drama. Nor are these experiments confined to schoolchildren. At the Midlands Arts Centre, the age limit is twenty-five to thirty. Marjorie Sigley, who is so successful in this field, works equally effectively with children and adult education classes. Victor Corti, who reduces the role of the director to that of a technical adviser, has described what is almost a Highway Code for adult learning-through-drama: including some slightly dubious phrases – 'self-criticism would be encouraged, but always related to the community and not of a personal nature'. It is hard to see how self-criticism cannot be personal. Brecht painted a rather over-simple view of community drama at the beginning of *The Caucasian Chalk Circle*, where the workers lay down their tools in a spirit of comradeship and divert themselves with an ancient legend. Joan Littlewood has advocated an adult 'fun palace'. All these wider visions seem rather improbable – and undesirable if they could be realized: partly because they underrate the amount of sheer technical expertise needed to transform drama from a pastime to a truly satisfactory and creative activity. And indeed, although community drama may be a vitally important adjunct to the art form which we call theatre; I do not see how it can replace the art form itself. The pressure for higher standards, for a more effective realization of an original idea, comes from within, and a democratic production may frustrate the need to present something which is perfect.

What usually happens with community drama is this: the Theatre starts by ostentatiously taking off its robes and ermine, the gauze and coloured glass, and puts on jeans and a sweater. The Play – instead of being a performance conceived secretly as a baby and presented after birth with a maternal pride, flounces and frills around the cot – is organized into existence in a very public way. Citizens raise problems, which are discussed and improvised into small scenes. And then there is either a dispirited running-down of this process, when everyone feels that ideas have been superficially expressed but nothing has been properly synthesized, or someone takes over control – a director, a writer, a leading actor. He is suddenly fired with enthusiasm and determination: and in the vital last weeks before a production he is the driving-force which organizes the random ideas into a coherent production. He may pretend for ideological reasons that this is not so, but nobody in the group is fooled. Indeed community theatre can lead to a production tyranny, which few directors working in a more conventional way would dare to attempt. Joan Littlewood, for example, rejects most forcibly the idea of a genius director: 'my belief is in the genius of each person'. Having founded the Theatre Workshop in Stratford, she has since opted out of the professional theatre system, preferring to work with groups of young people. In the midst of a professional production, however, she was always determined, even ruthlessly, to get her own way: rewriting the scripts, staging a scene differently at the last moment, supporting her decisions with a most eloquent invective. At Lincoln, it is true, where the company has developed slowly, trained at the E.15. Drama School and was inspired indirectly by Joan Littlewood, the sort of decisions which are normally associated with a director are taken by the Company as a whole – from the interpretation of the play to the planning of moves. The director stands by, watching the total effect, asking questions rather than formulating answers, and keeping his fingers crossed. This system works well at Lincoln, because the Company is a closely knit team, have trained in a similar way and bear certain rules in mind. Their 'freedom' is comparable with that of improvised jazz – where within a strict tonal structure players can be given certain themes to develop, certain areas in the music for display. The value of such productions is that the fusion of outlooks imparts a variety and richness of texture:

every actor contributes a slightly different interpretation of the basic ideas, thus adding a new window to the room. But the weakness lies in the fact that the original structure cannot be questioned too deeply, for fear that the ensemble will break up: a jazz musician who totally rejects tonality will have difficulty in being part of a band. Hence, community drama which starts with such admirably democratic ideals can easily become more formal, conformist and unchallenging even than tea-cup or kitchen-sink theatre.

Indeed, the value of community drama is not that the process in *itself* produces exciting theatre: but rather that the discussions, at the beginning, unearth rich and varied material for drama, and that the creativity of the actor is stimulated at an early stage, before the basic pattern of a production has become settled and decided. His performance, therefore, has deep roots. *After* these initial discussions and improvisations, then the director or writer takes over, and moulds the various ideas and outlooks into an interesting play or production. He rides these separately kicking horses, and drives them towards his particular home. It is this combination of freedom in the early stages of a production and control in the later ones which has produced exciting theatre – not only Joan Littlewood's productions at Stratford, but also Peter Cheeseman's work at Stoke-on-Trent. The regional documentaries at the Victoria Theatre include gobbets of local history, researched by members of the Company, taped recollections from men in the street, dramatized versions of local battles – from the pubs to the council chambers. While this material is being assembled, the writers, the actors and the directors work together in a very democratic way, simply to discover along what lines the production should proceed: but then Peter Terson or some other writer produces a script, and Peter Cheeseman decides on the dates of the production, and the process of daily discipline, centralized around the director, begins. Of course, a company which has worked together for some time, which drinks together at night, which visits schools together, will become more of a team: the decisions will tend to be collective ones. This would happen whether or not there is any ideological commitment to the idea of group productions. The days of the autocratic actor-manager are past. But equally a commitment to total democratic discussion and decision-making through all the stages of a production is equally frustrating. It doesn't work. And nothing destroys a company more quickly than the feeling that the final production will not live up to their hopes and expectations.

I must here declare an interest in that I have taught drama both in schools and adult education institutes, and that to play down the importance of learning-through-drama would be to knock something on which I have spent much time. One very commonplace and familiar incident stays in my mind. For a short, rather shattering time, I taught English in a secondary modern school in North London. It was a tough area. The classes were large, the children usually bored, counting the days like old lags before the moment of their final release. The school always seemed to be about six masters short, and I was a supply teacher, filling in time before university and taking the place of someone who, after years of solid coping, had just had a nervous breakdown. Naïvely, I tried to teach the third and fourth forms the sort of clause analysis, précis and essay-writing, and literary appreciation which had formed so large a part of my own education. The lack of response was startling. They didn't even bother to riot. The senior English master advised me to try out some class improvisation, based on any subject which might appeal to them. One of the third forms chose to act out a robbery, which had actually happened in the area the previous week. We swopped the roles around to give all the children a chance to watch and take part, to act the Law, the Victim and the Culprit. With comparatively little prompting from me – although it is hard to assess the extent of my initiative – the class became involved in the improvisation, which differed so little apparently from the games which they were playing outside, in the playground and streets. Again without my having to ask too many questions, although I asked some, the class became concerned with the accuracy of details. Did the robbers' car pull up with a screech of brakes? Was there an alarm? Most of them started out with vague sympathies which became more clearly defined – and more diverse – as the game proceeded. The child who was most self-righteous as the policeman, couldn't at first make the criminal seem human. He was a monster, a brutal thug who wouldn't open a door if he could knock it down first Then, after watching other interpretations, he changed clichés: the criminal was now hard done by, a poor man struggling against the odds to earn a bit of bread for his wife and starving children. The form bully became terrified as the Victim. Some saw the incident as heroic, others wanted to know what factually had occurred: and, as the children discussed the event – and tried different ways of doing it – the heroism became less arbitrary, the realism less cold. Later they were able to write the sort of essays about the incident which I had despaired of seeing from them – lively, involved and longer than two sentences.

Plato, of course, who thought most forms of fiction were harmful because people were lured into fantasies, would have disapproved. He might have argued that by encouraging children to improvise a robbery I was teaching them to rob. Aristotle might have sprung to my defence, retorting that, on the contrary, the impulses towards robbery were being siphoned off into a game. The children afterwards would not feel emotionally inclined to rob. Remnants of this old dispute – harmful stimulation versus useful catharsis – linger on still beneath so many other controversies – about censorship, pornography, violence on television and so forth. I am not convinced that this debate is relevant. What seemed to happen was this. The children came to the improvisation with some general impressions of the incident – derived partly from what they had heard about it, partly from similar stories which they had seen on T.V., partly from the conversation of their family – which the acting helped to bring into focus. For some, a one-sided view became a many-sided picture. In this incident, they needed less prompting from me, because the story was fresh in their minds. Certain limits were placed on the improvisation – the size of the floor, the time-length of the class – and since we wanted to compress as many impressions as possible within these limits we had to decide where to begin and end, where certain happenings should take place and what they should be. And so the incident was not allowed to wander without limit in the mind, attaching itself to streets, to places and times of day, to professions, classes and races. Through the improvisation, we gave the story a defined scope. If there is any direct purgation in acting, it comes not only by unloading excess feeling into drama, but also by giving these emotions a definite place, an area which can be temporarily isolated and examined. By undertaking this activity as a group – not simply by writing about the story during homework – the children became more aware of each other – and of me – imitating one another, criticizing, showing off and wincing away through shyness.

Different age groups, of course, respond differently. Younger children, it is said, are more uninhibited. They're certainly more malleable. Older children have more to contribute and also more need to assert their points of view. In the report which Michael Barry compiled for the Gulbenkian Foundation, there is an interesting survey of the reactions of children who watched Brian Way's *The Tramp and the Signpost*. They were asked, 'Whom did you like best in the play?' and the three most popular characters were the ones who most noticeably represented moral forces – the Spirit (the main driving-force for good), the Queen (a proud female baddy, who was converted to good in the end) and the Monster (a fearsome male baddy also won over to good). Boys seem to like the Monster, the girls the Queen. Among the age groups, the Spirit did well with the six- and seven-year-olds, and so did the Monster. The Queen was most popular with the nine- and ten-year-olds. The Monster's Assistant, a clown figure, did best with the nine- to ten-year-olds. Most of the children interviewed were under thirteen, indicating the strong attraction of black-and-white morality for the young: it was also interesting to see the fluctuation in sexual loyalties between the various age groups.

Among older children, the Edinburgh Royal Lyceum theatre-in-education team tried out a programme, *Something about a Soldier*, which began with classroom discussions, where one child was asked to persuade another to become a soldier and to kill. These discussions were linked with word-association games, with a documentary programme about the Army and eventually with a professional production of Brecht's *Trumpets and Drums*. One interesting conclusion that the team came to was that the children simply couldn't imagine situations in which it was right to kill. Working among adult students at the City Literary Institute in London, I found that playwriting was regarded as a private, personal activity in which emotions and experiences could be expressed with the freedom of isolation, but that acting was a 'public' activity, in which 'self-expression' gave way to 'the assumption of a role'. Group-playwriting was hard, but stimulating to handle. The discussions were long, heated and intense, drifting into the pubs when time was called in the classroom. The atmosphere was sometimes like a group therapy session, with the same problems of transference, the struggles for ascendancy and the sudden intimacies. The writing group became a very closely knit bunch, whereas in the acting class the students always seemed to maintain a certain detachment both from the activity and from each other.

It would be impossible to generalize from these random observations – misguided even to try – except perhaps to remark on the degree of involvement and enthusiasm which they seemed to arouse. From three classes, at the City Literary Institute and at Marylebone Institute, we were able to mount a full-scale musical, with an original script (by ten writers), original music, and a cast and stage staff of seventy-two people. In the same year – indeed both productions were mounted in the same production fortnight – the group presented two original one-act plays, one of which afterwards transferred to a professional theatre. But were there any useful results from this whirlpool of enthusiasm, and are they checkable in any way? It's hard to say. Some members of the cast and a couple of writers found their entry into the professional theatre, which might be regarded as a mixed blessing. The psychological and social values of the exercise are, in my opinion, quite impossible to check. Even if trained observers had been constantly present, or the whole proceedings tape-recorded, the very presence of this external eye would have altered the nature of the activity. And for participants to try to assess the value is quite impossible. It is like looking at the back of your eye. You can sometimes see what makes you blind, but not what makes you see. It is all too easy to see where the discussions broke down, where the productions and scripts failed, but not why the process developed and assumed an importance in our lives.

But should repertory theatres venture into this territory? The Arts Council on the whole thinks not. The Arts Council gives money basically for teaching-about-theatre, not for learning-through-drama, which it leaves to the education authorities. My own feeling is that this demarcation is increasingly hard to make. Writers are writing plays which use audience involvement: directors are directing them. The design of theatres is changing to meet the demand for closer audience–actor contact. Theatres are becoming arts centres: and the old gap between professional and amateur drama is narrowing – not necessarily the gap in skill, but in the approach to drama. Amateur companies, like Questors, no longer stick to plays well-tried on the professional stage: they are no longer imitative of professional achievements. Questors runs a new-plays festival. Touring 'professional' companies – like Portable Theatre – tour around the universities and even sometimes private houses, receiving in payment literally what they can get. There is a welcome tendency to regard drama – and all art – not as something which the few can practise, but as an activity for everyone interested, and as an activity which has a definite social value, however hard it may be adequately to define this value. This tendency may lead in some cases to a messy unprofessionalism, poor improvisation sessions, weak scripts and a rather lazy approach towards drama. But on other occasions both professional and amateur standards seem to benefit from the cross-fertilization – and from the recognition that art must emerge from human relationships and not be superimposed upon them.

The next generation will have more leisure. Our existing social structures seem to be breaking down. My own opinion is that the theatre in the future, and not far ahead, will become the place where leisure is used creatively – and particularly to experiment with those relationships which will form the basis of future social structures. The theatre will not reflect social change, but initiate it. This is why learning-through-drama programmes seem to me potentially of such importance. It is a vital extension of democracy, away from political parties and the vote, into something more fundamental – into discussing and developing the circumstances in which we live together. The following theatres run theatre-in-education programmes:

Birmingham Repertory Theatre	Teaching about theatre
	Learning through drama
Octagon Theatre, Bolton	Learning through drama
Theatre Royal, Bristol	Teaching about theatre
Everyman Theatre, Cheltenham	Teaching about theatre
Gateway Theatre, Chester	Teaching about theatre
	Learning through drama
Civic Theatre, Chesterfield	Teaching about theatre
Colchester Repertory Theatre	Learning through drama
Belgrade Theatre, Coventry	Teaching about theatre
	Learning through drama
The Derby Playhouse	Teaching about theatre
Dundee Repertory Theatre	Teaching about theatre
	Learning through drama
Edinburgh Royal Lyceum Theatre	Learning through drama
Northcott Theatre, Exeter	Teaching about theatre
	Learning through drama
Castle Theatre, Farnham	Teaching about theatre
Citizens' Theatre, Glasgow	Teaching about theatre
	Learning through drama
Theatre, Harrogate	Teaching about theatre
Queen's Theatre, Hornchurch	Teaching about theatre

Arts Theatre, Ipswich	Teaching about theatre
	Learning through drama
Century Theatre, Lancaster	Learning through drama
Thorndike Theatre, Leatherhead	Teaching about theatre
	Learning through drama
Phoenix Theatre, Leicester	Teaching about theatre
Theatre Royal, Lincoln	Learning through drama
Playhouse, Liverpool	Teaching about theatre
	Learning through drama
Everyman, Liverpool	Teaching about theatre
	Learning through drama
Library Theatre, Manchester	Teaching about theatre
'69 Company, Manchester	Teaching about theatre
University Theatre, Newcastle	Learning through drama
	Teaching about theatre
Theatre Royal, Northampton	Teaching about theatre
Playhouse, Nottingham	Learning through drama
	Teaching about theatre
Meadow Players, Oxford	Teaching about theatre
Little Theatre, Rhyl	Teaching about theatre
	Learning through drama
Playhouse, Salisbury	Teaching about theatre
Playhouse, Sheffield	Teaching about theatre
	Learning through drama
Victoria Theatre, Stoke-on-Trent	Teaching about theatre
Royal Shakespeare Theatre, Stratford	Teaching about theatre
Civic Theatre, Watford	Teaching about theatre
	Learning through drama
Connaught Theatre, Worthing	Teaching about theatre
	Learning through drama
Theatre Royal, York	Teaching about theatre
	Learning through drama
(Youth theatre only)	
Midlands Arts Centre, Cannon Hill, Birmingham	Teaching about theatre
	Learning through drama

8

Buildings, Areas and Actors

THERE are very few good theatre buildings in this country, and the recent spate of building and renovating has not added appreciably to their number. I am not using the word 'good' to mean 'aesthetically pleasing' – there are plenty of pretty theatres – nor, they tell me, is there such a thing as 'pure architecture'. I mean simply that few theatres fulfil adequately the purposes for which they were intended, that fewer still anticipate sensibly the sort of technical demands which directors and writers are likely to make in the future, and that almost none relate together the predictable demands of a community with the opportunities which a modern, well-equipped theatre can offer. And this is rather sad because although plays and productions *can* be performed almost anywhere, 'on a rug at the end of a room', the physical facts of the building in which plays are staged do profoundly alter performances – down to the very details of movement, voice projection and stage mechanics – and, therefore, poor theatres are not only frustrating for actors to play in, but also condition the productions we see. A good production can be staged in a badly designed theatre, but the impact is likely to be muffled. This has two consequences for the director – either he adapts his original ideas to fit in with the known limitations of the theatre, or he may wish to stress them too strongly in order that they will not be lost, out there beyond the proscenium arch. In both cases, poor theatre-design leads to unsubtle productions.

Expense is not the main problem – nor shortage of architects. Several new theatres have cost too much for what they offer the public and the director. Architects, too, have responded with style and ingenuity to the tasks which they have been set – but they've been set the wrong tasks. The basic problem which has resulted in poor theatres is a certain confusion of aim, and a slowness to realize how a decision in one direction can influence the course of events in another. A choice of a site can affect the shape of an auditorium and a stage, can therefore limit the opportunities open to a director and his choice of plays, his selection of actors and so on. A site can also affect audiences, limiting them perhaps to those who have cars or live in a certain area of a town. The problem with building a new theatre is that to start with there are too many imponderables. How large should it be? How will the public react? Will So-and-So, the famous director want to work in a theatre like this? New theatres can be cursed with all the opportunities they offer to different people – to local authorities, who want to leave a monument to their régimes, to directors who want to work in this sort of theatre or that, to architects who want to add something to a skyline. As soon as a new scheme for a theatre is announced, a circling hawk swoops, followed by fifty others, and attacked from all sides an unruffled building is not likely to emerge.

This central confusion as to what a theatre should be and what it should be able to do accounts partly for the erratic history of theatre buildings since the war: total inertia from 1939 to 1958, a controlled boom since then. Nor does this chequered pattern only apply to new theatres; renovations and conversions have suffered from the same over-all uncertainty. I have already pointed out that since 1939 there has been a general decline in the numbers of theatres in use: from about 300 (in 1939), to about 120 (in 1960) to about 100 (in 1970). This decline is due almost solely to the unprofitability of commercial touring. During the same period, there was a steady rise in the number of repertory theatres, from about 12 (in 1939), to 44 (in 1960), to about 60 (in 1970): and many of these reps simply took over the touring-theatres which commercial companies no longer visited. But the *needs* of a repertory company are very different from those of touring. Reps manufacture as well as sell the product, and probably offer services to the community, such as theatre-in-education and clubs, as well. A good repertory theatre is a complex unit, with workshops, rehearsal rooms, wardrobes, offices, paint frames, studios and club rooms: a touring-theatre need only have an auditorium, a well-equipped stage, high scene-doors for portable flats and a box office. Theatres may have declined in number since 1939, but those that survived often had to be used more fully and for purposes which were not anticipated in the design of the buildings. This led in the fifties to a number of tatty and makeshift conversions: the Salisbury Playhouse, for example, has no fly-tower and disastrously poor workshop facilities. The Harrogate Theatre has converted the area under the stage into a very inadequate workshop. And this tattiness spread into the image of repertory theatres, which at one time seemed doomed, not because the services they offered were not valuable, but because they aroused all the wrong public reactions: ranging from interested condescension to a pitying contempt. Therefore, when money was made available for theatre improvement – from local councils and from the Arts Council Housing the Arts programme, too much of it was spent on the external image of the theatre, and too little on improving the stages and basic dramatic facilities. Foyers were redecorated: restaurant extensions were added, improved box offices, bars and bookstalls, thick carpets on the stairs; while in the auditoriums acoustic problems were not solved, and backstage the scenery flats still had to be stored in open sheds, covered with tarpaulins. And so at a time when the repertory movement was growing at an unprecedented pace, and when more public money than ever before was being invested in the theatre, too much attention had to be paid to the philistines and too little to developing better facilities for repertory productions.

This is one paradox – that while the whole principle of public patronage was always under attack and fresh funds were particularly hard to find, so much money had to be wasted on inessentials. Another paradox was that from 1958–70, at a time when television is generally assumed to have had the greatest detrimental impact on the live theatre, eighteen major new theatres were built (in Billingham, Bolton, Canterbury, Chester, Chichester, Coventry, Croydon, Guildford, Exeter, Hull, Leatherhead, Leicester, Manchester, Nottingham, St Andrews, Southampton, University of Sussex, and Worcester), there were thirteen significant developments of older theatres (in Canterbury, Cheltenham, Derby, Dundee, Greenwich, Harrogate, Ipswich, Lincoln, Liverpool, Oxford, Stoke, Worthing and York) and plans were laid to build at least twelve more (at Birmingham – for the Rep and the Midlands Arts Centre, Bromley. Colchester, Derby, Dundee, Lancaster, Leeds, Manchester, Newcastle Sheffield and Stoke). A major conversion of the Theatre Royal, Bristol, has also started. The new theatres are not all purely reps: some are university theatres, which include visits from professional repertory companies. The conversions range from large-scale redevelopments – such as the Liverpool Playhouse – to more minor improvements, such as the Harrogate Theatre: and the plans are in different stages of development. The new Birmingham Rep is being built –

and the new Sheffield Playhouse: whereas the new theatre at Stoke is (I understand) in the process of being shelved. All these new theatres, conversions and plans do reveal, however, that the twelve years from 1958–70 were almost a 'boom' period for theatre building, exceeding the hopes outlined in the 1960 Arts Council Report, *Housing the Arts*, which stated that 'it is unlikely that in the next ten years more than six or seven major provincial repertory theatres will be built, either as new theatres or as replacements of existing theatres'.

This report reveals another slight irony, in that of the seventeen major cities, mentioned by the Arts Council as the first targets for adequate repertory accommodation, only five had new theatres during the ten years. University theatres were built in Manchester and Southampton, and there were extensive alterations at the Liverpool Playhouse: but of the seventeen named cities, only Coventry, Croydon, Hull, Leicester and Nottingham built new theatres, and of these only three were repertory theatres. The Arts Council expected, hoped perhaps, that the major cities would have good repertory theatres first of all: but these were also the strongholds, of course, of the touring commercial theatres. Leeds and Manchester in particular were slow in thinking about new repertory theatres, partly because the commercial theatres in the town weren't doing too badly. Smaller towns, however, such as Bolton, Chester, Exeter, Leatherhead and Worcester, seized the repertory idea with unexpected enthusiasm: and yet here lies another paradox. Since 1956 the trend in the theatre has been, I suppose, away from purely middle-class drama: the plays from the Royal Court and Stratford, the regional documentaries, the social dovetailing of community needs with repertory programmes. And yet many of these new theatres simply do not reflect this change of direction. They have stayed almost flamboyantly bourgeois. One of the largest chandeliers I have ever seen hangs down the main staircase at the Yvonne Arnaud Theatre, Guildford. The walls of the theatre at the Billingham Forum are piled high with family boxes. Most of the new theatres are experimental only in propaganda, traditional in fact. They claim to be more adventurous in design than they are. Peter Moro, who designed the Nottingham Playhouse and helped with the Festival Hall, asserted that the plans for the Playhouse stage broke new ground, because they provided either for an 'open' or a 'picture frame' stage – not an advanced form of adaptability. At a time when so many of our ideas about drama – and our hopes – have changed drastically, when the class bias in drama has shifted, when the techniques of Brecht and Artaud, not to mention Piscator and Littlewood, have occupied so much of our attention, when the possibilities of the theatre as a machine have been so enormously enlarged, the pattern of theatre building has stayed traditional, even conservative.

This is partly because the impetus towards new theatres has not come from the 'revival' of British drama during the fifties, but from an imitation of – even a rivalry with – the great German civic opera houses and theatres. Time and again, these theatres are cited as models of what British theatres should be doing – in the size of their grants, the elaborateness of their stage machinery, the opulence of their financial resources. But, of course, the German opera houses follow a very traditional pattern – the proscenium arches and fly-towers, the lush auditoriums. Brecht was disgusted by them. The idea dies hard in England, too, that a theatre should be like a London club, padded, with good bars and restaurants, plushly secure and solid. The first *environmental* impression which we receive from most theatres is one of lulling (and artificial) wealth. It is an impression which few seemed prepared to relinquish in favour of greater variety and excitement, and those civic authorities in whose hands the decision may rest as to whether a new theatre should be built are particularly fond of it. An opulent-looking theatre gives a certain tone to the town: it demonstrates prosperity. And councils are always more prepared to invest in something which looks permanent rather than in something 'experimental' – and how can one tell that a building will be 'permanent', unless it follows, at a distance perhaps, a model which has lasted for nearly a hundred years?

But what is the weakness of these 'bourgeois' theatres, apart from this very generalized accusation, lack of imagination? Isn't it better to have a 'bourgeois' theatre, rather than none at all? Yes, it is, I suppose: but theatres designed in this way are often expensive both to build and to maintain, and there may be a misuse of resources. The Yvonne Arnaud Theatre in Guildford, for example, compares favourably with several other new theatres in the country: and yet from many points of view it's simply inefficient. It has an almost perfect site, close to the town and the railway and bus stations – yet slightly apart from it, on the banks of the River Wey, next to a weir, with fields and woods on the opposite bank. The building is from the outside, neat and well proportioned – a bit like a concrete beer-barrel perhaps, and marred slightly by the large scenery-doors, which had to be placed by the side of the entrance foyer, facing the road. The architects, Messrs Scott, Brownrigg & Turner, rightly chose to place all the public lounge areas – the restaurant, coffee bar, bar and foyers (on two levels) – overlooking the river: so that in winter one can look through the windows and see the lights on the water, and in summer can walk out on to the balcony and down to the lawns and terraces below. The auditorium and stage are less successfully designed. The stage is a large one – with a proscenium opening of 36 feet and a depth of 33 feet – dimensions which are admirable for large productions, musicals and so forth. Unfortunately, the seating capacity of the theatre – 568 seats – is too small for such productions to be economic. The director, Laurier Lister, told me that in his opinion two hundred more seats would have been desirable. This could only have been achieved, however, by sacrificing the upper foyer level. When the theatre was built, the public response to it was hard to foresee: it seems small now – but then it seemed over-large. There are other problems too. The fly-tower is only forty feet high, so that flats of over sixteen feet dangle over the top of the stage. The front row of the audience sits so close to the stage that masking is always a complicated business. And so, although the Yvonne Arnaud Theatre is a very pretty one and managed most efficiently, the weaknesses in design and planning are already beginning to show: only five years after the theatre was opened, the authorities are appealing for funds to raise the fly-tower. Also, the seating capacity is too small for the productions which Laurier Lister would like to present – and indeed is presenting.

There are those who would argue, moreover, that 'bourgeois' theatres, like the Yvonne Arnaud, are failing in ways which lie beyond these important details described. Firstly, the size and capacities of the theatres are too rigidly fixed. If the theatre is to fulfil a new role in an Age of Leisure, these bourgeois theatres will be too small: equally, if audiences drift away from the live theatre, they will be too big. The very air of permanence prevents them from adjusting to circumstances. Secondly, the proscenium arch and fly-towers, the positioning of the stage, also rigidly determine the productions which we are likely to see. *Adaptable* theatres in this country usually mean that the relationship of the stage to the auditorium can be varied according to the play and the demands of the director. At Bolton, at the Northcott Theatre, Exeter, at the Manchester University Theatre and elsewhere, the stage can either be placed behind a proscenium arch, without a proscenium arch ('open end'), thrusting out into the auditorium (as at Chichester) or in the centre of the audience, as an 'arena' ('theatre-in-the-round') stage. Four new theatres are adaptable in this sense and there are also several studio theatres which, by altering banks of seating, are capable of these variations – the Traverse, Edinburgh, the Close, Glasgow, the Theatre Upstairs and the Open Space theatres in London. But even this interpretation of *adaptability* is a comparatively limited one, for it's not hard to imagine a theatre where, say, sections of the floor can be raised or lowered at will (so that the audience looks down on the stage sometimes and sometimes looks up), where sound and lighting effects – and film projection – can come from all sections of the room, where the scene dock, if needed, can cover the entire auditorium ceiling, where the walls of the auditorium are part of the set – where in fact, the theatre has become a controllable environment, 'a box for sensations'. This need not exclude traditional plays, but it would extend the range of opportunities available to the director, writer and actor. At present, it is argued, we only watch plays within an artificially lulling atmosphere, which can easily conflict with the tone of the play. The third and perhaps main argument against 'bourgeois' theatres is that they provide a fixed social environment – elegant dresses to match the staircases – which can so easily seem both out of date and awkwardly inappropriate.

The designs of theatres *are* becoming more adventurous, of course. One has only to compare the Ashcroft Theatre, Croydon, or even the Belgrade, Coventry, with the Octagon Theatre, Bolton, or the plans for the new Sheffield Playhouse. Even this daring, however, has waterproof boots on, protection against the ill-weather of disapproval. It is easy to blame this timidity in abstract – in practice, however, building a theatre is such a difficult adventure that to take any chances with an experimental design seems merely to increase the likelihood of disaster. Nor is it possible simply in theory to hang one's hat on an adventurous scheme – for under certain circumstances a rigidly fixed, proscenium-arch, 'bourgeois' theatre may be the best solution. Any general rules about theatre design are always liable to have their toes stubbed on exceptions. It is much more important that architects and councils are aware not of any 'correct' design for theatres, but of the foreseeable consequences which their decisions are likely to have.

Where should a theatre be sited? 'Between Woolworth's and Marks & Spencer's,' John Wackett, the former manager of the Octagon Theatre, Bolton, told me – in the centre of the market, with the shoppers, cars and advertisements, a screaming, cosy scrum. But Bolton is a lucky town, in that the main shopping-area flanks a broad, traffic-less square with fountains and some stately municipal buildings to cushion the commercial aggression. In the corner of this square, the Octagon Theatre sits snugly, both in the centre of things and slightly detached from them, like grandmother's lap. The idea that a theatre had to be in the main shopping-street came firstly from economic necessity. The theatre was a side-show in a market place. Actors had to go where their public was. In some country towns still, market day is the day for a matinée. Nowadays, however, it is no longer *economically* necessary to build a theatre in a town centre: enough people have cars. But many managers believe that it is socially desirable to site the building centrally, within the daily stream of events – partly so that audiences won't be limited to those who have cars, partly so that the theatre doesn't become a place simply for a pleasant evening's excursion, but can be used during the day as well – as somewhere to sit and drink coffee, to hold an art exhibition and lunchtime recitals – an all-purpose leisure-area.

Unfortunately, land prices in town centres are high: good main-street frontage is hard to find. Town theatres usually have to be built on a smaller patch of land than those situated in parks or university campuses: and even a fairly wide mainstreet frontage is usually too narrow for a 'square' theatre. When architects have to design a building which packs as many people as possible into a small site, the problems of sight lines and audibility become crucial. A long, skinny auditorium poses all sorts of problems. At the back, the audiences have difficulty in seeing and hearing – even if the floor is steeply raked – and so actors have to project 'out front' more vigorously than they might otherwise wish to do – thus also distorting the effect for the front rows. To avoid a long auditorium, most theatre architects preferred to lessen the number of rows on a single level, by piling one block of seats on top of another in circles and galleries. Limited land space – for theatres as for flats and office blocks – usually means building upwards. With the audience on several levels, the stage has to be placed where it can be seen by everyone, not on ground level, where the gallery would see an unrestricted view only of the top of actors' heads, but in a raised 'window' position on one wall – hence, the proscenium-arch or 'picture-frame' stage.

The critics of the proscenium-arch theatre sometimes argue as if the sole justification for the proscenium arch was that it enabled a director to produce 'naturalistic' effects and to change scenery efficiently – advantages which they rightly regard as being outweighed by other weaknesses. Historically, it is true, the proscenium arch was introduced into European theatre in the seventeenth century to help the development of elaborate stage-effects. It was originally merely an inner stage framework. The main action was on the forestage in front of the proscenium arch. In the nineteenth century in England, the forestage dwindled in size and the proscenium-arch stage, as we now know it, took over. However, the reason for this change was largely economic. There was no other way to ensure good sight-lines in a town theatre where too many people had to be packed into a small land-area.

Even today when planners generally seem to be aware of the importance of leisure areas within a town centre, councils who want to have a theatre – and have a choice of site – usually have to decide between a small town site – which often means a proscenium-arch theatre and a tall building with galleries – and a more spacious 'country' or park site. Bolton is a lucky exception to this rule: it has a spacious town site. The problem with setting a theatre outside a town is that access and advertisement immediately become more difficult. It is outside the flow of events. People can't drop in for coffee. They don't see the hoardings and photographs. The new and pretty Adeline Genée Theatre, near East Grinstead, had all its other economic problems increased by the fact that it was simply hard to find: down a long, winding country lane. It had to be tracked down carefully, and snared. A theatre has to have a fine reputation to lure audiences either into the country or to a small country town. Chichester, Glyndebourne, Stratford and Pitlochry are Meccas – Malvern and East Grinstead are not.

One advantage of having a theatre on a wide area of land is that all the offices and workshops can be accommodated in one complex – instead of having (as so often happens) the workshops somewhere on the other side of the town. But another gain, which some would say is more important, is that the theatre can then have a different sort of stage, a different relationship between audience and actors, perhaps an 'adaptable' theatre. 'Thrust' stages – and 'theatre in the round' – usually occupy more land space than a proscenium-arch theatre, and narrow auditoriums are impossible. The audience has to sit around the acting-area on three or four sides, rather than one. The Chichester Festival Theatre, which has a 'thrust' stage, can seat 1360 and no member of the audience is further than sixty-five feet from the stage. The sight-lines and acoustics are excellent, and there is an intimate atmosphere, unusual in so large a theatre, and impossible in a proscenium-arch theatre of this size.

The nature and positioning of the stage has never been so rigidly fixed by tradition that there were not rebels who wanted it otherwise. Even at the end of the nineteenth century, at the height apparently of the proscenium-arch tradition, William Poel tried to reconstruct an Elizabethan theatre for Shakespeare productions, and in 1921 the Maddermarket Theatre in Norwich, based on Elizabethan models, with a wide 'open' stage and no proscenium arch, was opened – by an *amateur* company. Yeats talked about a theatre being 'a rug at the end of a room' and Gordon Craig experimented with a variable proscenium arch, to change the size of the picture. And yet, in a sense, the stage has always seemed above theatrical fashion – until today perhaps – because the building was so permanent, longer-lasting than any director or company, and also because so many other theatre techniques rested on the shape of the stage and its place in the auditorium.

The stage was the cornerstone of an art. It couldn't be moved around without so much else giving way. In a proscenium-arch theatre, every significant line and movement had to be projected in one direction – out front, towards the audience. Hence, you only had to turn your back on the audience to fade out of the picture – to snub the patrons – or, as Sir Donald Wolfit used to do, to emphasize by contrast the next line, delivered frontally. Sir Donald Wolfit would turn his back on the audience in moments of great passion, shoulders heaving, and then turn round to confront the audience with some massive line, such as 'Woe to the honest! Woe to the honest!' (from *The Master of Santiago*) or 'Never, never, never, never, never' (from *King Lear*). It was, in short, one of those effective tricks which could be played with frontal acting, which after a time seemed dull and melodramatic, particularly after the coming of television, when cameras could move with such infuriating ease among the actors.

There were many such tricks, which were sometimes dignified with the word 'technique'. One rule was – always to include the audience in any conversation: therefore, one foot should point at the audience, the other to the person to whom you are talking. Peter Terson is one of many dramatists who would now find such a rule totally depressing – as would many actors too: 'I really couldn't imagine those actors who seem to sidle on sideways, crab-wise, saying my words: it all seemed so phoney to me, so false.' Another rule: always gesture (except for special effect) with the upstage arm – which somehow always gave the impression that actors on the O.P. side were left-handed. The very term, 'upstaging', refers to the pictorial effect of a proscenium-arch stage, where the audience's line of vision is always drawn into the heart of a grouping – in other words, to the upstage actors. The classic retort to upstaging is, of course, *masking*, another cardinal sin. It's almost impossible 'in-the-round' to mask or upstage. And so on – the groupings, the gestures, the delivery of lines, the ways of directing a scene so that the climax receives a strong pictorial impact – all these lumps of know-how ultimately rest on the assumption that the actors are playing in a proscenium-arch theatre. And so, to alter the shape of the stage – and its relationship to the audience – is a very significant step, not to be taken without due care and thought.

Frontal acting obviously has limitations: but so do all styles of acting. And the arguments against the proscenium arch usually concentrate on the separation between the actors and the audience – they work, as Stephen Joseph pointed out, 'in separate rooms'. One way to avoid this separation is simply to do without the actual arch, to lower the stage to the ground level and to raise the seats in a steep rake. This is usually called an 'open-end' stage, and an example would be the Mermaid Theatre in London. The 'thrust' stage brings the forestage into the centre of the auditorium – with the audience sitting on three sides – and an arena stage is simply in the centre of the auditorium with raked seats on all four sides. The main stage at the new National Theatre will be an 'open stage' – and the new theatre replacing the old Sheffield Playhouse will be 'thrust'. Sir Bernard Miles strongly attacked the thrust stage at Sheffield, which he described as a theatrical 'freak'. The main basis for his argument was that 'acting is a frontal activity, because the actor's means of expression, his eyes and his mouth, are in the front of his face. An actor can only control as many people as he can see, as he can control with his eyes and that we know is no more than a 160-degree angle of audience.' His objection is a more sophisticated version of that old complaint against 'theatre-in-the-round' – that half of the audience is condemned to the back view of an actor, which is a less expressive direction than his front. The key word is, I think, *control.* Actors often feel that they are 'controlling' the audience when the auditorium is quiet and attentive, the eyes trained in one direction, the hands neatly folded across programmes. Audiences, however, are only controlled by what interests them, and no amount of frontal staring will fix their attention if the basic material is dull. But, if the material is good, does frontal acting increase the interest? I think not – or, rather, I believe that the direction of the audience's attention towards the face of the speaking actor does not in itself increase the interest. In 'theatre-in-the-round', when the audience cannot see the face of the speaking actor, they should always be able to see the face of the actor to whom the speech is directed. Hence, in 'theatre-in-the-round', the *reaction* is as important as the *delivery,* which is not always true of frontal acting. The acting has to be 'in-the-round' as well: every actor on the stage has the same burden to carry. Nor have I noticed that audiences generally are less attentive during 'thrust'-stage or 'in-the-round' productions – a conclusion which should follow from Sir Bernard's arguments. But it is true that the weight of the audience's interest has to be spread more evenly among the cast, and that it is obviously less easy to obtain silhouetted and spectacular visual effects. And indeed an actor has to act with his whole body, not simply with his face and hand gestures: his shoulders also must be expressive. The performance has to be multi-directional, and what holds the audience is the cast's ability to present before them a situation in which there are no distractions, no lapses in concentration. In frontal acting, actors are – or used to be – told to stand still when someone else is speaking: to freeze, not to distract. Stillness, the rigid block-like physical and emotional silence of the second attendant, just isn't good enough for theatre-in-the-round. Stillness has to be a reaction to a situation, properly motivated and sustained. No supernumeraries can be carried. This is why so many actors find the challenge of theatre-in-the-round both formidable and exciting. This is also why there are no stars at the Victoria Theatre, Stoke-on-Trent.

If the cant word for the frontal actor is control, the cant word for thrust- and arena-stage actors is *contact*. It is sometimes assumed that simply by bringing the actors closer to the audience there is greater contact and therefore *involvement*. This is rather like suggesting that you can't seduce a girl without having an arm round her waist: it is a technique which works well in some situations, but is quite counter-productive in others. This idea is again based on one of those actors' illusions which isn't necessarily shared by the audience. On a proscenium-arch stage, with the spotlights glaring down, the audience merges into a black haze. An actor can only hear them, dimly aware that they're shuffling in boredom or quietly listening. On a thrust stage, firstly, the lights do not provide such a blinding barrier, secondly, the actors are physically closer to the audience and, thirdly, no tricks can be concealed. No prompt can sit helpfully behind the curtain to cover up mistakes. The actor is more vulnerable to the audience, more likely to be distracted by a disturbance in the third row. No curtain can be brought down in the event of a real catastrophe. But this does not necessarily mean that the audience has either a greater involvement in the play or contact with the actor. In a proscenium-arch theatre, the audience can concentrate so much on the stage that they lose a sense of their own presence. This was the reaction Brecht disliked so much – all those people sitting there, eyes glazed, forgetting their own problems in the mythical situations on stage. This selfless concentration is encouraged by the dark auditorium, the hypnotically brilliant lighting on stage, the glamorous costumes and high make-up. This situation in the 'Aristotelian' theatre, Brecht concluded, encouraged escapism, a profound form of audience involvement of which Brecht, a puritanical man, disapproved. To bring the actors in front of the proscenium toned down the hypnotic glamour. The audiences and actors are in the same room, on the same level. To lower the stage to floor level and to raise the seating in tiers around the central or thrust stages, also topples the actor from his pedestal – the raised, brightly lit and isolated podium which can give such a heroic glow to the proceedings on stage.

Some writers and directors believe that this heroic glow is rather important to the theatre. We are watching not ordinary men, but raised and elevated characters, deliberately separated by art from life. John Whiting, for example, attacked the whole idea of intimacy in the theatre: 'But, my God, there is power in the remote, isolated figure neither giving nor asking for understanding or love. Isn't it perhaps the power of the theatre to which a return must be made sooner or later?' Well, yes, it may – but it will not be entirely a *dramatic* decision if a return is made. We live in a society which is sceptical of hero figures: even our stars have to be ordinary. 'Unhappy is the land that has no heroes' – 'No, unhappy is the land which has the need of heroes.' Peter Cheeseman, perhaps the leading 'theatre-in-the-round' director, once wrote that 'forms of theatre differ in their techniques of performance, but also philosophically and even politically in the relationships implied in the human structure of the event they create. People form the partial or total background to the action presented in a thrust or round stage, each spectator can see almost the entire audience, the drama is played out in a space cleared in the middle of a community.' Yes, audiences are certainly more aware of their own presences – and yes – this does give a greater sense of *community*: but it would be wrong to suggest that this necessarily brings greater involvement. By becoming more self-aware, an audience can also become more self-conscious. There is a certain calm, controlled way of watching an 'in-the-round' production – not less attentive, but less ready to betray feelings. Laughter (I would have thought) is harder to obtain: glowing adoration impossible. Precisely because the audience is, like the actor, unable to hide or ignore the presence of the other, and is also more vulnerable, emotion is harder to express – perhaps even to feel. At best, 'in-the-round' productions provide the atmosphere of a serious, well-balanced discussion in which everyone is expected to take part – actors and audiences alike – even if that part is of quietly reserving judgement. It's hard for the audience to let go – to fall in love with the leading actress, to roar with laughter or watch tense with expectation: and indeed these may be juvenile emotions, not to be encouraged. However, through indulging these fantasies, one can sometimes learn something about the emotions for which these fantasies are substitutes. Theatre-in-the-round has an anti-cathartic effect: and, of course, to some directors, the unemotional honesty of 'arena' productions is a great mark in its favour. Brecht, who remembered the Nazi rallies all too vividly, was strongly opposed to catharsis. At best, he believed that it wasted emotional energy which could be more usefully spent on intelligent revolutions – and, at worst, that it could lead to blind hysteria. The local documentaries at Stoke owe much to Brecht – the short scenes linked together by social argument, the snatches of *théâtre trouvé* – tape recordings and newspaper cuttings, the casually intent and concentrated atmosphere.

Clearly, therefore, one has to resist the temptation to give any clear-cut, no-nonsense decision as to which type of stage is The Best: proscenium, thrust or arena. Such a choice depends firstly on the size and shape of the site, secondly on the intended role for the theatre within the town – is it to be a display or touring theatre? is it to be a community forum theatre? – thirdly on whether there are funds available to subsidize a permanent company, and fourthly on the ideological commitments of the director. Most 'standard' rep plays – Shaw, Ibsen, Rattigan and Christie – have been written for proscenium-arch stages, and therefore work better in that setting. Brecht and Shakespeare – and Euripides – succeed better on a thrust stage: although certain Brecht plays were written for arena stages – *The Man Who Said Yes* and *The Man Who Said No*. We have yet to see the best of Peter Terson's work in London, because we have not had (until recently) a good arena theatre.

But am I, perhaps, in failing to give a clear opinion on this matter, betraying myself yet again as a wishy-washy liberal? 'You'll give yourself piles,' one director told me, 'sitting on the fence so much.' I'm prepared to risk this discomfort, partly because this argument has generated more heat than light in recent years, and it's better to be sore than singed. Few directors would, I believe, wish to commit themselves fully to the picture-frame stage. After the productions at Chichester and Stoke, the value of arena and thrust stages has been proved. But fewer still perhaps would want to commit themselves so firmly to what David Rudkin has called the 'austerely egalitarian' atmosphere of the Victoria Theatre, Stoke – 'the only sort of theatre I willingly go to, now'. Nor is it really *necessary* to take this sort of decision. If the site for a theatre is reasonably spacious, it's usually possible to build an adaptable theatre, which can be transformed from a proscenium arch to a thrust to an arena. In some small theatres, this can be done simply by changing the seating – as at the Close Theatre, Glasgow, or the Traverse, Edinburgh. Of course, such an adaptable theatre has to have adaptable lighting as well – to cover every point of the theatre: sound and lighting boxes have to be carefully positioned. With larger theatres, the problems increase. At Bolton, the seating retracts or extends from under the first-floor balcony to alter the shape of the stage. Bolton seats from 338 to 422 and the system takes about half-a-day to transform, with a conventional stage team of six and helpful schoolchildren. At the Vivian Beaumont Theatre, Lincoln Center, New York, the stage can be transformed from a proscenium arch to a thrust with true American efficiency: a touch of a button, the seating retracts, the stage extends, and the whole process is over in a minute.

But are even *adaptable* theatres as we know them good enough? There are three quite distinct arguments against them. Firstly, because the shape of the stage and the relationship to the audience *is* so important, then perhaps directors and companies shouldn't be expected to change from production to production. Too many opportunities in art offers the temptation of superficiality. A director switching from one type of theatre to another will not properly master the skills of either. There is something to be said for a theatre which cannot be altered to suit the mood of the moment. Furthermore, if the ideological arguments are at all valid, then mightn't we be ducking out of taking far-reaching decisions about the purposes of art in society if we settle for this changeable compromise? If the public does not know what sort of theatre to expect, will it be able to adjust either to the community forum idea – so admirably suited to the arena stage – or to the display drama – which favours perhaps the picture-frame stage?

Secondly, it could be argued that we are concentrating on the wrong sort of adaptability. What really matters is not the nature of the stage, but the size of the theatre. Nobody knows, when a theatre is built, what the public response will be, and so the size of the theatre has to be guessed at. And usually, too, these guesses are conservative ones. I have already pointed out that the building of a new theatre in a town which already has a loyal theatre-going public generates a rapid new growth in audiences: that the theatres at Nottingham, Leatherhead and Guildford – which were thought to be uneconomically large when they were built – now are too small. If the theatre, in an age of leisure, is also expected to be a focal point for community activities, then obviously none of these new theatres will be able successfully to adjust. They were all built at a time when the Arts Council was stating rather too confidently that the ideal size for a repertory theatre is 800 or 900 seats: and they are all smaller than that. The new Sheffield Playhouse will be far larger. But oughtn't we perhaps to be thinking of theatres which can be built cheaply and then increased in size to meet the demand? This may mean that the solid 'bourgeois' theatres with their chandeliers and velveteen curtains are rendered obsolete: but mightn't this perhaps be a sacrifice not too hard to make? Victor Corti, who works with Inter-Action, a community theatre project in London, has suggested in *Gambit* (vol. 4, no. 15) that pre-fabricated arts-centres and theatres should be cheaply erected on stretches of under-used land, such as railway yards. 'Such short (or long) leases are available in every municipality having rail yards, where there are at present acres of disused coal bunkering. Even in the capital these sites occur with regular frequency. They are open, large and next to public transportation.' He proposes a design for an extendable box-theatre, with room for workshops, discussion lounges and performance areas, which could be erected cheaply – for under £100,000 and could be extended if necessary. Forty large ones, covering an area the size of the National Theatre, one acre, could be built for £250,000 apiece: therefore the total cost of them all would be that of the National Theatre. And assuming that most local authorities would not want theatres of this size – but only perhaps half as large – eighty or more of these theatres could be built for the cost of the National Theatre – thus covering the country with theatres ideally suited for an Age of Leisure. Within the box structure, there could be fully *adaptable* theatres.

The third argument against adaptable theatres as we know them is that this is merely one step towards controlling the environment into which the audience is plunged: and that we should explore this direction far more adventurously. The walls of the auditorium could be screens on which anything can be projected: every section of the floor should be raisable – so that the actors can surround the audience on platforms or be able to sink into pits: the sound and light effects of a theatre should be able to pinpoint a moth anywhere in the auditorium – or they should be able to sweep across the audience in waves: we should be able to induce an atmosphere of conversational intimacy in the auditorium – or of heroic expanse: every theatre should be able to have an electronic workshop for sound and music effects, should be able to link the sound with kinetic art, should be able in other words to explore that variety of environmental effects which is so conspicuously absent from our theatres, not because we lack the technical knowledge or even the money, but because we are not really thinking along these lines. Our assumptions about *theatre* too easily get in our way. We accept too readily the lulling atmosphere

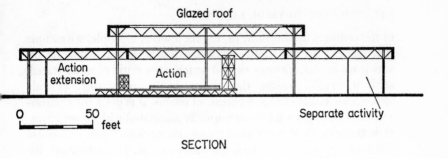

SECTION

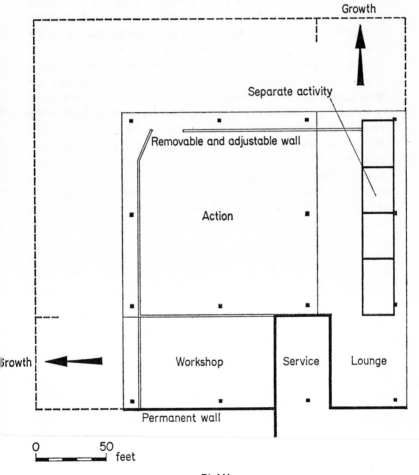

PLAN

Proposed design for a community theatre by Victor Corti and John Olley

of the ordinary auditorium: or, to take another example, we assume that *spectacle* in the theatre must mean a built set, brilliantly lit, which we in the audience sit and watch. One critic recently stated, as if it were a truism, that theatre-in-the-round can't provide spectacular visual effects, whereas, of course, it is good for environmental effects, poor for those normally associated with proscenium-arch theatres. And sometimes these assumptions make us misuse the very opportunities which are offered to us. Laser lighting, for example, has only as yet been used in proscenium-arch theatre, not in theatre-in-the-round, where the greater potentiality lies. Laser lights, very low-powered ones, provide thin beams of colour which do not diffuse noticeably on the stage or in the auditorium, therefore do not dim or diminish in power. They can be 'bounced' from reflectors and mirrors, providing – should this be desired – a cat's-cradle effect on the stage or in the auditorium: with lenses, the beams can be widened, though with a loss of power. A laser room, as a form of environmental sculpture, has already been built in the United States. Svoboda has used lasers in a production of *The Magic Flute* in Germany. But *The Magic Flute* was staged in a proscenium-arch theatre, where the laser lights would not necessarily have been more effective than coloured streams of paper or pinpoint spots. In theatre-in-the-round, however, the environmental possibilities are very exciting. The audience can be plunged into a complex pattern of colours, lines and angles, a three-dimensional set mysteriously hanging in the air, which can be changed by the flick of a switch. There are still some technical problems to overcome before all these possibilities can be realized. At present, in Britain, only weak lasers – up to eight milliwatts – have been used in the theatre, and these are only effectively seen in a dark auditorium or when beamed through smoke or a dust-filled atmosphere. Another problem is that the angle from which the beam is viewed alters the apparent intensity of the colour. Hence, it is difficult to design a pattern of laser lighting which is equally effective from all parts of the auditorium. In spite of these difficulties, laser lighting in an environmental theatre could be an almost revolutionary development, so it is particularly sad that no theatre in Britain has yet tried to experiment along these lines. The I.C.A. has sponsored an exhibition of laser sculpture and there have been several exhibitions of holograms, photographs which give a three-dimensional effect when a laser beam is directed upon them.

There have, however, been other forms of experimental theatres, built or projected. The theatre designed by Buckmaster Fuller for St Peter's College, Oxford, has movable lightweight screens for the auditorium walls: the seats at the Gardner Centre, Sussex University, can swivel individually around to face different areas in the auditorium – which is necessary because there are three stages set in the auditorium walls, which can either be used separately or joined together as one vast proscenium stage. Neither of these theatres is unduly expensive – the Buckmaster Fuller Theatre, which hasn't yet been built, is estimated to cost £160,000 and the Gardner Centre, £300,000: but equally, they, too, are really compromise theatres, more technically elaborate than the others, but still only scratching the surface of possibilities of environmental theatre. Oughtn't we to want to build at least one theatre which aims to be ahead of its time, a symbol of technological progress and an exciting machine for drama, something to stimulate creativity in others and not merely to act as a setting, into which creativity can be poured?

But isn't all this talk about adaptable and environmental theatres too idealistic? Don't the real problems lie elsewhere? How to persuade a council to build a theatre at all – and then, with this decision having been taken, to prevent them from making thoroughly stupid mistakes. Consider two separate examples. The Citizens' Theatre, Glasgow, which has a grant of £55,000 from the Scottish Arts Council and a grant of £8500 from the local council, has one of the worst theatres and sites in the country – an old touring-theatre set in the Gorbals, now a demolishers' yard. It's easy to point to the attendance figures of such a place – 25 per cent during the 1969 season – and to argue that this proves that there is no demand for the theatre in Glasgow or that the Company is not good enough to attract audiences. But, in fact, it takes a considerable effort to get to the Citizens' Theatre, and the journey is a depressing one. To attract an average audience of 250 is, under such conditions, an achievement. There seems little point in subsidizing such a theatre so heavily, if there is not also a serious attempt to find better accommodation.

At Hornchurch, where there have been plans for a new theatre for many years, the present Queen's Theatre has a rather run-down site in a side street, and it is in any case due for demolition when a road-widening scheme takes place. Originally, there were plans for a theatre in a park, the Billet Lane cricket-ground. When the Council changed hands, however, from Labour to Tory, this idea was shelved – and instead the Council put forward a scheme for a new theatre as part of a redevelopment project in Romford. The management at the theatre was dismayed. To begin with, the proposed town site ruled out the possibility of an adaptable theatre and, secondly, Romford is the commercial half of Hornchurch, which is a suburban, commuting district. The change of site meant that the image of the theatre would have to change as well – and the management knew well that the audiences, so carefully built up since 1953, might not transfer their loyalties to the new area. In both these cases, a considerable amount of public investment in the theatre was jeopardized by what really amounts to careless ignorance on the part of the authorities.

In both these cases, I would have liked to have seen a more positive intervention on the part of the Arts Council – but this would have exceeded the terms of its charter and would have established precedents which might involve it in all sorts of minor controversies. But isn't there perhaps a case for amending the Charter anyway, so that there can be a more positive attempt to use arts centres and theatres for some limited social engineering? Were the demonstrators massing outside the American Embassy in Grosvenor Square meeting in the right place? Shouldn't those protests, which are unlikely to have a direct result but which are aimed at altering a climate of opinion, really take place in a theatre? Not to *devalue* them – but simply to ensure that there is an acceptable place for argument and protest within our society, that there is some place to go when we feel indignant and want to change the circumstances under which we live. The argument against this idea is that the authorities might not take seriously a protest which does not involve social disruption and the threat of violence. This may at present be so, but it would be sadly short-sighted to ignore the possibility of a civilized forum for protest in an age when we face so much social change: short-sighted incidentally, for the authorities, the demonstrators and for the community as a whole.

Very few of the new theatres in this country take into account the possibility of social change: few attempt to exploit new dramatic opportunities for the theatre; few try to explore the technological possibilities for the theatre. And yet the picture as a whole may not be too depressing. More theatres have been built more quickly: and this spate of building has outstripped our expectations in 1960. Furthermore, our theatres have become more imaginative in design. If in the last resort we must feel dissatisfied with them, it is because the potentiality for drama within communities has so greatly changed over the past ten years: the opportunities have not yet been matched by the buildings.

9

Theatre for Whom?

THE very act of writing a book about the repertory movement places me among the enthusiasts. This enthusiasm, however, is not universally shared. Sometimes, indeed, there seems to be a hostility towards local theatres which can't be explained by normal indifference and isn't directed against other amenities in a town, cultural or otherwise.

The councils of Watford and Glasgow have subsidized their reps for some years – though not with undue generosity – which may give them the right to breathe fire against the walls they have helped to paint. But there are towns which do not subsidize their theatres and where managers still complain of an almost neurotic mixture of pride and resentment, excitement and bitterness. In Yorkshire, for example, the small town of Richmond has a theatre, built in 1788 and rescued from dereliction as a salvage depot by some local enthusiasts. This rare example of a Georgian touring-theatre would seem, from every point of view, to be an asset to the town. Financially, it places no burden on the rates. Richmond contributes to the Northern Arts Association, which in turn subsidizes the theatre: but the size of the grant greatly exceeds the original contribution, which is no more than other small towns in the area give. The productions, by outside companies, are usually excellent, and so are the recitals of music. Tourists come from London or further afield to sit in the gallery for six shillings and watch perhaps a Prospect production or listen to Yehudi Menuhin. But in Richmond itself, the attitude towards the theatre is one of cautious suspicion, which sometimes becomes almost aggressive. 'We could never fill the theatre from the town,' the Borough Treasurer, Mr Fairbrother, told me. 'Not fill it by half.' The theatre is a small one (238 seats), the season is short (from April to September) and Richmond has 7500 inhabitants. Shopkeepers and hoteliers are reluctant to advertise in the brochure, which goes all over the country. On one occasion, when the Queen Mother was paying a visit, a fellow councillor approached Mr Fairbrother (whose wife runs the theatre) for a couple of complimentary tickets. He was refused them on the grounds that there were none available and, in any case, he had never shown interest in the theatre before. 'I wouldn't be seen dead in your theatre,' he replied, 'on principle.'

Incidents like this are not rare or isolated, although they may seem trivial when set against the wider achievements of the repertory movement – the brilliant productions at Nottingham, Chichester and Bristol, the enthusiasm at Leatherhead and all the new theatres. But they do reveal that even well-established reps can be ambushed by a pack of enmites, whom they were tempted to ignore when things were going well. Reps are still vulnerable – as swimming-pools and libraries are not – to shifts in the political mood, squeezes and freezes, the shocked snort of a Grundy in power. Their existence can be threatened by a small setback. For years, the Belgrade Theatre, Coventry, has been one of the best reps in the country – adventurous programmes, good audiences, a model theatre-in-education team – but in 1969 a hot summer coincided with a change of political control on the Council, and the ominous rumours began. The audiences – probably lured away by the sun – were *dwindling*. The Belgrade was becoming an expensive luxury. Shouldn't the Council sell out to a commercial management? Warren Jenkins, the director, reacted with desperate professionalism. He quickly scheduled Agatha Christie's *Murder at the Vicarage*, explaining with a tight smile that 'we're playing it as a period piece, of course'. One actor with ideals resigned from the Company, but the smell of this familiar dumpling stew wafted over the Sunday suburbs, drawing in the older audiences to whom the sun was less of an attraction.

In short, the time has not yet arrived, which has been predicted for so long, when a theatre can be accepted as part of the normal life of a town, not to be opposed in essence – just as libraries are rarely opposed – although grants may be raised or cut. This state of happy stability has never happened. Even in Nottingham, perhaps the most theatrically alert town in the country, whose audiences have been enlightened by the best schoolmasters available, by Val May, Frank Dunlop and John Neville, there were some gloomy fears when John Neville left, which were fortunately dispelled when Stuart Burge arrived. Even in Leatherhead, where the old theatre club had sixteen thousand members, a council grant (before the new theatre was built) was bitterly opposed, although it was only for

£500. The local library (which issues annually 10,000 tickets) received a grant of £40,000, without much question. Clearly, libraries have a social status even in Leatherhead, which theatres do not possess and may never perhaps be able to claim. One is regarded as a necessary amenity, the other as a disposable luxury. For the past twelve years, rep managements up and down the country have been trying to prove their usefulness to the community in all sorts of ways – by staging local documentaries, by running theatre-in-education teams, by turning foyers into art galleries and presenting folk concerts and poetry readings on Sunday nights, by trying in short to demonstrate that the theatre can become a kind of cultural service station, filling up everyone with nearly everything.

I don't wish to imply that I am against these efforts. On the contrary, they seem to me very valuable. However, I have sometimes received the impression that reps are trying to justify their existence by any possible means: and sometimes the different claims set up gear-crashing juxtapositions. Shortly after Hugh Jenkins M.P. wrote in the *Sunday Times* that the reps were becoming the churches of the future – which may be all too depressingly true – Prince Charles spoke at the 1969 CORT Conference and said that 'drama was just as important, if not more so, than new bingo halls' – and was *applauded*.

Assertions like these reflect a chronic state of nervous introversion among repertory theatres. In private, the doubts range from 'How can we keep these places open with television around?' to profounder dialogues about the essential value of drama: but they don't always rise to the surface as sensible discussions. There is always the temptation to silence the philistines for ever with some clear-cut justification for the live theatre. Unfortunately, since nobody can decide what this justification should be, the new images are as confused as the old ones. The doubts are beaten back with too many good arguments which don't quite tally with experience. Nor is the antagonism so crass that it can be met simplistically. To some, the very phrase, *repertory theatre*, has an unfortunate ring, bringing to mind the living embarrassment of weekly tat. The possible verbal alternatives are just as bad. *Civic* theatre suggests an amenity listed somewhere below the golf course on a municipal brochure, while *community* theatre, or *Everyman's*, *People's* or *Citizen's*, sounds like sociological soap-opera, conveying altogether too optimistic a picture of the way in which people live together. What, for example, is a *community*, a word which I have used so often in this book? *Repertory* at least distinguishes one sort of company from another, but even Miss Horniman disliked the word, because it sounded pompous, and it only came to be generally used when the Pilgrim Players, Barry Jackson's amateur company, moved in 1913 to their theatre in Station Street, turned professional overnight and wanted to show just how professional they had become.

In any case, are the poor associations with the word all that misleading? The National Theatre and the Royal Shakespeare Company may, strictly speaking, be repertory companies, but they are national prestige efforts, supported so lavishly by the Arts Council that they can't be regarded as representative. Nor is a fine provincial company, such as the Nottingham Playhouse, exactly typical – with its splendid new building financed originally by a windfall to the local council when gas was nationalized and since maintained by the Arts Council as one of the major reps. Wouldn't the Grand, Wolverhampton, provide a more accurate image, where for years a small non-resident company has been struggling along, in the face of local apathy, shortage of cash, and a great sad barn of a touring theatre, which could seat 1400 and can make even a large audience of 500 feel despondent.

Isn't it inevitable, in other words, that most local reps will provide third-rate theatre? That the better actors will be lured away to the West End and television, to the larger subsidized companies, to films? The audiences are potentially so much smaller, that to fill the theatre – or even to achieve respectable attendance figures – programmes have to be changed every fortnight or so, thus reducing the time for rehearsal and the standards of production. Whereas thirty or forty years ago, these poor productions may have been worth supporting, nowadays one can probably see similar plays – in better productions – on television. Of course, the *human contact* in the theatre is a pleasant ornament to drama: but does even this argument hold good in the case of a small provincial rep? Some people find the presence of actors on a stage rather embarrassing, particularly if they're not very good. You can't walk out of a theatre without being offensive. You can't switch them off. And so you just sit there, enduring them politely. Far from participating more in the dramatic experience, which is how the theory runs, you stifle your reactions firmly, giving the cast a polite round of applause at the end, and walk out, feeling dutiful perhaps, but not exactly elated. At a boring production in the theatre, you are stuck with the boredom, and after several tedious evenings, if you continue to go, the habit acquires a stately stoicism, in which excitement is neither expected nor tolerated, should it accidentally crop up.

If this seems to be an accurate picture of what the *normal* rep provides, should a council feel any obligation at all to prop up a local theatre with a grant? Should even the Arts Council do so? The objects of the Arts Council are 'to develop and improve the knowledge, understanding and practice of the Arts' – but does, say, the world première of *Sincerely Yours* at the Theatre Royal, Northampton, really qualify? Hasn't the theatre become simply entertainment for a minority, a dwindling minority perhaps, and if it can't survive on ordinary commercial terms shouldn't it be allowed to die in peace? Since there are local reps which survive without subsidies, such as the Theatre Royal, Windsor, mightn't we be protecting incompetent companies – or hopelessly uneconomic ones – with our grants, merely postponing expensively the moment of closure? When enthusiasts talk about reps 'raising the quality of life' in a town, what exactly do they mean? The public can't *use* a theatre, as it uses a library – a production can't be stored or borrowed or studied. A theatre is not exactly an amenity – something like a park which increases environmental pleasure. It is simply an agreeable way of spending an evening if your tastes lie in that direction. Why then should a rep be subsidized, and not a cinema, a dance hall or bingo? Isn't there a concealed snobbery behind the very idea – since theatres were once a middle-class preserve and now seem to be swinging in a different direction? Aren't we straying on to very dangerous ground when we suggest that one man's amusement is superior to another's – and back up this opinion with public money?

The theatre has always managed to arouse some lively and concerned opponents – Puritans, censors, councillors protecting ratepayers and vice versa. A theatre manager can't brush them aside by alluding vaguely to Shakespeare, to Athens in the time of Pericles. From a lofty vantage point, Parnassus perhaps, these controversies may seem all to the good, stiffening fibres, testing morale, weeding out the weak, but at sea level, where a rep may be fighting for its life in a small town, the philistines seem a formidable bunch, unfairly snatching up any crude weapon which lies around – citing the weak productions happily, forgetting the good ones which they probably didn't see, waving some poor box-office figures as irrefutable evidence of a decline, dismissing the favourable ones as luck. And some of the shields, snatched up in defence, are crude as well: 'Of course, our rep could survive as a commercial proposition, if only we didn't live in a mixed economy. If people could spend their money freely, we'd have a full house every night. But they can't. And so we're *entitled* to state subsidies . . . it's only fair.' But this argument, of course, ducks the central question – is the theatre worth subsidizing from society's point of view – whatever that may be. Even a mixed economy has a scheme of values, though the anomalies may distress the Powells amongst us. To many people, even those friendly towards the theatre, the theatre sits uncomfortably astride that barbed wire fence which separates in our mind worthy causes – such as libraries – from unworthy ones – such as pubs and bingo halls. Not all rep managers, as we have seen, agree that the theatre should be subsidized: and those that do give different reasons why. Some point to the better standards of subsidized reps – comparing Sir Barry Jackson's company with those commercial companies at the time which were offering bloodbath melodramas and musicals like *Oh! Oh!! Delphine!!!*: some believe that reps provide social therapy, others an essential art form – and so on.

Thus, the views of the hostile – familiar though they are, unfair though they may seem to be – rub against at least one sensitive area. Another is that drama can't be easily institutionalized. Without sheer administrative incompetence, a grant to a library is usually well spent. There is an obvious value for money. But there is no such guarantee when money is given to a theatre. However big the grant to a company may be, however splendid the resources, exciting productions can't simply be handed over the counter, for drama is a human activity and subject therefore to the ebb and flow of concentration, commitment and the unconscious. It would be easy to defend the repertory movement if all the ebbs could be made to disappear, by waving a subsidy over them, leaving the flows unchecked. But this can't be done. Subsidies can raise the technical standards of a company, but sometimes these polished, lifeless productions seem the more useless because of the care and attention which has gone into them. Just as grants, fine facilities and public support can't *guarantee* good drama, so poor surroundings and local apathy don't *necessarily* destroy it. Peter Cheeseman's company at

Stoke plays in a converted cinema a mile from the town centre – in a building which looks at first sight like a forgotten Woolworth's. A theatre can be the space beside the counter in an Off-off-Broadway bar. When we give grants to local reps, we are simply trying to improve the environment, physical and economic, in which the activity of drama may grow. The soil can be watered and tilled, but the plant can't be forced to flower.

And so the gardening *may* be wasted – but it is not *likely* to be so, for drama is not a rare and delicate orchid. With a little encouragement, it spreads rapidly and develops some exotic blossoms. As I have pointed out, the West End is currently filled with flowers from the reps, and the influence of the Birmingham Rep spread to London, Malvern, Stratford and even to Canada. I was quite prepared to find, when I started to tour around the local reps, that the gloomy opinions were nearer the mark than the cheerful ones. In fact, the standards of production were higher than I had expected, the audiences younger and more enthusiastic, the attendances better. Even in the little Byre Theatre in St Andrews, where the manager switches on the tape-recorder before hurrying to do his stint of acting, I saw an excellent production of *The Boston Story* before a packed house. Too many reps perhaps were showing, like some art galleries, 'greeny-yellowy' plays – the equivalent to water-colour landscapes – in competent, naturalistic productions which did not reflect the lively rebirth of abstract drama. But there were many signs of a certain willingness for change – a concern and an interest in *avant-garde* drama – even where this concern was considered too daring to influence the actual programmes.

If asked to defend the repertory movement, however, I would not do so by praising adventurous programmes and good productions, by listing the West End successes, by citing box-office figures and selecting them carefully, by counting the new theatres and examples of community involvement – not because these achievements don't exist or are too significantly rare, but because they are not entirely relevant. I could have been lucky. The late sixties may have been vintage. The real justification for repertory theatre, or indeed any theatre, lies in the nature of drama itself – is it a valuable activity? – and the only proper defence for the reps is if we can be persuaded that people benefit from coming into contact with this activity locally, in their own towns, not simply by piling into a coach at Christmas to visit a London pantomime.

Value – benefit: two awkward, abstract words, very close to mere opinion. Decisions rest shakily on them. What is the *value* of a theatre compared to a new wing at a school? No one can say, and it's tempting to duck these two words altogether, substituting *usefulness* and *moral persuasion*. Drama can be thoroughly educational and useful, I'm afraid, and it's necessary sometimes to stress this over-solemn fact, simply to meet the accusations of frivolity. We learn, as adults and children, both from acting ourselves and from watching others act – though how and what we learn is another matter. Zola once said that in the theatre we make models of the 'real' world to demonstrate the cause and effect of human behaviour. He lived in a society – not dissimilar from our own in this respect – which had a high opinion of science, and if the theatre could take on some of the functions of a laboratory, the formal case for drama could be allowed to rest. In a laboratory, we can build a test tank to show the impact of waves on a sea wall: in the theatre, we can produce (and write) plays like *The Cherry Orchard* which demonstrates how one small, impoverished family of minor Russian aristocrats reacted to the impact of social change – the arrival of railways, the breakdown of the feudal system, industrialization and the rise of the bourgeoisie. My history master at school was convinced that we'd learn nothing about the Russian Revolution without seeing *The Cherry Orchard* and *Battleship Potemkin*, nothing about the Weimar republic without seeing *The Rise and Fall of the City of Mahagonny*, nothing presumably about venereal disease without seeing *Ghosts*. Plays may lack the precise measurements of truly scientific tests, but with honest observers like Chekhov they are as illuminating as most social-science case-histories, and far more interesting.

But no one who has appreciated *The Cherry Orchard* would call it a useful play. The word is not exactly wrong, but inappropriate, as if we were searching for a *raison d'être* where none is needed. Shaw and Brecht wasted much time in the moral defence of the theatre. Drama was a way, *the* way, of persuading people to take the right course of action. And, of course, the theatre *can* be morally influential, as it *can* be pernicious: the same play can have both these effects – when I leave the Westminster Theatre, which is run by Moral Re-armament, having being re-armed for an hour or so, I always feel very inclined to be evil, just to take the taste of goodness away. A play can provide catharsis for one person, harmful stimulation for another: just as one person can be convinced by a Shavian argument, another merely irritated. In other words, what we in the audience morally do with the experience of drama is our own responsibility. The dramatist cannot take moral decisions for us, which would make him an authoritarian. The poet, as Sir Philip Sidney wrote, affirms nothing and therefore he cannot lie: equally he only exhorts at the expense of losing his dignity, for the parallels between an invented situation and a similar problem in real life are rarely so close that the solution to one can be transferred to the other without displacing an important hair. The chief merit of drama is that it can illustrate clearly the process through which moral decisions may be taken, and this is more enlightening perhaps than doling out the decisions themselves.

The activity of drama, therefore, *may* be useful: I believe it is. It may make us better people. But useful or not, moral or not, drama can't properly be defended in these terms, or indeed attacked. Art is a self-justifying activity, and this is why the theatre is both hard to protect from its critics and rather easy: hard because none of the obvious justifications are relevant, and easy because the attacks miss the targets as well. Drama is a response to a human need. It is a way of forestalling our fears, anticipating hopes and of giving a shape and an identity to all those formative rhythms of feeling which would otherwise wander at random through the mind. Even sitting in a theatre, as the lights go down, mirrors an inner dream, which we both long for – and dread. In a moment where will we be? In Mexico? In a Bavarian cave? In life if we were snatched out of our daily routines and dumped – anywhere, like a refugee who has forgotten what war he has fled from, the experience would be traumatic. We wouldn't know where our loyalties lie, what friends will help us or who they are. We would search every street corner for a sign of protection or hostility. It would be an ordeal similar to (I hesitate to add) the moment of birth. In the theatre, we go through this experience, but in the form of a game. We want to know from the start of a play which characters are on our side – or trustworthy – and why. Every scrap of information we hoard for the future, and when all the secrets are known, and the struggle is over, we lose interest. The normal progress of a play leads from uncertainty to knowledge, and has, however sad the outcome, a reassuring effect. We have learnt to cope with the game: we may now be able to cope with life.

Some directors and dramatists would regard this, however, as an over-romantic approach. On the contrary, they would say, audiences aren't uprooted from their daily lives when they come to the theatre: they're not plunged into insecurity as the lights go down. They've come glowing with optimism: they've paid for their seats – which are comfortably cushioned: they've bought chocolates, a programme and ordered Scotch for the interval. They're sitting with friends. To reassure the already smug would be a futile game – and difficult as well, for the complacency is skin and dust deep. The audiences know this, however much they may smile and hold hands. Because they are comfortable, because this is time out and only a game, they can be confronted with what inwardly disturbs them, but which in real life they would try to reject. It is the time to discover 'the weasel in the cocktail cabinet', to move the play gently from calm to inner disturbance, from certainty and knowledge towards doubt and insecurity. Other directors would say that the very concept of progress – even from security to insecurity – is somehow misleading. Inwardly we are not aware of change – only of sensations moving around a static state of being.

Whichever approach a director may favour, whatever form he may choose, naturalism, expressionism and so forth, the nature of the activity remains the same – which is, to bring our objective and subjective experiences into focus, to give them a place and a definition.

> Hands, do what you're bid.
> Bring the balloon of the mind
> That billows and ebbs in the wind
> Into its narrow shed.

The theatre is that narrow shed.

I have suggested that there is a basic need for drama: and, by implication, that the value which a theatre has for us is related to the intensity by which we feel this need. Or at least secretly so – for just as some of the severest critics of Christianity are those who feel that the wealth of the Church mocks the religion of love and poverty, so some of the hostility against the theatre comes from those who feel that drama is being debased. The most violent critics of reps are usually not those councillors who want to keep the rates down nor those who aren't interested in the theatre at all, but those people who are interested in the theatre, go along to the rep to see a production, say, of *The Homecoming* and feel affronted. These are the people who badger the councillors with questions about rates being devoted to 'kitchen-sink rubbish' – who write indignant letters to papers – who try to start a snowball of a complaint down the slope to become an avalanche of disapproval which will bury a rep. It is not their apathy towards the theatre, which provokes this destructiveness: but their concern. It is as if an important part of their lives was being attacked.

In school, during class improvisations, some children who have been watching for a time will be impatient to take part: they may not want to act exactly – but they want to say what the others are doing wrong and why. In education, of course, we rather encourage this process of criticism, when it hasn't become too automatic, because when a child is trying to say what is wrong he is also searching for words and actions which are right. He is trying to improve the game, to bring it closer to his vision of reality. Adult theatre is partly an extension of these improvisatory games – if the word 'extension' can be held to cover a gap not only of years but of needs as well. As we grow older, our attitudes become more complex, the roles subtler, the indecisions harder to conceal. We want to be right. And so we stick to the script, we plan in advance, we distrust the unprepared. As the game develops in complexity, so it requires professional skills, voices and bodies trained to be supple: and those of us who have to push drama to the fringes of our lives give way to the more dedicated and expert. The gap between the performer and the audience widens. They are now the ones who act: we watch – and cannot interfere too much. The critical side of the game ceases to be important, because we cannot directly influence the pattern of events. And so, we assert our frustrated criticism when we can, with more emotion. Instead of saying, 'He should have done this!', we say, 'He's a bad actor!' As children, we are all actors, but this right is usually snatched away from us at adulthood. When our advice even as critics is ignored – or seems to be, we start to shout, 'She's marvellous!', 'He's terrible!' 'Rubbish!' 'Close the place down!' It is the only way to be heard. The door to the party is nearly shut.

Many, for example, disliked *Oh What a Lovely War!* because the officers were shown to be callous, snobbish brutes – true products of an unfair class-system. Some dismissed the play as one-sided, mere propaganda. But there's no reason why a play *should* present every

shade of opinion, like the B.B.C. news. 'A poet affirms nothing –
therefore he cannot lie.' A play is always a personal statement, in
which accuracy is merely one of the attributes of a good dramatist.
Those who criticized *Oh What a Lovely War!* felt that the game was
wrong: they wanted to change it, and because they couldn't do so
they felt frustrated. If this frustration builds up from play to play,
we're tempted to dismiss the whole activity as corrupt. The Puritans
can't always be blamed for this image of the theatre as a sex- and
money-mad place. Nor indeed can the theatre. It is an offshoot of
our concern for drama. The present pope, as Cardinal Montini,
wrote to defend Pope Pius XII from the allegations expressed in Rolf
Hochhuth's play, *The Representative*, which he had neither seen nor
read, only heard about from someone. Hochhuth, he stated, was only
a dramatist – and therefore only interested in sensational scandal,
which would bring audiences in, not with historical accuracy, which
would not. Cardinal Montini wasn't just shielding a reputation – he
was attacking the theatre for being basely commercial, for pandering
to low tastes in the interests of profit. He seemed, in short, a bit too
heated: a lesser man would have been accused of indulging in vulgar
abuse. Hochhuth of all dramatists tries to prove his case historically –
even when he needn't do so – and audiences came, not because a
scandal about a pope is good box-office, but because *The Representative* asked important questions, not just about the role played
by the Roman Catholic Church during the war, but about the nature
of the Christian witness. It was indeed a play for Christians, appealing more to the believers than to those agnostic critics who do not
share the opinion that Christians ought to behave better than the
rest of mankind.

Cardinal Montini's remarks on this occasion – unfair, ill-judged
and illogical – reflect a frustrated irritation with the theatre which
rises up from subterranean motives. Dramatists, actors and directors
are abnormally inclined towards idealism. Whatever drives a man
into the theatre, it isn't often sheer greed. Economic insecurity, it is
true, may force a dramatist to lower the aims with which he began –
may drive an actor into a cops-and-robbers serial – but only someone
unnaturally naïve and stupid chooses drama as a career simply to
make a fortune. If this were so, then the case for a state-subsidized
theatre, with fixed salaries and a civil service hierarchy, would be
proved. If economic security alone could raise standards, the solution is simple. We would only have to pension off our actors, so that

they could remain like high-court judges, way above the struggle – the Impartial Spokesmen of our Community. But grants don't ward off this sort of criticism. They may increase it. A rep director may be above the pull of the market, when he earns forty to sixty pounds a week, but *really* (the rumour then runs) he's not good enough to be employed in the *commercial* theatre. The theatre is attacked for being commercial and for not being so. And this is because the underlying cause for the frustrated impatience has nothing to do with commercialism at all. We appoint professional actors as our surrogates – and grumble at them, not only because they don't do the job properly, but because we want to do it ourselves – differently, in our own way. With the other arts, we can accept our place on the touchlines with good grace – but not with the theatre. Drama is an activity which we have all abused from time to time – if only perhaps by rehearsing a speech or running through a vital interview in our minds. We can all claim a little knowledge – enough to be impatient with rivals.

If drama were centralized in London, if people throughout the country only came into contact with plays through films, television or the national touring networks of commercial and subsidized drama, we might well feel that the whole activity of drama were gripped by establishment forces, monolithic and unchangeable. The sense of impatient frustration would grow, for we would have no means of altering an activity of which we could all claim a share, but in which our personal influence was being denied. A situation like this occurred at one time in New York where the production costs on Broadway and indeed Off, were so high that the seat prices were more than most people could afford. The example of the repertory movement in Britain led to the establishment of the Lincoln Center Repertory Company at the Vivian Beaumont Theater: where the prices, under the subscription system, were still high – but not prohibitively so for the averagely successful business man. But even among the economically dispossessed drama didn't drip to silence. A poor people's theatre grew up in back yards and restaurants. The Off-off-Broadway movement began, a rebellious and anarchic movement, very lively and muddled. Drama, which can become a means of helping a society to become more self-aware and therefore more united, became another weapon in the class war: with Broadway hating La Mama – and vice versa.

A society, in my view, has to find some area in which different levels and types of culture can meet, quarrel peacefully and marry. The theatre is that area.

The repertory theatres in Britain provide a vital link between the personal need for drama, its local flowering in the professional theatre and the national network of plays and productions. Repertory directors *are* influenced by their local audiences. They have to be. Actors, too, are sensitive to the joke which doesn't work, to the pause which can be prolonged, to the audiences which crowd in or stay away. The enthusiasm and the hostility is part of the scene. If the theatre were less important, it would be easier to run. As it is, every visit to a school, to a factory or a Women's Institute raises fresh questions, new praise and complaints. To close a theatre is one way of denying a deep and personal freedom, an access to a realm of possibilities which most of us crave for, without always knowing why. To open a theatre quite simply extends this freedom.

10

An Alphabet of Reps

BETWEEN the completion of this typescript (in autumn 1970) and the publication of the book, at least one new theatre will have opened, the policy of the new Conservative Government towards the arts will have been revealed in practice, and several artistic directors will have lost (and gained) jobs. The situation in repertory theatre is always changing – not in an arbitrary way, which would invalidate the whole idea of a guide, but in one of those complex evolutionary patterns which always seem predictable after the event. The reader should bear in mind that the information in this guide was (systematically) gathered in the years 1967–70, and (haphazardly) from the early sixties. During this period, each theatre was visited at least once, most twice, and some many times. Inevitably, however, some of this information will quickly be out of date: not every company is included, and factual information – the dimensions of the stage and so forth – is not all that one would like to convey. There are fine companies working in poor theatres, and vice versa. But to undertake fair and sensible *qualitative* descriptions is an almost impossible task: if I had visited each rep three times a year for the past five years, I would still have seen only a fraction of the work; and during this time my own standards will have been changing, often without my realizing how much they have. The prejudices in my mind when I began the research will have tightened or slackened: the examples will have altered and, with them, the hopes and opinions. With any subject, absolute objectivity is clearly impossible: but with a subject like this even that coolly pragmatic attitude of mind, beloved by businessmen and scientists, which is sometimes described as 'objective', is a sort of con-game – an attempt to persuade by seeming disinterested.

I mention these very obvious points, not to forestall criticism, but to indicate why and how the pattern of these short sketches has been affected by the fluid nature of the material. I have tried to separate the factual information about each rep, which can be checked, from my comments, which cannot. Each description will consist of at least two paragraphs. The first will be concerned with basic facts – the size and dimensions of the theatre, a very brief summary of its history, the size of the 1969/70 grants, the seasons, the nature and size of the 1969/70 company. The second paragraph will basically be concerned with the way in which these facts modify the programmes offered by the various companies. From my assessment of the productions I've seen – and from past programmes and press reviews – I hope to indicate how various companies have managed to tackle the various opportunities and difficulties, and the extent of their success: topics which clearly run closer to the wind of subjective opinion. The reps are listed alphabetically, according to the towns where they are situated: and the full address and box-office numbers are given beneath the heading.

Ayr, *The Graham Players*
Civic Theatre, Craigie Road, Ayr. B/O: Ayr 63015
A converted church hall, owned by the local council. The auditorium, with balcony, seats 352. The small stage has a P/A (proscenium arch) opening of 22 feet, a height of 12 feet, and a depth of 15 feet. There is no flying and little wing space: but, if necessary, the workshop and store behind the stage can be used for a change of set in the interval. A rep company, unsubsidized, was formed in 1951: and Rosemary Leach was the first manager to persuade the Council that the rep was a social asset to the town and should be subsidized. For the past thirteen years, the Civic has been leased by the Council to The Graham Players, which is run by the actor/manager, Victor Graham. There are eight members in this acting team: and the Company receives a small subsidy from the local council. Ayr is a holiday resort, and the repertory season runs from June to September: the programmes change weekly and there is no Monday performance. The 1969 ticket prices ranged from 4s to 6s.

Victor Graham's company is caught in a too familiar cycle of inadequacies. The theatre – and the area – is just large enough to sustain a small rep company, but no risks can be taken. The Council subsidies barely underwrite the small fluctuations in the weekly attendance-figures. The stage and backstage facilities can cope with a simple one-set play: but a production with a more elaborate scenic plot would be hard indeed to tackle. The Company can just cope (in numbers) with small-cast plays. There is no theatre-in-education programme: there isn't time for one. Students from Ayr College don't come even to the more ambitious productions, such as *Who's Afraid of Virginia Woolf?* The programmes lean heavily on farces and thrillers, which are well attended, by Ayr residents – not apparently by tourists. The Company depends rather too much perhaps on its star, Victor Graham, a pleasant light comedian, whose performance as the comic parson in *Pools' Paradise* (August 1969) was the most successful feature of a rather slipshod production. Victor Graham is popular locally: and he would like to change from weekly to fortnightly rep, but he daren't do so unless the Council is prepared to stand the possible initial losses in attendance. Such a change would undoubtedly raise the production standards and would lift the burden somewhat from the manager's shoulders: but equally why should the Council spend more on a theatre which lacks the basic facilities to tackle a more ambitious repertory programme and where the Company pleases the Ayr residents?

References: 30, 61, 72, 75

Bexhill, *Theatre South East*
De La Warr Pavilion, Bexhill-on-Sea. B/O: Bexhill 2022
A large theatre, built in the 1930s, as part of a seaside entertainments centre. The auditorium can seat 1150: but the balcony, seating 500, is usually closed for straight plays. The stage (P/A opening, 28 feet; height, 14 feet; depth, 25 feet) is well proportioned, has good flying and wing space, and a 10 foot apron. The foyers, bars and restaurant belong to the complex. The workshops are adequate, but situated half-a-mile from the theatre, in a disused railway station. The Company (formerly known as the Penguin Players) was established in Bexhill in 1950: it is run by Richard Burnett and his wife, Peggy Paige, who in the past have run companies in Margate, Clacton and Eastbourne: and have recently taken over the Leas Pavilion, Folkestone, and the Esplanade, Bognor Regis. Although the company at Bexhill is a non-profit-distributing enterprise, there are no local or Arts Council subsidies: each year, the Council and the Company decide on what percentage of the box office each will receive. The acting team at Bexhill varies from 12 members (during the slack season) to 25, at the height of the summer. Sometimes, a straight play alternates with a summer show; the policy is weekly rep with a change of programme mid-week.

The facilities at the De La Warr Pavilion are comparatively good. The only problem is that the theatre is too large for the productions which Theatre South East can supply or for Bexhill, with a population of 35,000. It is nevertheless hard to understand why the selection of plays over recent years has been so unambitious: mainly mysteries and farces, rising to the occasional peak of a Noël Coward season (summer 1968). The problem may partly lie with the Bexhill audiences, who are apparently intolerant of all modernity. *The Killing of Sister George* did well in the Theatre South East production at Eastbourne, badly in Bexhill. There

are no student audiences at Bexhill to relieve the pressure of all that retirement: and the absence of subsidies over the years must have deterred all incentive towards experiment. There was a plan to lengthen the run of each production, by touring them around the other theatres run by the Company on the south coast: but since the stage dimensions of these theatres varied direct swops were hard to make. There is no doubt that Richard Burnett has fought hard and long to maintain the Company in face of competition from television and the beach. But the production reviewed, *Portrait of Murder*, seemed, alas, to confirm the reputation of most seaside reps: it was dully staged, with mediocre performances, in a poor box-set.
References: 15, 67, 68, 107

Billingham, *The Forum Theatre*

The Forum, Town Centre, Billingham, Teesside. B/O: Stockton 52663
A new theatre was completed in March 1968 as part of the Forum, a sport and cultural centre within a new town square, and shopping-area. The whole project swarms with examples of enlightened self-interest. Billingham is an area on Teesside made rich by I.C.I.: the town centre was built by the Council, partly to attract residents to an industrial area. The Forum is financed by the commercial development of the town centre: and contains, in addition to a wide range of sporting facilities, a concert hall and (near by) an art gallery. The theatre itself seats 637, or 578 if the forestage is used. The auditorium is hung with family boxes. The stage (P/A opening, 44 feet; height, 23 feet; depth with forestage, $56\frac{1}{4}$ feet; with apron, $49\frac{1}{4}$ feet; without apron or forestage, $40\frac{1}{4}$ feet) is very well equipped, with excellent flying (counterweighted) and good wing space. The lighting board (with 79 ways) may be a little small for the size of the stage. The theatre has been heavily subsidized by Teesside, which is giving more to the theatre than any other council in the country (£60,000 during the 1968/9 season). The Northern Arts Association has given £7000 and the Arts Council £5000. The audience attendance-figures during the first two years were reasonably good, for an area without a tradition of live theatre: 50 per cent. There is no permanent company, and the former artistic director, George Roman, used to cast from London. The programmes have been mainly fortnightly rep, with a third week devoted to films: each production therefore has had a three-week rehearsal period. Outside companies, such as Prospect have also visited the theatre, and attracted capacity business. The play policy was, under George Roman, very ambitious – ranging from Pinter's *The Birthday Party* to *Macbeth* and *Guys and Dolls*: but the theatre, in spite of the heavy subsidies, lost money – £7000, and there was a crisis in its affairs in November 1969, during which the artistic director left.

The Forum Theatre seems to have been inspired by the great German civic theatres. The stage is splendid but it requires a spectacular product to fill it: and the theatre is too small for such a product to be economically run. Hence, the project requires either heavy subsidies, or a management prepared to build a company slowly up to fill the demands of the theatre. The audiences in Billingham, too, needed to be prepared for what their theatre could offer. Sadly, too much was attempted too soon. George Roman was undoubtedly right to look for large-scale productions to reveal the full glories of the stage: and his *Macbeth* was, by all accounts, splendid. However, the lack of a theatre-in-education team and the policy of casting from London – without building up a permanent acting team – prevented that interaction between a community and a company which has been so significant a feature of the current repertory movement. The theatre too, with all those family boxes, is condemned (I suppose) to family entertainment. *Billy Liar*, a production during the period of retrenchment, illustrated the futility of staging a small, box-set production on a stage forty feet wide. Because the production was planned to tour, the scenery had to end five feet at least from the proscenium arch. The production was adequate, and Michael Percival gave a goodish performance as Billy: but it was sad that this fine dramatic machine should be used for a play which can be adequately staged in a church hall.

References: 30, 35, 56, 74, 96, 106, 108, 119, 132, 133.

Birmingham, *Alexandra Theatre*

Alexandra Theatre, Station Street, Birmingham 5. B/O: 021-643 1231

An Edwardian touring-theatre, built in 1901. The auditorium seats 1562: and the stage is proportionately large – P/A opening, 39 feet 4 inches; height, 16 feet to 24 feet; depth, 31 feet 10 inches. It was originally intended as a popular theatre, staging melodramas, pantomimes, music-hall and revues: but in 1927 Leon Salberg, whose family have owned and managed the theatre since 1911, decided to follow the example of the Birmingham Rep, down the road. A repertory company was established: but gradually a system of mixed repertory and touring seasons was evolved, which still survives. The theatre received no grant until 1968, and faced a constant struggle for survival. The pantomime was a famous annual event, in a traditional formula although newly written each year: the costumes and the scripts were hired out to other companies the following season, and through the pantomime profits, and through staging only small-cast plays, the Company eked through. In 1969, the theatre was bought by Birmingham Council, who are maintaining it as a theatre, under its present manager, Derek Salberg. The acting team has a seasonally permanent nucleus of 6–7 members: stars, such as Adam Faith, assist on occasions. Policy: fortnightly rep, touring and pantomime.

This theatre is obviously old-fashioned, uneconomic to run and disproportionately large: the backstage facilities aren't bad, but they leave

much to be desired. The flying, for example, has no counterweight system, which must mean that the Company requires a team of heavy-weight wrestlers for the pantos. It is hard not to feel much affection and respect for this theatre, with its dignified family management, so much outshone by the reputation of the Birmingham Rep. Nevertheless, this was where the National Theatre presented for the first time Laurence Olivier's *Othello*. The production of *Alfie* (June 1969) was fairly good, and the theatre was full. The scenery was obviously restricted by cost considerations. The Alexandra is one of the theatres proposed by the Arts Council to be part of the touring-grid.
References: 28, 42, 85, 116.

Birmingham, *Midlands Arts Theatre Company*
Studio Theatre, Cannon Hill, Birmingham 12. B/O: 021–440 3838
The Studio Theatre is planned as part of an arts-centre complex for young people. There are two further theatres planned: the Cygnet and the Swan. The Studio Theatre was originally intended to house experimental and amateur productions, but it has been used by the professional reper-tory company since 1965. The auditorium seats 200: the stage has variable dimensions, but is basically an open-end, which could be adapted to thrust. The width is 24 feet. There is also a small, but attractive, puppet theatre: the Hexagon. The acting team of about 20 members works in both theatres, receiving training therefore in puppet techniques as well as in rep. There is an Arts Council subsidy of £24,000 under the Grants for Young People scheme. The repertory season runs from September to June: and the policy is basically repertoire. In 1970, for example, Henry Livings' *Eh?* ran with *Hansel and Gretel*.

The Midlands Arts Centre could well become the model for com-munity arts projects. The professional acting team works side by side with the amateurs, swopping advice and (in theory) attending each other's productions. The scheme is intended for the young – but the play policy is intelligently adult, and family parties can come. The puppet theatre for very young children is admirable. The productions of *Eh?* and *Little Malcolm* were both fairly good, although the Company is working within the rudimentary conditions of the studio theatre. It will be interesting to see how, in the future, the rep company will co-operate with the film studio, the music workshop and the other facilities which are planned at the arts centre. The severest social criticism of the arts centre has been that the project has not yet touched the poorer children in Birmingham, and that its situation (in Edgbaston, opposite the cricket ground) tends to defeat proper class integration: the artistic objection to the scheme could be that, surrounded by amateurs and children, the professionals can't get on with their main task, of presenting good productions of worthy plays. I found the whole atmosphere, however, lively and enlightening: and it

was interesting to note that four-fifths of the cost of the project had come from private sources, particularly industry and the trade unions.
References: 28, 105, 113, 121, 129, 132

Birmingham, *Repertory*

(1970–1) Station Street, Birmingham 5. B/O: 021-643 2471. (Autumn 1971) Broad Street, Birmingham

This theatre (in Station Street) was completed in 1913 and was the first to be built specifically for repertory purposes. Sir Barry Jackson and S. N. Cooke designed it for Sir Barry's amateur company, the Pilgrim Players, who turned professional – after the first performance on 15 February 1913: and the success of this company established the modern repertory movement and altered the course of British theatre. Unlike, say, the Alexandra Theatre, also in Station Street, Birmingham, which was built twelve years before, the Repertory Theatre was intended to be intimate, seating 450, in a single steep rake with a proscenium-arch stage. No pillars, no cupids, nothing to distract the concentration away from the production and the text. The stage has little wing space, little flying: the front-of-house and backstage facilities are (by Edwardian and modern standards alike) austerely inadequate. A new theatre is being built in the heart of the Civic Centre area, a monument in concrete and glass, with all those improvements to theatre design which the old building so patently lacks. There will be a high fly-tower, a studio theatre, fine foyers, a restaurant and good backstage facilities. The stage itself will be of a conventional pattern: and the auditorium will seat 900 in a single, rising arc. There is now a large (seasonally) permanent company, befitting its status as an Arts Council major rep: and the subsidies include £46,000 from the Arts Council and £8000 from the local authorities.

For many years, the Birmingham Rep has been fighting to maintain its extraordinarily high reputation in the face of many difficulties – and flamboyant competition from the Nottingham Playhouse not so far away. The generous patronage of Sir Barry Jackson was not immediately replaced by an equal local and national generosity, and there was an awkward gap between the time when one source of subsidy began to falter and when new ones were still to be found. The old theatre is too small to function economically. In the twenties and thirties, the Birmingham Rep was famous for attempting productions which (though undeniably exciting) few other companies would tackle: Shaw's *Back to Methuselah* was first produced here, and here as well Sir Barry tried out the first modern-dress productions of Shakespeare. The public really expected the Birmingham Rep to maintain higher standards, even during the difficult fifties, than those usually associated with what is really a rather small provincial theatre. The new plays had to be of undoubted quality: the revivals had to be exciting and indeed lavish. The two fine *Hamlet*s in the 1969 and 1970 seasons received almost less publicity than they deserved (although they starred Richard Chamberlain and Alec McCowen) – because such triumphs are associated with the theatre. Equally, the poor productions are more harshly criticized. Under Peter Dews, the present artistic director, the Company has been consistently interesting to visit – and yet perhaps it has seemed a little disappointing, somewhat unadventurous. I asked Humphrey Stanbury, formerly the general manager, from which modern dramatist would he seek a new play? Whom did he most admire? He replied – in 1967, in an age of Pinter, Osborne, Bond and many others – 'Peter Ustinov'. The most successful new play to have been premièred by the Birmingham Rep in recent years was that pleasant, middlebrow comedy, *Hadrian VII*, which is still running in London. The production at Birmingham was splendid, in surroundings particularly unsympathetic to the mock pomp and ceremony. Alec McCowen as Rolfe gave a most brilliant performance. There was also a visually spectacular production of Linney's *The Sorrows of Frederick*, which Peter Dews managed to stage in defiance of the limitations of the theatre. The new theatre should provide him with the opportunities he – and the Company – and the ghost of Barry Jackson clearly all deserve.

References: 13, 23–4, 28–9, 32–3, 43, 44, 47, 57, 59, 73, 88, 95, 128, 132, 155, 157, 158

Bolton, *Octagon Theatre*

Octagon Theatre, Howell Croft South, Bolton. B/O: Bolton 20661

An adaptable theatre, completed in November 1967, only eighteen months after the campaign to build it began. The stage has three basic shapes – as an 'open end', the dimensions are: width, 54 feet; depth, 23 feet 6 inches; as a 'thrust', the width is 26 feet and the depth 32 feet; and 'in the round' the width is 26 feet and the depth, 17 feet 9 inches. The seating alters with the shape of the stage, and banks of seats disappear under the first-floor/balcony level. For 'in-the-round' productions, the theatre holds 422 – for 'open end' 356 – for 'thrust' 338. There is also a false proscenium arch for productions which require it. The lighting board is possibly too small for the theatre: only 60 ways, and with a grid that covers the ceiling. The theatre cost £95,000 to build, and the sum was raised largely by public subscription in under a year. Bolton Council gave the site, which is an excellent one: and also £3000 in subsidy. The Arts Council gives £12,500 and the local authorities, other than Bolton, £850. There is a seasonally permanent acting team of about a dozen: and a permanent theatre-in-education team. In the 2½ years of its existence, the attendance figures have been very high, between 70 and 80 per cent capacity, and the theatre-in-education team has achieved a fine reputation. The project was originally conceived by the present artistic director, Robin Pemberton-Billing, and the money was raised largely through the efforts and the help of the present chairman of the Trustees, Thomas Markland. The rep company plays throughout the year, except in July, when a Children's Theatre Festival was staged in 1969. Monday nights are reserved for concerts and other activities. The seat-prices range from 5s to 9s 6d.

The Octagon Theatre is very much a 'new-style' rep: inspired more by Joan Littlewood than Sir Barry Jackson. The theatre was cheap to build and is marvellously serviceable, perhaps the best for its size and capacities in the country. The atmosphere in the building is a curious blend of youth club, arts centre and theatre, with the coffee bar crowded with teen-agers and the manager sweeping the yard at the back. The permanent company has been chosen to take part not simply in 'scripted' plays, but in local documentaries and with schools as well. *The Bolton Massacre* was a good local documentary: but, strangely enough, a second documentary about the *Bolton Wanderers* was both less successful and less well attended. The play policy is both ambitious and sensible, ranging from *The Home-coming* to *The Shaughraun* and *Oedipus Rex*. The standards of production appear to vary rather disturbingly: sometimes, as with *Oedipus Rex*, they are high – and apparently Alan Plater's *Charlie Came to Our Town* was splendid. At other times the productions can be thoroughly disappointing. The programmes vary from 1 to 3 weeks in length of run: and, with all the social services which the Octagon Theatre manages to offer, a short run in the main theatre must cause awkward complications with the timetable. References: 36, 45, 60, 69, 73, 85, 99, 118, 119, 120, 128, 132, 136, 137, 138, 144.

Bournemouth, *Bournemouth Theatre Company*
Palace Court Theatre, Hinton Road, Bournemouth. B/O: 0202 23275
The Palace Court Theatre was built in 1931 by an amateur company, the Bournemouth Theatre Club, which still owns it and leases it to the pro-fessional company. The auditorium, with a balcony, seats 553: the stage (P/A opening, 28 feet; height, 18–20 feet; depth, 23 feet) has adequate wing and flying space, although the general backstage facilities are rather old-fashioned. The storage and workshop facilities are 1½ miles from the theatre. There is, however, a good rehearsal room, with a small stage. There is a seasonally permanent acting team – ranging in numbers from 6 to 10. During the summer season, there is a policy of repertoire: in 1969, the three plays offered in repertoire were *Say Who You Are*, *Private Lives* and *Make Me a Widow*. For the rest of the year, between September and May, the professional company offers fortnightly rep, alternating with amateur productions. There are grants of £9000 from the Arts Council and £3000 from Bournemouth Corporation, which are not, how-ever, sufficient to protect the Company from the vicious circle of low attendances, subsistence plays and short runs. The audience attendance-figures in recent years have ranged between 35 and 40 per cent: and these

are clearly disappointing. The worst-attended plays during the 1968/9 season were the 'serious, modern' plays – by, say, Pinter or Orton. The best-attended were the stock thrillers and farces. The ticket prices range from 5s to 12s 6d.

During the summer, the Bournemouth Theatre Company is trying to compete for its share of the tourist trade with larger and much better-positioned theatres offering star productions, the Pier Theatre and the Winter Gardens, which starred in 1969 Bob Monkhouse and Ken Dodd respectively. The Palace Court Theatre is hard to find, tucked away beneath an enormous hotel, the Palace Court. And quite clearly it is being pushed out of the market. But perhaps the Company should opt out of a race where it is so handicapped. The Bournemouth Theatre Company ought instead to direct its attention towards the residents of Bournemouth: offering theatre-in-education and attempting to convey an image of local concern and permanence. There is a case for a larger subsidy to allow the Company to break through the barrier of local apathy with some more ambitious productions: and the Southern Arts Association has recommended a new publicity campaign. The production of *Say Who You Are* (summer 1969) was efficient.
Reference: 28

Bristol, *Bristol Old Vic Company*
Theatre Royal, King Street, Bristol. B/O: 0272 24388
Little Theatre, Colston Street, Bristol. B/O: 0272 21182
The Theatre Royal is the finest example of an eighteenth-century town theatre in the country. The auditorium, which seats 681, almost miraculously combines a fair size with intimacy. Slender pillars carry two elegant circles – it would be undignified to call even the second circle a mere balcony. The seats are harder in this second circle, but the acoustics and visibility are still very good. The stage (P/A opening, 25 feet 3 inches; height, 16 feet) had until the 1970 redevelopment programme very little wing or flying space: the foyer was inadequate, and so were the workshop and storage facilities. The development programme will leave the auditorium intact; but the stage will be transformed in sheer efficiency. There will be good flying and storage space; a studio theatre; decent dressing-rooms and good communications. The programme will cost over half-a-million pounds; and while it will undoubtedly provide Bristol with one of the finest theatre complexes in Britain – perhaps in Europe – the result may not be entirely satisfactory because the auditorium may prove to be too small for a major company, which the Bristol Old Vic undoubtedly is. The acting team at Bristol is seasonally permanent and consists of about 30 members, who play both at the Theatre Royal and at the Little Theatre, which is run together with the main theatre. During the eighteen months of alterations, the Company will only be playing at the Little Theatre. In

the past, the Little Theatre has been reserved not exactly for experimental programmes, but for those which are likely to appeal to a younger audience. The annual Arts Council subsidy in recent years has been in the region of £40,000 and the local subsidies amount to £10,000 annually. The money for the development programme was raised partly from the Arts Council (£125,000), partly from the Council and private subscription, and partly also from transfers of successful Old Vic productions to London. The seasons run from September to January, and February to June: the ticket prices (at the Theatre Royal) range from 3s to 12s, and (at the Little Theatre) from 4s to 8s 6d.

The Bristol Old Vic (which was founded in 1946) has a curiously diverse reputation – widely admired, but with strangely assorted achievements. During the early fifties it was famous as the company which gave birth to *Salad Days*, that light-hearted and now perhaps rather faded hit by two members of the acting team, Julian Slade and Dorothy Reynolds, which ran for 2283 performances in London. The Company pioneered the now familiar collaboration between rep companies and universities: the Bristol University Drama Department has always worked closely with the Old Vic. More recently, with Val May as its artistic director, the Old Vic has become celebrated – some might add, notoriously so – for 'naturalistic, well-made plays': superb productions of sensible, middlebrow comedies and dramas, such as *Conduct Unbecoming*, *Poor Horace* and *Mrs Mouse, Are You Within?* all of which transferred to the West End. Val May is one of the best directors in the country of ordinary, apparently unexciting, proscenium-arch, naturalistic plays. Simply to watch his lighting-plots or his sense of timing within a scene is quite fascinating. In *Mandrake*, a rather gauche musical set in Renaissance Italy, he used the set to provide almost a *son et lumière* in a Florentine square, lighting a wall through the windows of a church, showing the passing of the day by deepening the shadows under the arches. The Theatre Royal whose proscenium arch will presumably never give way to an experiment in thrust, is the ideal theatre for his work: and the reputation of the Old Vic Company is now internationally known. Clive Barnes, for example, regretted that the Lincoln Center Repertory Theater in New York could, with all its resources, only compare with the Bristol Old Vic in England: a backhanded tribute, but a very telling one. The Lincoln Center was at one time intended to provide a sort of American National Theatre.

References: 12, 13, 28, 41, 44, 47, 57, 59, 73, 95, 115, 128, 132, 153

Bromley, *Bromley Theatre Trust Ltd*
New Theatre, High Street, Bromley, Kent. B/O: 01–460 6677/8
The old 'New' Theatre is now known as the Little Theatre, to distinguish it from the new 'New' Theatre which is now being built on a site also in the High Street, some few yards along the road. The 'Little' Theatre seats

902, and it was originally a Victorian swimming-pool, converted into a long, skinny theatre. The stage is small for the seating capacity of the auditorium: the P/A opening is 29 feet and the depth is 15 feet. There is no wing space. The front of house facilities are poor. There is clearly a need for a new theatre: and a splendid one is now being built. The projected date of completion is in 1973. This new theatre will seat 778: and the stage will basically follow the proscenium-arch pattern. However, the P/A will have variable dimensions: the opening will range from 28 feet to 45 feet – from a picture-frame to an open-stage effect. The height will also vary – from 14 feet to 20 feet: and the depth – normally 40 feet – can be increased with the apron stage (10 feet). Therefore the stage will have a number of different effects, and to match this adaptability, the backstage facilities will be superb. The whole centre stage area will be on a lift, which can raise the stage or lower it to basement level. The wing areas are large enough to contain complete sets, which can be trucked across into the centre stage area. Thus, three complete sets can stand side by side on the stage: and to change from one set to another will take about half-a-minute. The stages 'in the wings' also contain revolves, and so it will be possible to have six complete sets, each occupying the same area which is used now on the main stage, all ready for quick display. The theatre will be housed in a big complex of buildings on a site which has been donated to the town 'for cultural purposes'. There will be a library above the theatre, and various other amenities (such as a restaurant) will also be included. The cost of the development programme will be in the region of £2,000,000, of which the Arts Council is supplying roughly £300,000.

The major obstacle to the development of the Bromley Rep Company in the past has been the poor theatre, which has limited both the productions and the outside services which the rep can offer. There is no permanent acting team – nor a theatre-in-education programme. The play policy has been broadly based – ranging from 'modern classics' (such as *Five-Finger Exercise* and *A Streetcar Named Desire*) to the occasional première of new comedies (such as Kenneth Horne's *The Coming-Out Party*). Stars (such as Cliff Richard) are often brought down from London. The standards of production are reasonably high, although I was rather disappointed both by *Five-Finger Exercise* and by *The Coming-Out Party*. Reference: 132

Bury St Edmunds, *Candida Productions*
Theatre Royal, Westgate Street, Bury St Edmunds. B/O: Bury St
    Edmunds 5469
A fine Regency theatre, in a small country town. The auditorium seats 333, with a dress circle and grand circle. The stage (P/A opening, 24 feet; height, 12 feet; depth, 30 feet) has fine proportions, but there is little wing or flying space. There are new workshops close to the theatre. The

theatre was opened in 1819, the third oldest theatre in the country with a continuous tradition of live drama. A non-profit-distributing company now runs the Theatre Royal, and has leased it for several seasons to Candida Productions, who use the theatre as a base for touring. There are also amateur productions, and other touring companies visit the theatre. Candida received a 1968/9 Arts Council grant of £5400: and the over-all attendance-figures for the same period were 55 per cent capacity. The ticket prices range from 6s to 10s, and (at the weekend) from 8s to 12s.

The population of Bury is 24,000, and the theatre seats 333. These seem to me the salient facts. If the theatre is to survive – and it is a fine theatre indeed – then clearly it has to be subsidized. The subsidies to Candida Productions were too small, and there is no Arts Association yet in East Anglia to protect the Theatre Royal as the Northern Arts Association has protected the Georgian Theatre, Richmond. There was a good production of Sheridan's *School for Scandal* in October 1969; but the standards of the touring companies have been uneven.

Cambridge, *Cambridge Theatre Company*
Arts Theatre, Cambridge. B/O: Cambridge 52000
(See PROSPECT)

Canterbury, *Canterbury Theatre Trust*
Marlowe Theatre, St Margaret's Street, Canterbury. B/O: 0227 64747
A neatly converted cinema, with a vaguely ancient façade and a pleasant auditorium (with a small balcony), which seats 645. The stage (P/A opening, 24 feet; depth, 20 feet) has little flying or wing space. The conditions backstage are generally cramped, with no attached workshops, wardrobe or scenery store. There is a seasonally permanent acting team of about ten; but Canterbury is close enough to London to attract guest stars. The Arts Council gives an annual subsidy of £15,000; and Canterbury Council, who own the building, annually underwrite productions to the tune of about £4000. There is no theatre-in-education team, and the Gulbenkian Theatre, attached to the University of Kent, attracts away the students. The Marlowe Theatre is really a regional rep for East Kent. The tourist trade is unreliable, because Canterbury itself – although a tourist town, of course – has few hotels. Most tourists stay on the coast, in guest houses which serve evening meals at (theatrically) awkward times. But the attendance figures are reasonably good: 57 per cent. The programmes change fortnightly, and the seasons last from Easter to mid-July, from mid-August to early March. The seasonal gaps are filled by amateur companies, such as the Old Stagers.

The Marlowe Company was founded in 1951 by the present manager, Peter Carpenter, and Christopher Hassall, the poet and librettist. Canterbury Council was one of the first in the country to take advantage of the

1948 Local Government Act, which allowed them to support the local theatre. In the past twenty years, the Company has gained an excellent reputation for reliable productions of sensible rep plays, avoiding both the *avant-garde* and the lewd. Sometimes, the definition of these forbidden categories may seem to exclude too much: Peter Carpenter stated that there was no direct interference with the artistic policy of director (currently David Kelsey), but that by general agreement plays which were not quite Canterbury would be avoided. He did not say exactly what these plays would be, but he reacted strongly against Pinter's *The Homecoming*. The absence of community activities narrows the Company down simply to the production of plays – and some would argue that this is a desirable restriction. *The Prime of Miss Jean Brodie* seemed to me very much a Canterbury Play in a Canterbury Production: the central performance by Penelope Lee was good, and the difficulties of staging a many-set play on a restricted stage were fairly sensibly overcome. Ray Lawler's *A Breach in the Wall* (premièred in the 1970 Canterbury Festival) was given an evenly balanced, though to my mind a rather unexciting, production.
References: 30, 60, 67, 73, 101, 110, 132

Cheltenham, *Everyman Theatre*
The Everyman Theatre, Regent St, Cheltenham. B/O: 0242 25544
A medium-sized, Victorian touring-theatre, designed by Frank Matcham, whose other theatres include the London Palladium and the Coliseum. The auditorium, with a dress circle, upper circle and balcony, seats 750. The stage (P/A opening, 24 feet 6 inches; height, 18 feet; depth, 40 feet) has good flying facilities, not counterweighted though, some wing space, a revolve and a rather inadequate lighting board of only 48 ways. The workshops are connected to the theatre but are inadequate. The Everyman used to be called the Cheltenham Opera House, and it was opened in 1891: Mrs Langtry and her company appeared in *Lady Clancarty* on that occasion, and the top price was 10s 6d – exactly sixpence more than the top price in 1969. The theatre closed in 1959 after several poor seasons and the closure caused a furore in the town. A non-profit-distributing company was formed to run the theatre, and a repertory company was established. The acting team is now a fairly large one – about 22 in number – although the seasonally permanent team fluctuates from about 8 to 24. There is a flourishing teaching-about-theatre team, which visits the local schools. There are two theatre clubs – the Young Everyman Group, which has 900 members, and a Theatre Membership Scheme, which exists for the purpose (I suppose) of raising funds. The Arts Council gives an annual grant of about £20,000, and the Cheltenham Corporation £5000. The attendance figures (1968/9) were 55 per cent capacity; and the seasons run from June to May. The policy is for fortnightly rep, although there are plans to change to three-weekly.

Salad Days is, according to Rae Hammond, the General Manager, Cheltenham material; but if this conveys too dull an image, Ann Jellicoe's *The Knack* also did well. The problem at Cheltenham – and elsewhere – is how to retain the interest of youngsters, without offending the traditional audiences, whose tastes are somewhat conservative. There are occasional Monday performances of *avant-garde* plays; but the programmes over the years have been very well balanced, to suit many tastes. The productions reach reliably high standards; but new plays are rarely included and there have been no local documentaries.

References: 15, 30, 43, 60, 88, 105, 106, 116, 128, 132

Chester, *Gateway Theatre*

Gateway Theatre, Hamilton Place, Chester. B/O: Chester 40393

A theatre was included in the general development plans for Chester: the Gateway Theatre opened in November 1968. The auditorium seats 500, and the stage (P/A opening, 32 feet; height, 15 feet; depth, 50 feet) has good flying and wing space. Modern facilities backstage, a studio theatre and fine foyers combine to make this theatre possibly the most attractive in the region. The acting team has a permanent nucleus of about 12 members, who are encouraged, by improvisation sessions, to become a closely knit team. There is a thriving theatre-in-education team, and experimental productions are offered at the studio theatre. There are plans to develop the whole site as an arts centre, and concerts are given in the theatre. The 1968/9 Arts Council subsidy was £5000 and local subsidies amounted to £6102. The attendance figures (1968/9) were a respectable 55 per cent capacity: and the ticket prices range from 5s to 8s 6d. The policy is for three-weekly rep throughout the year: on Monday evenings, however, there are concerts and poetry recitals. There is a flourishing theatre club, which helps to staff the theatre with various helpful attendants.

In its short history, the Gateway Theatre Company has won a deserved reputation for liveliness and intelligence. The programmes are very carefully selected to suit all tastes – but at the same time the really poor farces are usually avoided, together with the bad mysteries. The programmes also include at least one 'highbrow' production, which in Chester means Pinter's *The Caretaker*. If this seems timid, then there are more *avant-garde* plays, Pinget and Arrabal, offered in the Studio. The team is led by a young artistic director, Julian Oldfield, who has succeeded in developing a certain style and enthusiasm in his company. *The Merchant of Venice*, directed by Peter McEnery (March 1970) was a most lively version, updated not quite to today, and featured an outstanding Shylock (David Suchet). The *Boeing-Boeing* (July 1969) production was less successful, mainly because of a tinselly set and a lack of slickness in the timing.

References: 28, 77, 105, 107, 120, 128, 132, 133

Chesterfield, *Civic Theatre*
Civic Theatre, Corporation Street, Chesterfield. B/O: 0246 2901
A Victorian public hall, built in 1879 as the Stephenson Memorial Hall, and converted in the thirties to a cinema and in 1949 to a repertory theatre. The auditorium, with two circles, seats 622: the stage (P/A opening, 28 feet; height, 18 feet; depth, 28 feet) has little wing space, but reasonable flying – though with no counterweight system. The lighting system is old-fashioned, and the board is awkwardly placed, to obscure all view of the stage. There are no workshops attached to the theatre. The building is owned by Chesterfield Corporation and run by the Civic Theatre Trust. There is a seasonally permanent nucleus of an acting team, 6 members. The Arts Council gave a 1968/9 grant of £8000 and local subsidies amounted to £2750: there is a small theatre-in-education programme. The policy is for fortnightly rep, and the seasons run from the middle of July to mid-April. The ticket prices range from 5s to 7s 6d.

From the start, the Civic Theatre has had a hard struggle for survival: attendance figures in 1962 fell to 15 per cent, and now they hover around 36 per cent. The theatre may be a little large for the area: Chesterfield has a population of 70,000 but there is no tradition in the town for theatre of any sort, and those enthusiastic for rep would probably travel to Derby or Nottingham. The struggle is reflected in the various seasonal programmes: low-cast, single-set comedies, with the occasional mystery play or classic revival. The theatre is a gloomy building: but there is a chance that a new theatre will be included in the 1972/3 town redevelopment programme. The existing theatre will then be swept away probably by a road-widening scheme. *The Flip Side* (autumn 1969) was a competent production, but interestingly enough two productions of D. H. Lawrence's plays, *The Daughter-in-Law* and *A Collier's Night Out*, achieved good box-office figures during the 1968 and 1969 seasons: there are local associations with Lawrence, which, while not actually guaranteeing his popularity, at least ensure a certain interest in his name.
References: 28, 128

Chichester, *Festival Theatre*
Chichester Festival Theatre, Chichester. B/O: Chichester 86333
The Festival Theatre was opened in 1962, just before the current revival of repertory could be safely welcomed. It is situated in a fine parkland setting, Oaklands Park, just outside the town. The theatre whose design was influenced by Sir Tyrone Guthrie's Festival Theatre at Stratford, Ontario, is hexagonal in shape: the auditorium seats 1360, around a thrust stage (width, 32 feet; depth, 39 feet). No seat is further than 65 feet from the stage. Backstage, there is good dressing-room accommodation (17 rooms), a fine lighting board (78 ways) and there are various stores and small workshops, which are not entirely adequate for the policy of

repertoire. The theatre cost originally £170,000 to build, and there have been many additions – new heating and lighting – since it was opened. This sum was raised mostly from private and commercial donations by Leslie Evershed-Martin and others, whose determination drove the enterprise through to completion. The theatre is now almost self-supporting, partly through the ticket sales, and also through private patronage. The Chichester Festival Theatre Society numbers 8000 members, and half of their annual subscription (£1) is donated to the theatre. The audience attendance-figures are extremely high – now at about 86 per cent – and the ticket prices range from 5s to 35s. The revenue from the seventeen-week summer-season (1968/9) was an astonishing £161,458, at an average ticket-cost of just over a pound. There is no Arts Council subsidy as such, but there is a guarantee against loss, which in 1968/9 amounted to £7500. The policy is to play repertoire during the summer season (from May to September); and there is an acting team of about 37, seasonally permanent.

These bare statistics illustrate the gamble which was taken when the Festival Theatre was built: a gamble which conditioned the programmes to begin with and still (I suppose) does. There is no large city to support the theatre, which has to attract the tourists: but drifting tourist-trade would never fill the 1360 seats. It had to be a positive tourist attraction – somewhere like Glyndebourne or Stratford, with high seat-prices and an international reputation. This meant that the Company had to concentrate on providing not day-to-day productions, building up the reputation and audiences slowly, through consistently good work, but spectacular productions of classic plays in the first season. There were few grants to cushion the possible losses. The theatre was, moreover, of a shape and size unfamiliar in Britain. The Festival Theatre had to establish itself as a Mecca – by presenting *haute couture* productions during the first season in a strange theatre with a company brought together in the winter.

Sir Laurence Olivier took on this task, together with the early framework for a National Theatre Company. His failure then might have threatened not only the Festival Theatre, but also perhaps the National Theatre as well. His seasons there were triumphantly successful – and incidentally more ambitious during these uncertain early years than the programmes have seemed in days of greater security. This was where Albert Finney created his marvellous performances as Armstrong in Arden's extraordinary play, *Armstrong's Last Goodnight* and as the manservant in *Miss Julie*, where Laurence Olivier directed and played in *Uncle Vanya*, and so on. Every season, even after the departure of the National Theatre Company, has brought theatrical riches from Chichester – recently Alastair Sim in *The Magistrate*, Topol in *The Caucasian Chalk Circle*, Maggie Smith in *The Country Wife*.

If the Festival Theatre at Chichester is so successful and requires so little in the way of subsidies, why can't this example be imitated? There are several possible answers to this question, which in different disguises is often being raised. One is that the Festival Theatre gamble only worked because this is a comparatively wealthy area of the country: the ticket prices are higher than those of other reps, and is there another supporters' club in the country which raises £4000 annually? But this dependence on private patronage has an effect on the choice of programmes. Little is attempted at Chichester which could be regarded as controversial or *avant-garde*: Bolt's *Vivat, Vivat Regina* – yes, Bond's *Saved* – definitely not. Even *Armstrong's Last Goodnight* did bad box office. Chichester – like Glyndebourne – is a theatre for the wealthy, who will find nothing there to disturb them. It is not exuberantly posh: there are spaces in the car park for coaches as well as Lotuses; but one is aware of a certain easiness of manner which comes from having paid the instalments. The theatre is not really designed to serve the town near by – except by attracting the tourists. The site is given by the Council, but no other support. Hence, there is no theatre-in-education programme, no studio theatre, no attempt to reflect the aspirations of the people who live near by. It is not Chichester's local theatre, but a national theatre which has somehow landed in a park near a town. As a repertory theatre, it is therefore severely limited to its central task of presenting fine plays in admirable productions. It performs this task wonderfully well.

References: 12, 13, 28, 37, 38, 47, 53, 56, 57, 59, 68, 74, 85, 101, 107, 112, 132, 136, 138, 144, 152

Colchester, *Repertory*

Colchester Repertory Theatre, High Street, Colchester. B/O: 0206 73948
　(1972) Mercury Theatre, Colchester

A converted art-gallery, seating 368, with a small balcony. The stage (P/A opening, 28 feet; depth, 17 feet) has no flying or wing space: if a play requires two sets, one scene has to be built inside the other. There is no workshop connected with the theatre, and very small administrative offices. There is no permanent company: David Forder can cast from London, an hour's journey away. But there is some continuity between the casts, so that the audiences at Colchester are familiar with at least the names of various actors and actresses. The 1968/9 grant income was (from the Arts Council) £18,000 and (from local authorities and private sources) £5246. The ticket prices range from 5s to 8s: and the audience attendance-figures have dramatically risen in recent years – from about 30 per cent in the early sixties to 60 per cent and above in the late sixties.

In 1937, the late Robert Digby started the rep in the old Albert Hall and Art Gallery: but the resonant name and oil paintings on the wall can't really compensate for the dismal circumstances backstage. Fortunately, a new theatre is being built, the Mercury, which has an interesting hexagonal shape. The stage will be basically 'open-end', though it can be converted to proscenium-arch. It will be situated on a fine site close to the heart of the town and contain a studio theatre, workshops and a restaurant. It will cost £200,000, and the money has been raised.

The Colchester Company deserves this new theatre: it has been struggling for years with the sheer technical difficulties of the old building. They have managed to run a theatre-in-education team (visiting schools), and broadcasts of their productions have been relayed over local radio to the hospitals in the area. With the University of Essex near by, and a local radio station as well, the Colchester Rep is becoming a cultural centre for North Essex and indeed the region. The new theatre should help the Company to develop (as is the intention) as an arts centre. The present standards of production are high: *The Daughter-in-Law* (May 1969), although the change of set in the interval was hard to make, sustained the tension of Lawrence's play. The pantomimes are to my mind severely restricted by the stage, but they have enormous popularity in Colchester. References: 60, 62, 65, 106, 107, 117, 128, 132.

Colwyn Bay, *Prince of Wales Theatre*
Prince of Wales Theatre, Colwyn Bay. B/O: Colwyn Bay 2668
This theatre, now managed by the Borough Council, was in 1967 briefly managed by the Welsh Arts Council who were attempting to find a suitable home for the Welsh National Theatre. The plans failed for various reasons. The theatre is little more than a church hall, seating 518, but with a cramped P/A stage (P/A opening, 25 feet; height, 14 feet; depth, 18 feet): the 9-foot apron stage which was added by the Welsh Arts Council did little to improve the basic facilities. There is no flying and little wing space: there is a small workshop and scenery store beneath the stage. There is a seasonally permanent nucleus of an acting team. There are no grants as such, but the theatre is owned by the Council, who employ (currently) Rex Browne as theatre manager: they maintain and run the theatre as a civic amenity. The policy is for weekly rep, with a change of production mid-week. The seasons run from May to September: and the ticket prices range from 5s to 6s 6d. There are no other activities – such as theatre-in-education.

This is, I'm afraid, another theatre in a seaside town, which seems to have become stuck in an awkward rut. The programme policy – summer seasonal weekly rep, mysteries and farces – suggests that the Council is solely concerned with the tourist trade; but, unfortunately, few tourists seem to come. The audiences are mainly drawn from the residents of Colwyn Bay and the surrounding districts. Colwyn Bay itself has only 23,000 inhabitants, although there are several other tourist towns in the area, stretched out in a chain along the coast from Llandudno to Rhyl.

But the Prince of Wales theatre has neither the facilities nor (apparently) the desire to become a community theatre. The plays offered in the 1969 season seemed unadventurous; and the production I saw, *Two Faces of Murder* (August 1969) did not bear out the theatre director's proud claim that 'the standard here is particularly high'.

References: 30, 61, 108

Coventry, *Belgrade Theatre*

The Belgrade Theatre, Corporation Street, Coventry. B/O: 0203 20205
The Belgrade Theatre was the first new theatre to be built in Britain after the war, in 1958, and the first one whose design and conception reflect the changing role which a rep is now expected to play within the community. The actors aren't guest stars from London, nor on their way to higher incomes in films and television. They have flats built for them next to the theatre, as part of the complex. They are residents of Coventry. From the beginning, the Council recognized that the theatre would need subsidies: and in return for their support the Company was expected to provide an adequately balanced programme for the community – a mixture of 'popular' and 'serious' works – together with a theatre-in-education programme. The theatre seats 900: and the stage (P/A opening, 36 feet; height, 19 feet; depth, 29 feet) is very well equipped, although the flying capacity could cause awkward masking problems. The foyer is large enough to hold exhibitions of children's paintings, bookstalls, coffee bars, photographic exhibitions and so on: for art exhibitions, the lighting is probably not adequate. There is a good restaurant, and a most useful studio theatre. The workshops are not, unfortunately, attached to the theatre, but are well designed in a single complex with the wardrobe, paint shops, etc. The subsidies include £45,000 from the Arts Council and £12,000 from the Coventry Council; but the Company is slowly repaying the capital cost of the theatre. There is a seasonally permanent nucleus of an acting team, 16 members: with a full-time theatre-in-education staff of between 10 and 12 members. The average ticket-price is about 7s.

In some respects, the Belgrade Theatre is still a model to other community reps: the standards of production are consistently high (though without the spectacular successes of Nottingham). The play-selection policy neatly balances the many demands. Warren Jenkins gives a free ticket to every school-leaver who is also shown around the theatre and encouraged in the belief that drama is not for an intellectual élite, but a proper reflection of human hopes and aspirations. The Belgrade has been in existence for long enough now for us to be able to detect the flaws and merits of this idealism. One flaw is that the theatre really has to please too many tastes: *No, No Nanette* and Bond's *Narrow Road to the Deep North* in the same season is a startling assortment. This mixture prevents the company from evolving a distinctive style in any genre. Warren Jenkins, currently theatre director, is most experienced in all aspects of theatre, as an actor, singer and dancer; but even he must find his imagination taxed by so diverse a programme. The second problem is that there is still a tug between commercial theatre and a socially useful theatre: there were unfulfilled plans to transform the place into an arts centre, temporarily abandoned because of the cost. Nor has Warren Jenkins yet been able to afford to ignore the box office for half a year in order to build up a really exciting drama policy and acting team. Hence, the actors, who are underpaid though not by normal rep standards, drift back to London all too quickly. Actors have to be encouraged either by money or by the sense that they are tackling some really worth-while project. Some at Coventry rebel against the prospect of Agatha Christie during the slack box-office seasons, and turn with relief to the more exciting programmes in the studio theatre, which is nevertheless too small to be effective. Social altruism can have the unfortunate habit of sliding between the artist and his inspiration, so that he is diverted from the realization of an inner dream by some worthy external consideration, racial harmony in the town or the desire to present school-text Shakespeare. Warren Jenkins has steered a very delicate and canny course between the obstacles, but one wonders whether Coventry might not have enjoyed more exciting results if the theatre had not been burdened with so many worthy causes. An argument against community theatres? I think not. The Belgrade has achieved some excellent results as a pioneering theatre: it was not always possible in the early days to decide on the best course of action – say, in choosing seasonal programmes. The lack of decent storage space prevented repertoire. And so mistakes were to be expected, and from them the Belgrade and many other reps have learnt. The production of *Wind in the Sassafras Trees* (1968) starred Frankie Howerd and Barbara Windsor and was very funny in the style of the *Carry On* films. *Removal Day* (September 1969) by a Coventry author, Cyril Bolton, was an interesting new play about the destruction of a house and its furniture by a gang of removal men: excellently produced and acted.

References: 13, 28, 29, 37, 40, 41, 46, 47, 54, 59, 70, 71, 73, 74, 95, 120, 121, 128, 132, 136, 153

Crewe, *Theatre*

Crewe Theatre, New Heath Street, Crewe. B/O: 0270 55620
A medium-sized touring-theatre. As a touring-theatre, it could never be made to pay, partly because Crewe (population 52,500) is not a place with a large or wealthy middle-class population, and partly because the theatre seats (with circle) 900, which is too small to attract major companies. In 1955, the theatre was bought by Crewe Corporation, who firstly tried to run it themselves and then leased it to a small non-profit-distributing company, Crewe Theatre Trust, which now manages the

repertory company. The acting team consists of a resident nucleus of 10 members, who have partly been chosen for their all-round abilities: most of them can sing, dance, improvise and take part in local documentaries. One of these, *The Railway Town*, was very popular. Relationships with the local council are very good, and there are plans to extend the rather fragmentary theatre-in-education programme. The theatre is used on Monday nights for the occasional concert or experimental production. There are grants of £8000 from the Arts Council and £4000 from the local council, who also supply the theatre rent-free.

The present company at Crewe is headed by Ted Craig, a young, enthusiastic and talented artistic director, who (befitting a rep director) has a great admiration for the town and the public for whom his theatre is intended. His programmes are ambitious, ranging from *Hamlet* to *Oh What A Lovely War!*, but avoiding rep potboilers which (interestingly enough) normally do bad box office here. There seems to be in the town an attitude of concerned interest towards the theatre. Crewe is within that belt of Midland towns where the tradition of repertory has flourished strongly in the past. The audiences at Crewe are growing in numbers (52 per cent capacity in 1968/9) and the younger age groups predominate. Keele University is ten miles away. The stage (P/A opening, 31 feet; height, 18 feet; depth, 30 feet) is a little old-fashioned but quite serviceable. There is some wing space: reasonable flying, though no counterweight system. A small rehearsal studio/theatre has recently been opened. The facilities at Crewe – and the enthusiasm of both the team and apparently the town council – encourages the belief that the awkward transition between a failed touring theatre and a successful rep will be overcome. The production of Sardou's *Let's Get a Divorce* (November 1969) was a lively and intelligent one.
Reference: 28

Darlington, *Civic*
Civic Theatre, Darlington. B/O: Darlington 5774
An Edwardian touring-theatre, built in 1901 and converted into a smaller theatre by Darlington Corporation in 1966. The theatre now seats 601: the stage (P/A opening, 28½ feet; height, 14 feet; depth, 23 feet) has good flying capacity, but no counterweight system. There is no permanent acting team at the Civic: and the theatre is used for all purposes – by amateurs, by visiting small touring companies, by companies formed to provide an occasional season of rep, for pantomimes, variety shows and symphony concerts. The present manager, P. J. Hamilton-Moore, is rightly proud of the fact that his theatre has been redecorated and now looks splendidly inviting. But, alas, no consistent policy has evolved to use the theatre effectively. Even star variety programmes do badly: straight plays rarely achieve more than a 35 per cent attendance.

If this theatre is to avoid a sort of spiritual and financial stagnation, then clearly the Council has to decide what it wants to do with it. There aren't many good touring companies at all today, and the major ones would probably not want to visit this theatre, which only seats 601. Hence, the opportunities would seem to lie with the formation of a rep company, despite the low attendance-figures at straight plays. The Education Department seems at present uninterested in a theatre-in-education programme, and this theatre at present has little capacity to run one. More investment and a subsidy will be needed if a rep is to be provided for the town.

References: 30, 47, 48, 61, 74.

Derby, *Playhouse*

Derby Playhouse, Sacheverell Street, Derby. B/O: 0332 47929

A converted hall, with a balcony. The auditorium seats 396: and the stage (P/A width, 25 feet; height, $12\frac{1}{2}$ feet; depth, 21 feet) has limited flying space and little wing space: there is a huge but rather clumsy lighting board with 92 ways. The workshops are adequate and attached to the theatre; and the facilities front and backstage are efficient but lack glamour. There is a small coffee-bar and a small foyer. The rep was formed in 1948 – simply a half-professional company working in a church hall. In 1952, the Company moved to another small hall in Sacheverell Street, the site for the present theatre. In 1956, at a time when the live theatre all over the country felt under pressure from television, the old building burnt down; but such was the enthusiastic response from the town and from local industry (particularly Rolls-Royce) that the theatre was rebuilt and vastly improved. There is now a seasonally permanent nucleus of an acting team, 5 to 8 members. There are currently grants of £18,000 (from the Arts Council) and about £5000 from Derby and other local councils. The ticket prices range from 5s 6d to 9s; and the season runs from August to June. The policy is for fortnightly to three-weekly rep.

There are plans for a new theatre at Derby, although these have not yet been formally approved, either by the Arts Council, the local council or the Company. Clearly the present theatre is inadequate, particularly for a lively company which runs a theatre-in-education team, presents film shows on Sunday evenings and live concerts. Roger Clissold, formerly the artistic director, said that he would like to see the building 'bursting at the seams' with activity. The Derby Playhouse is (I'm afraid) in danger of bursting, without having a new suit tailored. The production of *Cat On a Hot Tin Roof* (October 1969) featured a performance of great power and intensity by Bill Maynard.

References: 27, 28, 29, 30, 31, 33, 34, 35, 73, 115, 121, 128, 132

Dundee, *Repertory Theatre*
Dundee Rep, Lochee Road, Dundee. B/O: 0382 23530
A converted church hall. The old theatre burnt down in 1963, but the disaster was converted very nearly to triumph, when the management discovered a rather unlikely hall, further from the town centre but nearer the University. The efforts to convert the place, the enthusiastic and improvisatory atmosphere attracted the students, who in turn influenced the selection of plays. The existing theatre is nevertheless poorly designed for repertory. The hall seats only 300, and the front-of-house facilities are poor. The stage (P/A width, 26 feet 11 inches; height, 10 feet 9 inches; depth, 18 feet) has adequate flying, though no counterweight system: there is a distinctive circular forestage, which greatly adds to the intimacy of the theatre. There are workshops connected to the theatre, but they are inadequate: there is a general shortage of space backstage. The grants include £20,000 from the Scottish Arts Council and £4000 from Dundee. There is a permanent acting team, about 8 members: and there is an extensive theatre-in-education programme. The ticket prices range from 4s 6d to 8s 6d; and the policy is for three-weekly rep, with occasional repertoire, throughout the year.

Over the past few years, the Dundee Rep has pursued a most ambitious and exciting policy, including many new plays, interesting revivals, local documentaries and controversial modern plays. The students have sustained the Company, in the face of some local opposition. The standards of production are very high. Even in a summer revue, *We Are Not Amused*, filling in that awkward gap in the year when the Edinburgh Festival takes most of the attention, the cast was efficiently polished, able to sing and dance; and the sketches, though rather lacking in bite, were amusing. The more ambitious productions, such as *The Homecoming*, were wholly admirable, and well received by the audience too. But the Company obviously needs a new theatre, and several years ago plans were accepted by the Council and the rep to convert the huge and unwieldy Caird Hall in the centre of Dundee, which seats 2000 people and reminded Sir Thomas Beecham of Euston Station. The Council, however, retracted its support for the scheme, and offered the rep instead a converted cinema, rather further from the city centre. The management of the rep refused; and this ex-cinema is now run in rivalry with the rep as a Civic Theatre, offering a mixed bag of entertainment. The University came to the rescue of the rep; the Principal, Professor J. Dreever, said that if the Corporation of Dundee will not accept responsibility for the town's cultural life, then the University must. There is now a plan to build a University theatre, seating (at maximum) 900 and (for daily purposes) 600. This will be made available to the rep, at a nominal rent.

References: 65, 114.

Eastbourne, *Eastbourne Theatre Company*
Devonshire Park Theatre, Eastbourne. B/O: Eastbourne 21121
This is one of the largest (and potentially most profitable) repertory
theatres on the south coast. The auditorium seats 1008: the stage is
reasonably convenient to run – the P/A opening is 28 feet – and does not
require a huge production. The backstage facilities are adequate. It is
now being leased (on a profit-sharing basis) to Charles Vance, who took
over in 1969 from Theatre South East. Charles Vance is one of the rare
commercial actor/managers. He used to run a commercial rep in Chelmsford, and, defying the general trend towards subsidized theatres, has
succeeded in running reps simultaneously at Tunbridge Wells, Whitby
and Eastbourne. He holds together a company of 20 at Eastbourne with
three resident producers, and he sometimes takes productions around the
various theatres he leases. He runs at present weekly rep at Eastbourne,
although he hopes to change to fortnightly rep and to move the Company
away from simply popular entertainment plays. He claims to have been
the first producer to have presented Shakespeare in commercial rep for
twenty years after the war; and he hopes at Eastbourne to set Monday
nights aside for experimental theatre. He also wants to run a theatre-in-
education programme.

Charles Vance has the sort of personality – indeed flamboyance – to
succeed where others have failed. He sailed single-handed across the
Atlantic in 1965, and in 1970 took over the title role in *Harvey* at ten
minutes' notice, when the star, Patrick Wymark, was rushed to hospital. I
saw a competent production of *Watch It, Sailor* (September 1969), which
was in fact Charles Vance's first production at the Eastbourne theatre. It
did seem better than the other seaside rep productions (with the exception
of Worthing's Connaught Theatre) which I saw during that season.
References: 15, 61, 68

East Grinstead, *Adeline Genée Theatre*
Adeline Genée Theatre, East Grinstead.
This theatre, completed in 1967, was originally conceived as a ballet
theatre for the school in whose grounds it stands. But the attractiveness of
the building has led to several attempts to run it on a professional basis.
The auditorium seats 330: and the stage (P/A opening, 34 feet; height,
15 feet; depth, 38 feet) is very well equipped, with an excellent fly-tower.
The first Arts Council grant was given in 1970: £850. There is no
permanent company. In 1970, a ballet festival was staged there.

The first attempts to use this fine theatre were very ambitious. I
remember the second production, a large-scale musical with an adventure-
story play, *Man from the West*, starring Edward Judd. If this musical
could have transferred to the West End as a smash-hit, the fortunes of the
theatre could have been made. Unfortunately, it didn't; and for a small

theatre, it was disastrously uneconomic. Only with large subsidies can this theatre be made to run successfully: it is hard to find, down a winding rural lane, and the stage is disproportionately large for the auditorium: it has so far lacked the continuous backing which it requires.
References: 44, 138

Edinburgh, *Edinburgh Civic Theatre Trust*
Royal Lyceum Theatre, Grindlay Street, Edinburgh 3. B/O: 031–229 4353
A fine Victorian touring-theatre, built in 1883 and named after Sir Henry Irving's famous Lyceum Theatre in London. The original managers, J. B. Howard and F. W. Wyndham, came to own a chain of touring-theatres, including some of the finest in the country. Irving's London Lyceum Company was the first to play in this theatre, in a repertoire which included *Hamlet, Much Ado About Nothing* and *The Bells* – three of Sir Henry's most famous performances. In 1964, the theatre was bought by Edinburgh Corporation; and in the following year, the Edinburgh Civic Theatre Trust was formed to manage the theatre as a repertory. For normal repertory purposes, however, the Royal Lyceum Theatre is far from ideal: the impressive auditorium, with two circles and a balcony, seats 1292, too many for the average company. The stage is rather small for the size of the theatre: P/A opening, 27 feet 1 inch; height, 16–22 feet; depth, 34 feet. There is a fixed proscenium arch and a small 8-foot apron. The backstage facilities are adequate: there is good flying, though without a counterweight system, and fair wing space. There are good workshops near the theatre, though there is an awkward entrance to the stage for the scenery. There are two small rehearsal rooms, but no studio theatre – which is a serious lack for a company with an active theatre-in-education team. The main grants come from the Scottish Arts Council (£45,000) and from Edinburgh Corporation (£32,000): and, while there is no permanent company, the casts are mainly drawn from a pool of 50–60 actors living in or near Edinburgh. The season runs from April to September in three-weekly rep: and the ticket prices normally range from 5s to 12s 6d.

Some would claim that the Royal Lyceum Company provides Scotland with a national theatre. No other Scottish company – although there are several good ones – can match its resources, financial and otherwise. For that reason, the production policy has concentrated on those plays which other companies might be reluctant to tackle: new plays, *haute couture*, ambitious revivals. I was very impressed by the 1969 *Uncle Vanya* and particularly by the performance of Cullum Mill in the title role – a Scottish actor who has, alas, not often been seen in London. *The Ha-Ha*, a new play starring Angela Pleasance, transferred from the Lyceum to the Hampstead Theatre Club in London: I enjoyed Miss Pleasance's performance – and Dorothy Reynolds as the matron – without feeling convinced about the play. Clive Perry is currently the artistic director at the Royal Lyceum, and his team includes the fine young director, Richard Eyre.

References: 120, 126, 127

Edinburgh, *The Traverse Theatre Club*

112 West Bow, Grassmarket, Edinburgh. B/O: Edinburgh 226 2633
A theatre club and studio theatre. The auditorium is a bare room, 60 feet by 40 feet, with a lighting grid covering the ceiling: the switchboard contains only 12 ways. Steps, arranged in triangular units, provide the seating which can be altered to change the shape of the stage: maximum seating, 120. The Traverse Theatre Club was founded by Jim Haynes (who afterwards started the Arts Laboratory in London) in January 1963: and perhaps no other small theatre in Britain has exerted such an influence. In six and a half years, eighty-three world or British premières were presented at the club: and a glance at the various programmes reveals the wide-ranging seriousness of the tastes, which were not limited simply to plays which could be quickly labelled '*avant-garde*': Jarry's *Ubu Roi*, Lawrence's *The Daughter-in-Law*, Storey's *The Restoration of Arnold Middleton* – three British premières, drawn almost at random from the list. The management brought the La Mama Experimental Theatre to Britain for the first time in 1967, and Grotowski's 13-rows Theatre in 1968. The Traverse Theatre Club within a couple of years of its opening proved the value of these small experimental theatres: soon, similar ventures were springing up all over the country – the Close, Glasgow, the Brighton Combination, the Arts Laboratory in London, the Theatre Upstairs and Ed Berman's Ambiance Theatre. In 1965, the Arts Council gave the Traverse its first grant, of £1500, a sum which has now risen to £12,000. There is also a grant from Edinburgh Corporation. The new studio theatre was opened in 1969, and there was an impressive list of tributes to the Company, from among others, Lord Snowdon and Miss Jennie Lee. Clearly, with this event, the Traverse ceased to lead the underground in the theatre, and became almost part of the Establishment. Jim Haynes at one time warned against the 'creeping professionalism' of the company. There is now a permanent team of paid actors, led by Max Stafford-Clarke, the artistic director. A growing number of dramatists, including Stanley Eveling, look towards the Traverse as a natural home.

The play-selection policy of the Traverse Theatre has been much influenced by the French Absurdists – Arrabal, Jarry, Ionesco and Adamov – whose work has been well represented in their programmes: modern British and American Absurdists – Ableman, Eveling, Beckett and Taylor – are also regularly included. The production methods – an emphasis on athletic teamwork – and the physical circumstances of the theatre resemble the Off-off Broadway movement. This fusion of genres has provided the Traverse with a style admirably suited to the conditions under which they work: cerebral and anarchic, young yet a bit academic, rebellious and eager to gain approval. There were signs during the 1969 season that the rebellious side of the Traverse Company's work was acquiring a distinctly middle-aged sense of responsibility: *Sawney Bean*, a play about cannibals by Robert Nye and Bill Watson, was a rather poetic study of the origins of language. The linguistic anarchy of Ionesco becomes with Stanley Eveling a rather witty and English form of non-sense, closer to Lewis Carroll than the Dadaists. The standards of production have lost their early unevenness, and are now far higher than those in other similar theatre clubs. It is, quite simply, the best theatre club in the country.

References: 45, 103, 109, 136, 144

Exeter, *Northcott Devon Theatre and Arts Centre*
Northcott Theatre, John Stocker Road, Exeter. B/O: 0392 54853
A repertory theatre, completed in 1968, and sited within the grounds of Exeter University. The stage is an adaptable one: as a P/A stage, the dimensions are – width, 51 feet; height, 21 feet; depth, 30 feet. Clearly, with this height and width, the normal objections to 'cramped' picture-frame stages are invalid. The 'in-the-round' stage is formed by constructing a seating bank on the main stage and using the apron stage as the playing-area. The apron adds an additional 18 feet to the main stage. Some of the effect of theatre-in-the-round is, however, lost – because the seats are not evenly distributed on all four sides: hence, there is a tendency for producers and directors to angle the production towards the main bank of seating. The auditorium seats 433 with a P/A stage, 580 for theatre-in-the-round. There is a good rehearsal room: and excellent flying space for P/A productions. The lighting board is slightly inadequate, but the backstage and front-of-house facilities are excellent otherwise. The real need at Exeter is for a studio theatre, partly for the theatre-in-education team, partly to present *avant-garde* plays. The acting team consists of a permanent nucleus of an acting team, 12–18 members; and for the past two seasons a resident dramatist has worked with the company. The grants include £20,000 from the Arts Council, £12,000 from local councils and £15,000 from the University. The Company has undertaken extensive tours of the whole region – Devon and Cornwall – and runs an ambitious theatre-in-education team. The seat prices range from 6s to 12s: and the policy is a limited form of repertoire – productions are held together over a longer period and presented in weekly runs. The attendance figures over the past two years have been high: roughly 70 per cent.

The first achievement of the Northcott Theatre Company was to establish in the first two years of its existence a viable regional rep in an area of the country where established theatres have often failed in the past. The second achievement was to construct an attractive arts centre open to the town, on the campus of a university. These two successes demanded rather different qualities from the management, which succeeded in being both tolerant of all visitors and well organized in themselves. The organization can be appreciated from the extensive tours, undertaken while the permanent company is still playing at the main theatre; by the scripts written for children by the theatre-in-education team; by the recitals and film shows arranged. The tolerance is shown by the friendly relationship with both the University and the town, the relaxed and helpful attitudes of the front-of-house staff. The programmes at the Northcott Theatre have been ambitious – new plays, local documentaries, *haute couture* and musicals – without being *avant-garde*. The productions are of a high standard: the regional documentary, *The Bastard King*, was relayed by B.B.C. Television, and Millar's *Abelard and Héloïse* transferred to the West End. The 1969 production of *Oh What A Lovely War!* was effective on the open stage.

References: 45, 57, 60, 94, 99, 109, 120, 128, 132, 133, 136

Farnham, *Farnham Repertory Company*
Castle Theatre, Castle Street, Farnham. B/O: 0251 3–5301
A medieval granary, converted to its present use as a theatre in 1939. The building itself has great charm, particularly in the quiet street where it is situated. The auditorium seats 167: and the small stage (P/A opening, 21 feet; height, 7 feet 7 inches; depth, 18 feet) has many limitations: no flying, little wing space, a 12-way lighting board. Although Farnham itself is a small town, the catchment area includes Farnborough, Basingstoke and Aldershot; and so the plans for a new theatre, seating 350, are not over-ambitious. The present grants include £8000 from the Arts Council, and £735 from the local councils. There is a semi-permanent nucleus of an acting team, 4 members. The policy is for fortnightly rep all the year round. The ticket prices range from 4s 6d to 8s 6d. There is a youth liaison officer, but no theatre-in-education team as such.

The reputation of Farnham grew in the sixties firstly with Joan Knight as artistic director and then with Antony Tuckey, both of whom have now moved to larger theatres. The sheer size and limitations of the stage impose tiresome restrictions on any director: plays with more than one set usually have to be avoided; the Company has to be small; and so on. Malcolm Griffiths took over in 1969, and tried to introduce an adventurous policy of three-weekly rep, new plays and interesting revivals, including Mrozek's *Tango* and Shirley's *The Cardinal*. He ran into trouble with the theatre board, and resigned, together with the theatre manager, Peter Evans. The exact cause of the trouble is hard to determine. The reason given – falling attendances – is not entirely supported by the figures,

which were respectably high and distorted in any case by the change from
fortnightly to three-weekly rep. The area, however, is somewhat conservative in outlook. Peter Evans told me that the Company would
attempt to bridge the class gap 'downwards' – to attract the agricultural
workers and students, as well as the Aldershot officers. The first season
included plays like *Loot* and *The Mighty Reservoy*, as well as familiar
comedies, such as *Odd Man In*. This policy may have been enlightened,
but it did fail to take into account the limitations both of the theatre and,
perhaps, of the area. The south of England has not generally taken the
idea of community theatres fully to heart.
Reference: 128

Folkestone, *Arthur Brough Players/Theatre South East*
Leas Pavilion, The Leas, Folkestone. B/O: 0303 52466
A converted hall, seating 460. There is a small balcony in the auditorium.
The stage (P/A opening, 22 feet; height, 10 feet; depth, 14 feet) is small
for the size of the theatre: and with no wing or flying space, and really
depressing conditions backstage, the theatre is not an inviting one for any
company – except for a Ruth Draper. The ancient lighting board has 20
ways. There are no subsidies, although in an extraordinary agreement the
Council apparently promised Arthur Brough to waive the £1500 rent for
the theatre, if he would stay open from Easter. Arthur Brough's policy
was weekly rep, and at the end of his long reign at the theatre, over forty
years, the seasons lasted from Easter to the end of October. The ticket
prices range from 4s to 10s 6d.

In spite of the enormous difficulties posed by the theatre and the
constant pressures of weekly rep, Arthur Brough and his wife, Elizabeth
Addyman, both of whom retired in 1969, won considerable respect and
affection in the town. The programmes which they presented over the
years balanced carefully stock plays of the thirties (*Damsel in Distress*,
The Amazing Dr Clitterhouse) with 'classics' (such as *She Stoops to
Conquer*) and 'serious, modern' plays (*The Queen and the Rebels*, *The
Confidential Clerk*). They could not, therefore, be accused of sticking to
seaside-entertainment plays. Nevertheless, the choice of plays was
restricted both by the theatre and by the rather conservative tastes of
Folkestone; and the production standards suffered by the sheer strain of
overwork. The eminent actors, Alastair Sim and Eric Portman, whose
careers began at Folkestone, left quickly for more lush pastures. When
Arthur Brough retired, his company was replaced by Richard Burnett's
company from Bexhill, Theatre South East.
References: 64, 65, 67, 68, 75, 107

Glasgow, *Citizens' Theatre*
Citizens' Theatre, Gorbals Street, Gorbals Cross, Glasgow C5. B/O:
Glasgow 429–0022

An old touring-theatre, the Princess's Theatre, was leased to a rep company, founded in 1943, by James Bridie and others. The auditorium seats 1004: the stage is large and clumsy, and the whole building is in that awkward stage of a theatre's life, when it ought to come down but no one will sign the warrant for its death. This euthanasia really requires several other matters to be settled before it can be satisfactorily dispatched. The Company using the Princess's Theatre is the Citizens' Theatre, a name to handle reverently in Scotland and with respect elsewhere. The Scottish Arts Council nurtured this rep through the tough fifties and sixties: it won a reputation for serious productions of worthy plays. Here Home's best play, *Now Barabbas* was premièred, and later *Armstrong's Last Goodnight*. Nobody, with the exception of some members of the Glasgow Corporation, would apparently like to see the Company fold; and so a new theatre really should be found or built before the old can be knocked down. The Corporation until recently refused to consider incorporating the Company's management into any redevelopment discussions. Gorbals was being knocked down around the theatre. This geographical insecurity was also a contributing factor to the far worse psychological insecurity: the theatre board has a tough control over the artistic policy, as well as the financial. Five artistic directors came and went in five years: Robert Cartland discovered that the Press learnt of his dismissal before he did. Giles Havergal found that his selection of Bond's play, *Saved*, was simply overruled. The theatre is heavily subsidized – £55,000 from the Scottish Arts Council and £8500 from Glasgow Corporation; and the Company has been under considerable attack, because its attendance figures have not seemed to justify the expense. There is a good theatre-in-education team, no permanent company except for the Close Theatre, and much of the money which is given to the Company in grants goes out simply in patching up the theatre.

The sad fact is that the Citizens' Theatre Company is a good rep, and it has maintained its standards in the face of much difficulty and bickering. Glasgow is a huge city, of well over a million people, which really ought to have its own rep. If the Citizens' is forced to close, then it will be by far the largest city in the country without a rep. At present, the Corporation also owns the Kings Theatre in the centre of Glasgow, and sometimes has been known to invite the Nottingham Playhouse Company to play in rivalry to the Citizens' Theatre. The 1969 *A Delicate Balance* was an excellent production of a difficult play; and, at the small Close Studio Theatre next door, an interesting production of a play by John Grillo was staged. Both productions confirmed the impression that Citizens' Theatre Company deserve the conditions under which it can survive: at present, in this old building and harassed by rumour, sniping and speculation, sheer survival from month to month is a hard enough task. There are indications, however, that this situation is changing and that a new theatre will be built nearer to the town centre. We must hope that this is so.

References: 45, 50, 75, 120, 128, 136, 144, 149, 152

Greenwich, *Greenwich Theatre*

Crooms Hill, Greenwich, London SE10. B/O: 01-858 7755

A new auditorium and stage, constructed within the shell of an old Victorian music-hall. The conversion, which opened in 1969, faced – and overcame – many problems: a tight budget (£120,000), an awkwardly shaped site, an area close to the West End without a tradition of live theatre. Money (and local enthusiasm) was raised over the years by various means: there was an extensive canvass of the area, led by professional fund-raisers, to see what support for the live theatre there was. A music-hall was started at the Green Man, Blackheath Hill, which still runs very successfully and profitably. The Bowsprit Company, a theatre-in-education team, toured the schools. In fact, long before the actual theatre was built, the Company had become well known in Greenwich. There were also grants from the Arts Council and the local council, which amounted to about half the total cost. Ewan Hooper, currently the artistic director, was the driving force behind this long campaign; and the design of the theatre reflects his experience as an actor and director. The auditorium, seating 426 in a single, steeply raked arc, sweeps down to an open-end stage, irregularly shaped but 48 feet wide (at its widest point) and 40 feet deep. The rigidity of the hexagonal stage flanked by the walls of the building is partly offset by traps in the floor of the stage, which enables the stage to assume many levels and heights. This use of levels was an effective feature of all the early productions. There is a good restaurant and an art gallery beneath the sloping auditorium. The ticket prices range from 6s to 24s.

The first few plays at Greenwich were (interestingly enough) new documentary plays – about Martin Luther King, the Spithead Mutiny and (later) Marie Lloyd. John Hale's *Spithead* featured a good performance by Ewan Hooper, as the intolerably restrained and strong-minded Valentine Joyce, leader of the mutiny. It was rather too straightforward a documentary for my tastes, clearly distinguishing between the goodies and baddies. A later musical about Marie Lloyd, *Sing a Rude Song*, transferred to the West End; but, to my mind, a more striking production was the fine *Medea*, with Katharine Blake. Greenwich promises to become one of the most exciting reps in the country, strategically placed moreover for West End transfers. Much will depend on the local council and Arts Council subsidies, which are in the process of formulation: the seating capacity is too small for the theatre to run on a purely commercial basis, without much sacrifice of style and standards. There is at present no permanent company, although there are plans to form one. There is however, a permanent theatre-in-education team.

Guildford, *Yvonne Arnaud Theatre*

Yvonne Arnaud Theatre, Millbrook, Guildford. B/O: 0483 60191

A new repertory theatre, on the banks of the River Wey, near to the centre of Guildford. It was completed in 1965 for the cost of £361,000, of which almost 70 per cent came from individual patrons: Guildford Corporation gave the site at little more than a peppercorn rent, and the Arts Council gave some money. The funds were raised by a professional Appeal Organizer, who worked with much voluntary help; Yvonne Arnaud was an active member of the Guildford Theatre Movement. The auditorium with balcony seats 568. The stage (P/A opening, 36 feet; 18 feet high; 33 feet deep) has a large P/A opening, designed originally to prevent the cramped picture-frame effect: the backstage facilities are generally good. There is a revolve (which is rarely used), good dressing-rooms, excellent workshops. There are several weaknesses in the stage design: the fly-tower is too low, which means that masking is always a problem. Only 16-foot flats can be hung for a stage with a P/A height of 18 feet. The front row of seats is also rather close to the stage. As a repertory theatre, it is hampered by lack of rehearsal space and a studio theatre. The grants include £17,800 from the Arts Council and £1825 from the local council. There is no permanent company: Laurier Lister, currently artistic director, prefers to cast from London, although he retains two or three young actors to provide a nucleus of a resident company. The ticket prices range from 5s to 15s: and the policy is for three-weekly rep, throughout the year.

Laurier Lister is in many ways the ideal artistic director for Guildford: a man of considerable West End experience, whose revues after the war (*Airs on a Shoe String*) were particularly successful. He also excels in modern French comedies: Anouilh and Giraudoux. He pointed out to me that he has to provide the local equivalent to a night out in the West End, that his public *did* go to the theatre and that they would willingly travel to London (half-an-hour away by train) if they could not find what they want locally. Hence, he tries to attract stars down from London, and offers a programme which avoids controversy: not *avant-garde*, not sensational, and not over-trivial. The attendance figures at Guildford over the past few years have been exceptionally high – between 75 and 80 per cent; and even those who originally complained that the theatre would be a white elephant, impossible to fill, are now worried that it is too small to run commercially. My own reservations about this admirable rep are somewhat different: the play policy is too conservative for my tastes, and also I can see few signs of the students at the University of Surrey par-

ticipating in the work of the rep, except during the 1970 Festival. The Yvonne Arnaud Theatre is less of a community theatre and more a subsidized outpost of West End 'boulevard' theatre.
References: 13, 28, 38, 50, 56, 60, 68, 102, 103, 107, 132, 133, 134, 135, 145

Harrogate, *White Rose Theatre Trust*
Opera House, Oxford Street, Harrogate. B/O: 0423 2116
A Victorian touring-theatre, opened in 1900. The auditorium seats 850, and there is a fine and unusual frieze in the foyer. In the thirties, the policy changed and a weekly rep was formed. The theatre is, however, not well equipped for rep. The workshop facilities are poor; the stage requires a large product; and the residents of Harrogate were (quite rightly) critical of the standards. The rep closed during the mid-fifties, opened in 1958 and closed again in 1960: there was an outcry in the town, and the Council bought the theatre, and a theatre trust was formed. Again, however, the rep fell into difficulties and closed in 1965. In 1966, it reopened, and there has since been a determined attempt to sustain the rep. The policy changed from weekly to fortnightly rep, which immediately raised the production standards: the Company acquired a seasonally permanent nucleus of an acting team, about 8 in number. The Arts Council provided a subsidy of £10,000 a year, which has now risen to £13,000; and the Council gave £1500. The attendance figures when expressed in terms of percentage of capacity seem disappointing: 37 per cent. When expressed in plain numbers, about 300 per performance, they seem very creditable – particularly for a town the size of Harrogate.

The new management at Harrogate seems to have succeeded where the others have failed: they can now genuinely claim to provide a regional rep for the Yorkshire dales. The Harrogate Festival of Arts and Sciences is now an annual event, and the contributions of Harrogate Theatre to the Festival have always been interesting. There was a fine production of Ibsen's *An Enemy of the People* (August 1969), directed by David Scase and starring Anton Rodgers. In the previous year, there was the première of Alan Plater's *Charlie Came to Our Town*.
References: 43, 60, 106, 107, 128, 132

Hornchurch, *Hornchurch Theatre Trust*
Queen's Theatre, Station Lane, Hornchurch. B/O: 49 43333
A converted cinema. The auditorium is long and narrow, seating 379: the stage (P/A opening, 20 feet; depth, 18 feet) has no flying or wing space. Percy Cox, a member of Hornchurch Urban Council, first realized that this was an area (well populated, just outside the eastern suburbs of London) where a professional rep company could be successfully established. There was a flourishing amateur tradition in the area, but no professional rivals. The Hornchurch Repertory Company opened in 1953,

and immediately faced all sorts of problems: productions were quite simply confined by the stage size to one-set, small-cast plays. During the fifties, in spite of the challenge from television, its local reputation grew with some fine productions of 'stock' rep plays – *Hay Fever*. Hornchurch cast its productions directly from London, and therefore could attract the occasional star. The grants are currently £18,000 from the Arts Council and £8000 from the local council. There is no theatre-in-education team. The policy is for three-weekly rep (no Monday performances) and the seasons run from mid-August to June, with a six-week pantomime season. Ticket prices range from 4s 6d to 10s.

The Hornchurch rep is severely limited by the theatre, which is in any case due for demolition. There are plans for a new theatre, which have not yet been finalized. The Company has been lucky over the years to have Paul Mayo as set designer. In the 1969 production of *Entertaining Mr Sloane*, I did not realize until the last Act that the set had been built subtly out of proportion to enhance the size of the stage. With this ingenuity, ambitious productions can be tackled – such as the admirable *Women Beware Women* (1968). The play policy is enlightened, and the standards are high.

References: 128, 149

Hull, *Gulbenkian Centre*
Gulbenkian Centre, Hull University, Hull.

An adaptable theatre, built on the campus of Hull University. The auditorium seats 200, in all its various patterns: there is one fixed block of seats, and three blocks of seats on movable bleachers. The dimensions of the arena stage are 31 feet by 28 feet: the P/A stage has an opening of 26 feet and a depth of 28 feet. There is a lighting grid across the ceiling and also on the movable proscenium periaktoi.

This university theatre, which has excellent basic facilities, opened in 1969 and should provide fine practical experience for the drama department. There is not, at present, a resident company; although we are beginning to find that a chain of university theatres around the country is unearthing a new kind of professionalism – academic-experimental. The opening production at the Gulbenkian Centre was a re-creation of the bill at Hull Theatre Royal (December 1820): surprisingly enough, the three plays, Planché's *The Vampire*, Mrs Inchbald's *The Wedding Day* and Dibdin's *Of Age Tomorrow*, managed to demonstrate the technical possibilities of the theatre, without offering any new insights into Regency drama.

Hull, *Hull Arts Centre*
Hull Arts Centre, Hull.

A converted church hall, opened in 1970. An arena stage. A small permanent company was formed to supply not only a community theatre for the new Hull city centre, but also to provide a touring company, which will link with the theatres at Lincoln and Bolton. The facilities at the theatre seem adequately functional; and the first two productions, *Don't Build a Bridge, Drain the River* and *The Daughter-in-Law*, both succeeded in raising local concern and response. *Settle Us Fair*, another local documentary, was astonishingly written only a few months after the strike with which it is concerned was settled. This use of the theatre, to be concerned with highly topical – and political – issues, suggests that Hull Arts Centre may be searching for a 'social-engineering' role for drama. But this general policy has yet to be developed. *Settle Us Fair* was carefully written, and well acted: and the scenes where the news comes of two trawler losses were unbearably moving. The Hull audiences watched and listened with a solemn intensity, as if it were a religious ceremony. The Hull Arts Centre augurs well for the future.

References: 132, 133

Ipswich, *Arts Theatre*
Arts Theatre, Tower Street, Ipswich. B/O: 0473 53725
A converted hall, rented from the Mechanics' Institute in Ipswich. The auditorium, with a small balcony, seats 345: the stage (P/A opening, 21 feet; depth, 19 feet) has little flying and no wing space. There is a seasonally permanent nucleus of an acting team, about 8 members: and the Company builds up to the larger productions, such as the 1968 *Beggar's Opera*. The Arts Council grant was £21,500, and Ipswich Council has recently changed its guarantee-against-loss policy (which gave £1000 in rough figures annually for ten years) for a straight annual subsidy of £3000. There is a very active theatre-in-education programme – centred around a studio theatre in Turret Lane, but also composed of a company visiting schools. The studio theatre offers a wide range of activities – including mixed-media shows and film evenings. The policy is for three-weekly rep (closed on Mondays), and the season runs from August to May. The ticket prices range from 6s to 8s 6d.

The company at Ipswich is working under poor conditions: the theatre is poorly equipped and the stage is small and cramped. Nicholas Barter, currently the artistic director, used to work with Theatre-Go-Round, the touring offshoot of the Royal Shakespeare Company. He has, therefore, much experience in working with schools under inadequate conditions, and in generating an enthusiasm which scorns and overrides practical difficulties. The Turret Lane Drama Centre is a thriving place, and Brian Way, whose Drama Centre in London pioneered this kind of youth club/workshop, admires the relaxed atmosphere which avoids being institutionally friendly. In the main theatre, the production standards are high, but not exceptionally so. Robert Chetwyn (artistic director, 1962–4) gave a fine production of Hauptmann's *The Beaver Coat*, starring Peggy Mount;

and Nicholas Barter's production of a new play written for the company, *I Learnt in Ipswich How to Poison Flowers* by Garry O'Conner, was admirable.

References: 60, 99, 105, 120, 129, 132

Lancaster, *Century Theatre*

(Touring theatre: headquarters, 35 South Road, Lancaster. Lancaster 64556)

A mobile theatre, constructed from five lorry-trailers. When placed side by side, these trailers fit together to provide an auditorium, seating 225, sloping down to a P/A stage (P/A opening, 23 feet; depth, 19 feet; height, 9 feet). In 15 years, the Century Theatre has travelled 6000 miles with their 100 tons of lorries and equipment, concentrating on the rural towns in the North West in general, and the Lake District in particular. The mobile playhouse was designed in 1952 by John Ridley, and built for the cost of £25,000. In view of the concern, expressed by the Arts Council and other bodies, for the rural areas of the country, it is surprising that the experiment has not been imitated elsewhere. The theatre is by no means ideal – the stage has no flying space and little wing space – but it is more convenient for a touring company to work within a familiar stage and auditorium than to swop from church hall to church hall. There is a seasonally permanent company of 15; and the grants include £30,500 from the Arts Council and about £7000 from other sources. The audience attendance-figures are remarkably high, although, of course, the theatre is small: 85 per cent capacity. The ticket prices range from 6s 6d to 10s 6d: and the policy is for repertoire. The Company normally spends the height of the summer tourist season at Keswick. In autumn 1970, a permanent headquarters is scheduled to open in Lancaster, the Duke's Playhouse. While there will be no change from the general policy of touring, there are plans to establish a larger permanent company, centred on Lancaster and playing both in the Duke's Playhouse and on tour.

Although the existing mobile playhouse is clearly inadequate, the Century Theatre has managed to solve the various problems admirably. The plays are selected carefully and remain in repertoire throughout the season. In 1969 Euripides' *The Trojan Women* played in one programme with Beckett's *Happy Days*; while on another bill Chekhov's *The Anniversary* and Shaffer's *Black Comedy* provided another neat contrast. The acting standards are high, and the permanency of the team improves the group acting. There is also a theatre-in-education team, centred in Lancaster; and strong links are being fostered with the University of Lancaster. The Century Theatre also occasionally visits other theatres in the area, such as the University Theatre, Manchester, and the Georgian Theatre, Richmond.

References: 94, 98, 120, 129, 132

Leatherhead, *Leatherhead Repertory Company*
Thorndike Theatre, Leatherhead. B/O: 537 5461/2
A new repertory theatre, built within the shell of an existing building. The auditorium seats 530, in one steeply raked arc. The stage (P/A width, 36 feet; height, 16 feet; depth, 30 feet) has excellent flying (counter-weighted) and wing space: the lighting board has 80 ways. The facilities, backstage and front-of-house, are generally excellent: the apron stage can have several different heights and dimensions. There is a studio theatre for the theatre-in-education team: there is a good restaurant, and club room. There is no permanent acting team: Hazel Vincent-Wallace, currently managing director, prefers to cast from London, but at the same time she likes to retain a certain continuity in the acting team. She tries to ensure that at least half the cast of any one production is familiar to Leatherhead audiences. The grants include £30,000 from the Arts Council and £1500 from the local council. There is a flourishing supporters' club. The policy is for three-weekly rep, and a repertory season from September to May. The ticket prices range from 5s to 12s.

In 1951, when the Leatherhead Rep was formed, few companies in the country could have faced a bleaker outlook. The theatre at that time was a converted cinema, the Ace, which had already failed once as a repertory theatre. The stage was small – the auditorium, little more than a church hall. Leatherhead was a small town – under 40,000 inhabitants; and the Company was young and (comparatively) inexperienced. Television, too, was beginning to be a threat. Eighteen years later, this small company, led from the start by Hazel Vincent-Wallace and Michael Marriott, moved into a new theatre, perhaps their finest reward for many years of solid achievement. This success is all the more interesting because it was achieved without much help from London. There were few triumphant transfers to the West End, although *The Matchgirls* (1965) achieved a certain success. Nor was the theatre associated with certain stars: Dame Sybil Thorndike never played in the old theatre, and the new theatre was named after her because of her long association with the repertory movement in general. She belonged, in fact, to Miss Horniman's Gaiety Theatre Company. The achievements of the Leatherhead Rep were based on reasonably high standards of production and a truly remarkable cultivation of local support. The real question now is whether that friendly, convivial atmosphere of the old theatre club can be transferred to the new building where the basic facilities are obviously so much better. There is also in Leatherhead a marked generation-gap. The audiences are predominantly in their late thirties and forties, although there is also a thriving Young Stagers club. But young married couples often find Leatherhead, which is in the gin-and-tonic belt of London, an expensive and rather dull place in which to live. Hence, the programme policy tends to be conservative in outlook and sometimes educational: there is an attempt, however, to include two or three new plays every season.

References: 43, 44, 56, 60, 67, 68, 107, 128, 132, 133, 145, 153

Leeds, *Playhouse*

Leeds Playhouse, Calverley Street, Leeds, LS2 3A3. B/O: 0532 42111

Leeds used to be the largest city in Western Europe without a repertory company. This situation has now been remedied. In September 1970 a temporary theatre was opened on a site given by Leeds University. This theatre was built for only £150,000 in about eleven months. The stage is a large, many-sided thrust stage, 'like a huge threepenny bit': each of the 12 sides is 30 feet. The auditorium seats 750, and no seat is further than 75 feet from the stage. There is a resident company of about 20 actors, a theatre-in-education team, and a theatre club with already 1400 members. There have been grants for the first half-year from the Arts Council (£12,000) and the local council (£5000). The ticket prices range from 6s to 14s. For a city without a repertory tradition and where the commercial theatres have recently been experiencing hard times, the audience reception for the first two productions was gratifying: Pirandello's *Henry IV* had attendance figures of just under 50 per cent, and some excellent reviews.

Leicester, *Leicester Theatre Trust*

Phoenix Theatre, Leicester. B/O: 0533 58832

Repertory theatre, completed in 1963. The building is a somewhat rudimentary construction, particularly in comparison with the other new theatres in the area: Nottingham and Coventry. The auditorium seats 274, in a single tier. The stage (width, 47 feet; depth, 32 feet) is basically an open-end stage, with a 5-foot apron. The grants include £21,000 from the Arts Council and £15,000 from the local authorities. There is a resident nucleus of an acting team, which is increased for various productions, such as Denis Potter's *Son of Man*, which transferred in 1969 to the Round House, London. The attendance figures in recent years have been roughly in the region of 70 per cent.

Robin Midgley is currently director of productions at Leicester: a novelist, dramatist and actor – as well as a director. His remarkably wide-ranging talents are well reflected in the choice of plays at the Phoenix. He started the late-night productions of plays which are regarded as too *avant-garde* for family audiences – and thus managed to retain, without the help of a studio theatre, the student audiences. His programmes for the main theatre neatly balance the various interests of his potential audiences – neither too dull nor too experimental; Alan Aykbourn's *How the Other Half Loves* transferred from Leicester to the West End. *The Son*

of Man featured a good performance by Frank Finlay, but was too much like a B.B.C. schools production for my tastes.
References: 11, 28, 29, 60, 71, 129, 132, 133

Lincoln, *Lincoln Theatre Association Ltd*
Theatre Royal, Clasketgate, Lincoln. B/O: 0522 25555
A Victorian touring-theatre, built in 1893 and partially converted for repertory purposes in 1930. The auditorium seats 392, although there is also a gallery, seating 150, which can be opened when necessary. The stage (P/A opening, 21 feet 6 inches; height, 16 feet; depth, 23 feet 6 inches) has reasonable flying – with a makeshift counterweight system and some wing space. The workshops are half-a-mile away from the theatre. The acting team is encouraged to develop as a closely knit ensemble. The productions are democratically discussed among the actors, with the director chairing the discussions. The grants include £35,000 from the Arts Council and about £3000 from local sources. The policy is for fortnightly rep, but there are no Monday performances. There is an active theatre-in-education team, and a thriving theatre club. The ticket prices range from 2s 6d to 8s 6d.

One feature of the Theatre Royal productions surprised me: despite the methods of rehearsal, the actual performances did not seem *greatly* to differ from those elsewhere. There is a difference, of course. The production of *The Lincoln Harlequinade* (October 1969) was a lively version of *commedia dell'arte*, happy, somewhat unpolished, and in a style which few rep companies could tackle. But Philip Hedley's production of *Live Like Pigs* possessed all the virtues of good rep productions – clarity, respect for the text and consistent characterization. I had been warned that the standards at Lincoln were uneven: sometimes brilliant, sometimes very ragged. This was not my impression. The real differences seem to me not to appear on the stage, but in the general atmosphere of the theatre, which is clearly a friendly and sociable place. The actors raise money for the theatre by taking music-hall to the pubs. They all work with the theatre-in-education team, and help backstage if necessary. Philip Hedley, and his company, have been much influenced by Joan Littlewood: indeed, many of his actors were trained at the E.15 Drama School, London. The Theatre Royal, Lincoln, has attempted to preserve the energy and outlook of the old Theatre Royal, Stratford; and while their productions lack the prickly authority of Joan Littlewood's – and her capacity to find and rewrite new scripts – the work is consistently interesting.
References: 51, 52, 60, 61, 69, 88, 99, 118, 119, 120, 122, 123, 129, 132

Liverpool, *Everyman*
Everyman Theatre, Hope Street, Liverpool L1 9BH. B/O: 051-709 4776
A converted cinema. The auditorium seats 450; and the stage (width,

25 feet; depth, 21 feet 9 inches) is an 'open-end', although with a small 'thrust' capacity. The backstage conditions are very bad. The workshops are small and cramped, beneath the stage: there are two small dressing-rooms. The front-of-house facilities are almost equally bad: there is a small coffee-bar, and a foyer. The seats remain from the cinema days, and are worse for wear. Peter James and Terry Hands (now with the Royal Shakespeare Company) started the rep in 1964, and concentrated on those serious, modern plays which he felt were being neglected by the Liverpool Playhouse. His efforts attracted the student audiences, and gradually his theatre came to be regarded as a drama centre for young people. The grant from the Arts Council (£18,000) is specifically for theatre-in-education. Peter James lectures at the University and there is a thriving theatre-in-education team. School parties are invited to visit the Everyman, and four matinées and four evening performances a week are devoted to school texts. There is a seasonally permanent nucleus of an acting team, 10 members: and the ticket prices range from 6s to 8s (for public perform-ances) – 3s per head for schools.

In spite of the extensive theatre-in-education programme, the pro-grammes of the Everyman are by no means solely for children. Indeed, they are highly ambitious: ranging from Bond's *Early Morning* to Beckett's *Endgame*. Neither of these plays was included in the schools programmes. The Everyman Theatre has really a divided role in Liver-pool: it is both a theatre which upholds the banner of experimentalism and a classroom where G.C.E. and C.S.E. set texts can be illustrated. The conditions at the theatre are hard to overcome, and yet the production team succeeds remarkably well. The acting team demonstrate the value of group permanence: there are improvisation sessions in the theatre every Sunday.

References: 28, 46, 47, 60, 102, 103, 110, 120, 129

Liverpool, *Playhouse*
Liverpool Playhouse, Williamson Square, Liverpool L1 1EL. B/O: 051–709 8363
A converted Victorian music-hall. The Liverpool Playhouse can fairly claim to be the oldest rep in the country with a continuous tradition of survival. It was founded in 1911, partly in friendly rivalry with Miss Horniman's Gaiety Theatre in Manchester. Basil Dean (from Miss Horniman's company) helped to nurture the Company through the difficult early years. The theatre was built in 1866 and was known as the Star Music-Hall: and, although the building was developed and reno-vated in 1968, the auditorium is still basically that of a spacious and elegant pleasure-dome, with wide circles and balconies, curving around a broad and deep stage, an orchestra pit and thick curtains. The austerity of the Barry Jackson theatres – the adaptability of post-war theatres – have

not touched its solid opulence. The stage (P/A opening, 32 feet; height, 17 feet 6 inches; depth, 36 feet) has no apron, no revolve, no capacity for back projection. There is, however a good, counterweighted flying system, and fine workshops. The development programme added a spectacular new foyer, two restaurants and a rehearsal room, which can also be used as a studio theatre. There is a seasonally permanent nucleus of an acting team, 10 members. The grants include £45,000 from the Arts Council. There is a small theatre-in-education programme. The ticket prices range from 3s to 12s: the policy is for fortnightly or three-weekly rep, and the season runs from September to July.

The reputation of the Liverpool Playhouse, now considered by the Arts Council to be a 'major rep', tended to be overshadowed during the twenties and thirties by the Birmingham Rep. William Armstrong was the director from 1923 to 1944, and his programmes tended to follow the almost conventional pattern for reps in the thirties: domestic comedies, mysteries and the occasional Shakespeare. He did, however, première *Toad of Toad Hall*. After the war, John Fernald took over for three seasons; and his production of *The Cherry Orchard* transferred to London in 1948, and was acclaimed by the critics. Antony Tuckey, currently the artistic director, took over the Company in 1968, shortly before the development programme had been completed. With the greater opportunities of the redesigned theatre, he has undertaken an ambitious and imaginative programme. There are plans to incorporate a resident dramatist, Barry Bermange, into the Company. There have been some notable premières – *Breaking the Silence* – and productions of 'controversial' new plays – *Saved*. But it is hard for Antony Tuckey to break away from the rather conservative image, so carefully fostered in the days of William Armstrong. The 1969 production of *Billy Liar* was thoroughly competent, although I wondered whether perhaps this sort of play should not have been left to lesser companies, since it neither requires the facilities of this theatre, nor needs the resources of a major rep to tackle.
References: 12, 13, 21, 22, 28, 38, 40, 46, 47, 52, 59, 73, 78, 102, 104, 107, 120, 129, 132, 133

Manchester, *Library Theatre*
Manchester Library Theatre, St Peter's Square, Manchester M2 5PD.
B/O: 061-236 7406
A converted lecture/recital hall. The auditorium seats 308. The stage (P/A opening, 30 feet; height, 11 feet 6 inches to 14 feet; depth, 20 feet) has no flying, but reasonable wing space. The backstage facilities are generally cramped, but there are workshops on the premises. The Library Theatre was built in 1933; and after the war was leased out to several different companies. In 1952 there was a disastrous season which forced the Libraries Committee in Manchester to consider either closing the

theatre down, or setting up a permanent company. They decided to start a company, which now contains a seasonally permanent nucleus of an acting team, 15 in number. There is an extensive theatre-in-education programme: the Company visits schools, and children also attend improvisation sessions in the theatre. The grants include about £9000 in concealed subsidy from the Libraries Committee which runs the theatre. The policy is for three-weekly rep. The season runs from August to May; and the ticket prices range from 6s to 10s (students, 3s 6d).

The general programme policy is for 'all plays which are good of their kind'. But unfortunately the nature of the theatre excludes those plays which require complicated staging or large casts. The 1970 *Macbeth* suffered under these conditions, and shared the curse common to many rep productions of Shakespeare – undue reverence for the text which leads to monotonous and heavy-handed acting. The 1969 production of Giles Cooper's *Everything in the Garden* was both more suitable for the theatre and better acted.
References: 28, 29, 57, 95, 120, 129

Manchester, *Stables Theatre Club*
Stables Theatre Club, Grape Street, Manchester 3 B/O: 061–834 5000
The Stables Theatre Club is an overtly experimental theatre club, connected to Granada Television. The theatre (in a converted yard with presumably stables) has movable seating, which therefore encourages different shaped stages. The auditorium seats 90: and the stage can be either open end, or thrust, or transverse, or in the round. There is a large acting team – 21 during the 1969 season – which also works for television and therefore contains some star names – Ewen Solon, André van Gyseghem.

The Stables Theatre Club is an excellent little theatre for trying out television plays. *Disabled* by Peter Ransley was staged there in a fine production. For large-scale works, such as John Bowen's version of the *Bacchae*, it had to battle against the built-in intimacy of a small room. There is a good bar and snack restaurant, adjoining the theatre.
References: 14, 28

Manchester, *'69 Theatre Company*
University Theatre, Devas Street, Manchester. B/O: 061–273 5696
A new university theatre, completed in 1965, which houses the '69 Theatre Company for 19 to 21 weeks of the year. The auditorium seats between 250 and 350, according to the shape of the stage. The stage is adaptable: as an open end, its width is 52 feet 6 inches and its depth is 23 feet. There is also, however, a movable proscenium, and lifts which can raise or lower a large forestage. The '69 Company like to use this forestage, and so for them the thrust stage is preferred. The lighting is excellent and there are

workshop facilities attached to the theatre. The University uses the theatre for most of the year, and in the summer the last-year students run a summer rep. I saw a pleasant but rather amateurish version of Thomas Morton's *Speed the Plough*, produced by the Summer (University) Company: there wasn't enough distinction between the (deliberate) gaucheness of the script and the less deliberate gaucheness of the Company.

The '69 Company is, however, one of the best in the country. It was originally formed from the old '59 Company which ran an artistically successful – though financially disastrous – season at the Lyric, Hammersmith. Michael Elliot was the artistic director then as now. The '69 Company is heavily subsidized by the Arts Council, when one bears in mind the size of the theatre and the length of the season: it receives £15,000 – which is equivalent to 12s 6d on the price of each ticket. The reason for this subsidy may be that the '69 Company is being held in reserve, to become the nucleus of a team which will take over a new rep (still to be built) in Manchester. Certainly, the present situation is thoroughly unfortunate for the Company, unless it is only temporary. The theatre is well equipped, but far too small; and the professional team is always being blamed for the inadequacies of the amateur productions. Recently two '69 Company productions transferred to London – *She Stoops to Conquer* (with Tom Courtenay and Juliet Mills) and *'Erb*, a new musical.
References: 13, 28, 29, 56, 57, 129, 132, 136

Newbury, *Watermill Theatre*

Watermill Theatre, Bagnor, nr. Newbury. B/O: Newbury 1288
A converted watermill, in a delightful village and by the banks of a river. The mill is owned by the Gollins family, and was converted over six years by David Gollins. The cost of the conversion was only £3500, but the labour was freely given. The auditorium seats 115: and the stage is a small one, rather on an eighteenth-century pattern. The depth of the stage is 22 feet. The policy is for fortnightly rep during the summer – from June to September: and the ticket prices range from 8s to 15s. There are no subsidies, and there is a small resident company of 10. The aim of the theatre is simply to cover costs, and to help in this worthy task there is a restaurant and a bar.

The programmes at the Watermill Theatre have been carefully chosen both to suit the Theatre and the Company. When I was there, I saw a production of *Ghosts*, which fitted the intimacy of the place. The standards of acting were fairly high. It is very much a theatre for tourists and summer visitors.
Reference: 28

Newcastle upon Tyne, *Tyneside Theatre Company*

University Theatre, Barras Bridge, Newcastle upon Tyne 1. B/O: Newcastle 23421

A new (1970) university theatre, with a studio theatre attached. The old Newcastle Playhouse, with its friendly, antiquated stage and bars, its tattered foyers and dressing-rooms, was clearly unsuitable for the ambitious repertory company which was using it. It was scheduled for demolition in 1970 as part of a road-widening scheme: and the Tyneside Theatre Company moved into the new university theatre in Newcastle, while waiting for (at some unspecified time) a new repertory theatre to be built. The main University Theatre seats 450 in a single steeply rising tier: the stage has a sort of proscenium arch, which deliberately fails to conceal the backstage workings. There is a promenade level to enable visitors to see above the proscenium arch into the wings. The opening is 44 feet, depth 36 feet and height (to the promenade level) 13 feet. There is a 40 feet fly-tower, an excellent (80 way) lighting board, and a 7 feet 9 inches apron stage. The studio theatre is an adaptable one, with a lighting grid across the ceiling and movable seating for 120 to 200. The plan is that the students will mainly use the studio theatre, but will also take over the main theatre for occasional productions: the repertory company, during the vacations, will also use the studio theatre for experimental productions. At the old theatre, the Tyneside Theatre Company received grants of £16,000 from the Arts Council, £10,000 from Northern Arts, and £3000 from the local authorities. They ran a wide-ranging theatre-in-education programme (now known as *Stage Coach*), had a seasonally permanent nucleus of an acting team of between 6 and 7 members, and worked closely with local dramatists, of whom Cecil Taylor is perhaps the best-known.

It is too early to hazard a guess as to the ways in which the new theatre will improve the work of this admirable company. The value of the studio theatre is that it will enable the company to continue its policy of encouraging new dramatists under conditions which will prevent great losses. Their local documentary, *Close the Coalhouse Door*, did well in the region, and transferred (less successfully) to London. I slightly preferred *The Wrecker*, a new play about a local mining village by James Mitchell, another Geordie writer. *Dr Faustus* was given a splendidly imaginative production in the old theatre: it was directed by Ann Stutfield, the artistic director of the company, and contained some marvellous lighting effects, and some carefully balanced acting performances.

References: 13, 60, 69, 99, 120, 129, 132

Northampton, *Repertory Players*

Royal Theatre, Guildhall Road, Northampton. B/O: 0604 32533

A Victorian touring-theatre, built in 1884, and converted to a rep in the 1920s. The auditorium seats 503, although a gallery (seating 100) can be opened. The stage (P/A opening, 20 feet 6 inches; depth, 24 feet) has reasonable flying capacity, though no counterweight system. There is also some wing space. The backstage conditions are generally old-fashioned; and the foyer is small. The theatre is nevertheless an attractive one, with an elegant circle. The grants include £18,000 from the Arts Council and £2100 from the local council. There is a resident company, 12 in the acting team; the policy is for fortnightly rep, and the season runs from August to May. The ticket prices range from 5s to 10s.

I was unfortunate enough to see a really poor production of *Lady Windermere's Fan* at this theatre, directed by the artistic director, Willard Stoker, who was at one time the director at the Liverpool Playhouse. This production was no doubt untypical of the standards at the Theatre Royal, and therefore a better indication can probably be gained from the programmes (which reveal some sensible though rather stolid theatrical tastes), from the reviews in *Stage*, which welcomed the production of *A Boston Story* as '*a pièce de résistance* for devotees of romantic comedy' and from the support of the Arts Council, which has helped the theatre loyally since the war.

References: 23, 28, 58, 60, 94, 129, 156

Norwich, *Norwich Players*

Maddermarket Theatre, Norwich, NOR 04H. B/O: Norwich 20917
A converted eighteenth-century chapel. Nugent Monck adapted an old hall in the early twenties, into an 'Elizabethan' theatre, with what would now be called a 'thrust' stage. The theatre is now used by an ambitious amateur company, the Norwich Players, which concentrates mainly on Shakespearian and Jacobean productions. In this theatre, some of the early acting techniques associated with thrust and in-the-round productions were developed – particularly the relationship (in Jacobean productions) between the soliloquy on the forestage and the spectacular scenes in the inner stage.

References: 31, 139

Nottingham, *Nottingham Theatre Trust*

Nottingham Playhouse, Wellington Circus, Nottingham. NG1 5AF. B/O: 0602 45671
A new repertory theatre, completed in 1963. When gas was nationalized, the compensation paid to the City of Nottingham was placed in a trust to be administered for various cultural purposes; and after some hesitation the trustees decided that a new theatre for the already buoyant Playhouse Company was one of these purposes. The new Nottingham Playhouse opened in 1963, and from the start the venture has been highly successful. The theatre (designed by Peter Moro, who helped with the Festival Hall) looks rather like a Scarfe cartoon of Sir Alec, a high bald dome above a

row of grinning teeth; but it faces a pleasant oval of grass and trees, a relaxing oasis in the desert of roads, one-way streets and half-completed developments around. The auditorium seats 756, with a wide circle. The stage (P/A opening, 32 feet; depth, 31 feet) has two forestage lifts. There is a spectacular lighting block (100 ways); and the backstage facilities include a 60-foot fly-tower, a recording studio, good dressing-rooms and workshops. There is a large browsing foyer, ideal for centenary exhibitions, *Poetry Under the Mural* and other bits of cultural flotsam. The productions under two artistic directors have reached reliably high standards: the tickets are cheap in comparison to London – 12s 6d maximum. The attendance figures for several seasons have been well over 80 per cent. Many productions have transferred to the West End, including the spectacular *The Ruling Class* by Peter Barnes. The Company, which contains about 30 actors, has also received the signal honour of being invited to play at the Old Vic, filling in for the National Theatre during the touring season. The Nottingham Playhouse may not be, as its posters claim, the finest theatre in England; but it is the most striking example of a local repertory theatre which has acquired a style and an identity, aroused local enthusiasm and pride and can offer to the West End productions which might otherwise not be seen in Britain.

The stage is a large one; and both John Neville (formerly artistic director) and Stuart Burge have decided quite rightly that ambitious productions, large in scale and concept, are needed to fill the area. This in turn has demanded a large company, playing in repertoire to reduce the risks of a single failure. Bearing the scale in mind, the subsidies from the Arts Council – £50,000 – and from the local council – £22,000 – are not unduly lavish, particularly since the local council receives back £27,000 in rent and loan repayment. The high attendance-figures are needed simply to maintain the solvency of the Company; and to economize on the productions would in a theatrically alert town like Nottingham increase rather than lessen the risk of failure. Stuart Burge has so far faced these uncertainties with admirable skill and panache. His play policy, inasmuch as it can be summarized, is for new plays 'rather way-out' and exciting revivals. Many productions linger in my mind, impossible to name them all: Leonard Rossiter's performance in *Arturo Ui*, which Michael Blakemore directed at the Playhouse – that marvellous moment at the end of *The Ruling Class* when the inner stage swings round to reveal a skeletal House of Lords – John Neville's performance as Shaw in *Boots with Strawberry Jam*, an otherwise dismal musical – the students in David Caute's *The Demonstration*. And so on. Each year has brought fresh flowers to the tree.

References: 13, 14, 25, 28, 29, 43, 44, 47, 49, 55, 56, 57, 59, 71, 73, 74, 88, 95, 96, 110, 112, 118, 132, 133, 145, 153, 155

Oldham, *Oldham Repertory Theatre Club*
The Coliseum, Fairbottom Street, Oldham. B/O: 061-624 2829
A pre-war theatre, seating 580. The Repertory Theatre Club was formed in 1938, and took over a medium-sized theatre, used both for touring and for rep seasons. The stage was rather small (P/A opening, 29 feet; height, 12 feet; depth, 20 feet), with adequate wing space but very little flying. The backstage facilities are generally in need of overhaul, although there are workshops connected to the theatre and an adequate lighting board. There is an apron stage (8 feet) which extends over the orchestra pit. The auditorium and front-of-house facilities were renovated in 1966, and now the theatre has a pleasant, friendly though still sedate appearance. It is no longer purely a theatre club: it became a public theatre in 1969, although there is still a club, attached to (though no longer running) the theatre. The Arts Council grant is £8000, and there are no other grants. There is a permanent nucleus of an acting team, 6 members: and the policy is for fortnightly rep throughout the year. The ticket prices range from 3s 6d to 8s 6d – with reductions for club members.

The programmes reveal the wide-ranging tastes of the administrator, Carl Paulsen, and his associate director, Kenneth Alan Taylor: they have succeeded in building up audiences both for ordinary family entertainment (such as *Uproar in the House* and *Hobson's Choice*) and for more ambitious projects. The company has performed all the major Pinter plays. A production of Ionesco's *Rhinoceros* was less successful in attracting the public. The small grants prevent the company from attempting a theatre-in-education programme at present, although there are plans to start one in the future. The production of *Aladdin* (January 1970) which was written by Kenneth Taylor, seemed lively – and wittier than most pantomimes attempt to be. The production (by Carl Paulsen) was slick and intelligent.

Oxford, *Meadow Players*
Oxford Playhouse, Beaumont Street, Oxford. B/O: Oxford 47133
A converted museum. The Playhouse has had a chequered history as a theatre: it was once indeed converted into a miniature golf course. J. B. Fagan's company struggled there from 1923-9; and Sir Ben Greet's company took over in the thirties. Another crisis threatened in 1956, when Frank Hauser was asked to take over the theatre. During some disastrous years for the theatre in general, Frank Hauser's Meadow Players acquired an enviable reputation for excellent revivals and good productions of serious modern plays. Several of these productions transferred to London – *The Hamlet of Stepney Green* (by the then unknown dramatist, Bernard Kops), *Dinner with the Family* (first British performance), *The Critic and the Heart* by the (unknown) Robert Bolt; and the venture was by no means lacking even in that tangible success which is revealed at the box office.

In 1960, however, the Playhouse was taken over by the University, who now let out the theatre to the Meadow Players, reserving several weeks in the term for University productions.

Thus, the Meadow Players, which the Arts Council regards as 'a major rep', has no permanent home; they share the Playhouse with the University and tour when the theatre is occupied. The theatre itself is not badly designed for rep, although there are many problems. The auditorium (with circle) seats 700, or 650 if the forestage is used. The stage (P/A opening, 28 feet; height, 15 feet; depth, 25 feet) has reasonable flying and wing space (though only 15-foot flats can be flown). The workshops unfortunately are seven miles away from the theatre. There is no studio theatre. The grants include £50,000 from the Arts Council and £4620 from the local council. There is no resident acting team: Frank Hauser prefers to cast each play separately from London; but, in any case, should he wish to develop an acting team there is no place for them to work.

To meet both the physical difficulties of the theatre and the problems of sharing, Frank Hauser has developed a complicated policy of repertoire – one production out on tour, while another plays at Oxford. The Meadow Players belong to DALTA (Dramatic and Lyric Theatres Association) which the Arts Council envisages as the basis for a network of touring companies. But it is hard to see how an effective touring company can be maintained without a more efficient base from which to work. One actress, appearing in *Peer Gynt*, had to travel daily from London to Birmingham, because the cast with whom she was supposed to be working were appearing there in *St Joan*. At one time, there was also the suggestion that the Meadow Players should become a regional rep for the Thames Valley area, touring within this limited range but building up a permanent centre at Oxford. The present dilemma facing the Meadow Players is whether all ties should be cut with Oxford and a company formed based probably in London expressly for touring, or whether they should seek to improve the facilities at Oxford. The Playhouse may become less attractive to students when the new Buckmaster Fuller Theatre is built at St Peter's. It is sad that a major company should face such uncertainty in its immediate outlook. The programmes in the past have reflected Frank Hauser's wide-ranging, scholarly and informed tastes. The Meadow Players could never be accused of being parochial in outlook. I remember with gratitude Santha Rama Rau's stage version of *A Passage to India* (which transferred to London), Mitchell's version of a Compton-Burnett novel, *A Heritage and Its History*, and more recently a fine production of Molière's *The Miser*; less gratefully, an incoherent production of Genet's exciting *The Blacks* and an uneven *St Joan*.

References: 12, 13, 30, 38, 44, 52, 54, 57, 59, 73, 83, 84, 85, 94, 95, 99, 129, 132

Perth, *Perth Repertory Theatre Company Ltd*
Perth Theatre, High Street, Perth. B/O: 0738 21031
A Victorian touring-theatre, converted in 1935 to a repertory theatre. The auditorium, with dress circle, seats 606: the stage (P/A opening, 24 feet; height (variable) 18 feet; depth, 26 feet) has good flying but no counter-weight system. There is good wing space on the O.P. side. Workshops and scenery stores are connected to the theatre. There is a rehearsal hall, which is also used as a youth studio; and the theatre-in-education team concentrates not on going out to schools, but on bringing the children into the theatre. Perth Theatre was originally owned by Marjorie Dence and David Steuart, who started the rep, which was the first in Scotland. Marjorie Dence left it in her will to the Scottish Arts Council who in turn sold it to Perth Council. The grants include £20,000 from the Scottish Arts Council, and £3000 from Perth. The policy is for fortnightly rep, from September to May: in the summer, there is a variety show. The ticket prices range from 3s to 11s; and the attendance-figures for a fairly large theatre in a comparatively small town (population 42,000) are good – 45 per cent. There is no seasonally permanent acting team: Joan Knight, currently artistic director, usually casts for two or three productions, using the same actors, and then alters the team for the following few weeks.

The Perth Rep is one of the few companies with a resident dramatist, William Corlett, whose official title is Publicity Officer. William Corlett wrote *Return Ticket*, which moved to the West End a few years ago. Joan Knight was at one time artistic director at Farnham and guest director at Watford: she manages to combine a great determination and artistic firmness, with a friendliness which overcomes the barriers which still sometimes divide repertory theatres from their public. She is the ideal repertory director, and her programmes reveal the range of her interests – from a Sunday reading of Weiss's *The Investigation* to Vanbrugh's *The Confederacy of Wives*. The production standards are high.
Reference: 113

Pitlochry, *Festival Theatre*
Festival Theatre, Pitlochry. B/O: Pitlochry 233
New repertory theatre, for a professional festival company formed in 1951. The original theatre was a large tent; and, although this has been largely replaced by a more solid construction, the shape of the tent still distinguishes the auditorium which seats 502. The stage (P/A opening, 46 feet; height, 12 feet; depth, 36 feet) has so wide an opening that it gives the appearance of being an open-end stage. The grants include about £20,000 from the Scottish Arts Council and various small sums from the local councils. There are good workshops and scenery stores. There is a large seasonally permanent acting team, about 30 in number; and the policy is for repertoire. Throughout the summer season, from

April to October, the Festival Theatre shows six plays in one week: Pitlochry is a very small town, about 2,000 residents, and the purpose of the theatre is to add another tourist attraction to a town which is already a popular Highland resort, with ski-ing, shooting, salmon-fishing, deer-stalking and golf. This catering for tourists conditions not only the unique form of repertoire – the slogan is 'stay six days and see six plays' – but also the choice of programme. Kenneth Ireland, O.B.E., the director of the theatre, chooses the programmes along this pattern: a low-lowbrow, a high-lowbrow, a low-middlebrow, a high-middlebrow, a low-highbrow and a high-highbrow. When I was there (in 1968) the high-highbrow was *Hamlet* and the low-lowbrow was *Boeing-Boeing*. The ticket prices range from 11s 6d to 25s: there is a fine restaurant, but none of the local services which many repertory theatres now provide – no studio, no theatre-in-education team. Concerts are held at the theatre on Sunday nights.

The Pitlochry Festival Theatre has grown significantly over the years, assisted by a publicity campaign which advertises in almost every programme in the country. The margin for error is slight: there are no built-in audiences at Pitlochry, and (rather like the Chichester Festival Theatre) it has positively to attract tourists. Pitlochry is undoubtedly a splendid place to visit; and the productions I saw at the Festival Theatre were *Hamlet* and *You Can't Take It with You*. The *Hamlet* was disappointing, a rep Shakespeare which succeeded in being both sentimental and wooden. The Hart/Kaufmann play, on the other hand, had some splendid moments, very well directed and acted. The Festival Theatre has attracted some good directors over the years: John Bowen came here to direct *The Fall and Redemption of Man*, his version of the mystery cycle of plays. References: 30, 74, 107, 138

Prospect *Productions Ltd*
Head Office: 1/6 Falconberg Court, London, W.1. Administration: 01–437 7365
Prospect is unlike the other major, subsidized touring companies (*Theatre-Go-Round, Meadow Players*) in that it has no permanent headquarters of a theatre – nor indeed a permanent acting team. In 1963, Toby Robertson (currently Artistic Director), Iain Mackintosh and Richard Cottrell were asked to form a summer season company at Oxford, to complement the *Meadow Players*. The success of this season led to a tour, which firstly included the smaller theatres: such as the Georgian Theatre, Richmond. During the general dearth of good touring companies, *Prospect* emerged as the one company which could adequately – and inexpensively – cope with the major problems: staging mainly classics or rare revivals, on an open stage, emphasizing brilliant costuming in place of elaborate sets. The acting standards were quickly recognized to be exceptionally high – not only in the major roles (Ian McKellen in *Edward II* and *Richard II*,

Timothy West in *Life of Johnson*) – but also in the ensemble acting. On tour, *Prospect* succeeded in attracting very high attendance-figures, between 75 and 80 per cent: and now is one of the companies forming the DALTA group. Hence, it no longer plays at the smaller theatres, concentrating on the chain of theatres envisaged in the touring-grid proposals. It has, however, particular associations with the Cambridge Arts Theatre: and one of its founder directors, Richard Cottrell is now the artistic director of the newly formed Cambridge Theatre Company. *Prospect* has also established a tradition of Edinburgh Festival appearances, where the productions which will form their seasonal repertoire are presented.

Each seasonal repertoire consists of three or four plays – usually a Shakespeare, a little-known classic (such as Otway's *Venice Preserved*), and either perhaps a 'modern classic' (such as *The Cherry Orchard*), or an anthology evening (*All the World's a Stage*) or, very occasionally, a new play (such as John Wilson's *No Man's Land*). This emphasis on *established* plays is perhaps one of the penalties of touring: *Prospect* wants to go to a town knowing that the public will have heard of the play, if not of the company. *Prospect* receives a substantial Arts Council grant – of £35,000: and in return it offers to parts of the country where good theatre is rare some marvellous productions of classic plays. There is no theatre-in-education, no experimental theatre, little attempt to relate to particular communities – not even to Cambridge, except by presenting good theatre and fine acting.

References: 13, 37, 41, 54, 59, 88, 94, 153

Richmond, *Richmond Theatre*

Richmond Theatre, The Green, Richmond, Surrey. B/O: 01-940 0088
A late-Victorian (1889) touring-theatre. It was designed by Frank Matcham (*Cheltenham Opera House, London Palladium*), and is one of the best examples of his work, with fine gold leaf designs in bas relief and panels round the dome of scenes from Shakespeare's plays. The auditorium seats 975, although the gallery (which seats 300) is not usually used for repertory productions. The stage has a P/A opening of 26 feet 9 inches, a maximum height of 21 feet and a depth of 30 feet: it gives the impression of being almost classically in proportion to the size of the auditorium. Since 1960, the theatre has been managed by Frederick Piffard, basically as a rep, although there is no permanent nucleus of an acting team. The policy is for fortnightly rep: and the seat prices range from 5s to 12s.

The Richmond Theatre is an attractive one, and well situated on the edge of the Green. The Arts Council have supported it over the years, both with the renovation programme and with an annual subsidy. There is a strong supporters club. The productions (I'm afraid) have often seemed disappointing to me. I remember happily Edward Woodward's

performance in *The Rattle of a Simple Man*, which was premièred at Richmond and subsequently transferred to London: and also an amusing farce, *Not Now Darling*, which also transferred. But the play-selection policy at Richmond has often seemed to stick unimaginatively to farces and thrillers: and the standards of production – particularly of those plays which are not aiming for a London transfer – have been uneven. Perhaps the lack of a permanent company is to blame – although Richmond is close enough to London for the stars (Jimmy Edwards, Derek Nimmo, Michael Dennison) to come down.
Reference: 68.

Richmond, *Georgian Theatre*

Georgian Theatre, Richmond, Yorkshire. B/O: Richmond 3021
A Georgian theatre, restored in 1962 from dereliction as a warehouse. The delightful auditorium with its small surrounding boxes and neat gallery seats 238. The stage (width, 24 feet; depth, 27 feet 8 inches) has a P/A opening of 17 feet. There is no flying or wing space. The theatre was built in 1788 by Samuel Butler, an actor/manager whose circuit ranged from Kendal to Northallerton and Harrogate. His company used to tramp across the ridge of the Pennines for each short spell at Richmond. The theatre is now owned by Richmond Corporation, and leased out to various touring companies, such as Prospect and the Century Theatre. There is a small grant from the Northern Arts Association, £1500; but no grant from the local council. The ticket prices range from the extremely cheap, 6s to 10s, to the expensive, 35s. In spite of the smallness of the theatre, where no seat is poor, the expensive seats are always apparently sold first.

The programmes at the Georgian Theatre in recent years have included many riches: the Century Theatre's production of *She Stoops to Conquer*, a recital by Yehudi Menuhin, Joyce Grenfell's one-woman show. The theatre is absolutely charming, and the only sad feature of the enterprise is that the inhabitants of Richmond are apparently cautiously critical of the venture. Tourists, however, have been known to come up from London to visit certain productions: an indication perhaps, that the reputation has leap-frogged local dourness.
References: 152, 153

Salisbury, *Salisbury Arts Theatre Ltd*

The Playhouse, Fisherton Street, Salisbury. B/O: 0722 22104
Converted church hall. The auditorium seats (with balcony) 406: the stage (P/A opening, 26 feet; height, 12 feet; depth, 28 feet) is poorly equipped with no fly-tower and little wing space. There is little foyer or bar space; and the workshops and storage are inadequate. Shortly after the war, the Salisbury Playhouse was run directly by the Arts Council as

the base for a touring company; but this policy was discontinued. The management was taken over by a local board in 1953; and the grants now include £20,000 from the Arts Council and about £1700 from local councils. There is a seasonally permanent nucleus of an acting team, 12 members; and the policy is for fortnightly to three-weekly rep. Monday nights are set aside for the occasional *avant-garde* production. The seasons run from mid-July to May. The ticket prices range from 3s to 7s 6d. There is an active theatre-in-education team.

Reginald Salberg, the general manager of the Salisbury Playhouse, belongs to the well-known Salberg family which runs the Alexandra, Birmingham. He has succeeded – despite the poor conditions at the Playhouse – in presenting very varied and interesting programmes, with the emphasis perhaps on serious 'middlebrow' productions, such as *Candida* and *The Royal Hunt of the Sun*. The attendance-figures are remarkably high – over 75 per cent: and there are plans for a new theatre, which have not unfortunately been bullied beyond the drawing-board stage.

References: 27, 28, 29, 30, 31, 32, 33, 34, 35, 60, 73, 94, 104, 129, 132

Sheffield, *Sheffield Repertory Company*
Sheffield Playhouse, Townhead Street, Sheffield S1 1YD
(1971) New Sheffield Theatre, Arundel Gate, Sheffield. B/O: 0742 22949
A converted British Legion hall. The theatre, which is to be replaced in 1971, can seat 546, has a reasonably sized stage (P/A opening, 28 feet; depth, 28 feet) with good flying but little wing space. Sheffield was one of the first towns in the country to have a permanent rep. In 1923, Herbert Prentice followed Sir Barry Jackson's example by transforming his amateur company into a professional one. But there was no single rich patron to protect the Sheffield Rep as Sir Barry protected the Birmingham Rep, and the following years were a constant struggle against insolvency. This is partly reflected in the worthy, though unadventurous, programmes of the thirties and forties: 711 plays were produced at the Playhouse between 1923 and 1958, of which only 30 were premières. Its reputation, however, grew; the audiences stayed loyal; and during the Second World War an offshoot company was started at Southport. From this strong stem and sturdy roots, the Sheffield Playhouse Company began in the sixties to flower. The Arts Council recognized it as a major rep; the grant is roughly £43,000. And in 1967 the New Sheffield Theatre Trust was formed to organize the building of a new theatre, scheduled for completion by 1971. This will seat 1000 around a thrust stage: there will be a revolve, excellent general facilities – backstage and front-of-house. The site commands a fine view across the city. A new studio theatre, seating 250, will replace the rather tatty, but thoroughly useful, Vanguard Theatre, which is at present the focal point of the Youth Theatre team.

The new theatre will be a well-deserved reward not only for the pioneering work of Herbert Prentice, but also for the young, talented and self-sufficient team which Colin George, the current artistic director, has so carefully fostered. Colin George believes in having a company which is chosen not by the season but which evolves over the years. He rarely invites guest stars, preferring to cast from the Company, which currently consists of 10 actors and 6 actresses. This mixture of security and opportunity for the acting team is reflected in the fact that the Playhouse can tackle 'group' plays, such as *The Cherry Orchard* and *The Caucasian Chalk Circle* with a fair degree of success. The local documentaries are also splendid: there is a resident dramatist, Alan Cullen, whose *The Stirrings in Sheffield on Saturday Night* was an excellent example of this genre. Colin George does not work towards London transfers of productions: his company occasionally tours and went to Belgrade in 1968. His main concern is to build up in Sheffield a centre of theatrical involvement and interest – through theatre-in-education, local documentaries and by encouraging the slow growth of a fine permanent company. He ignores, in his programmes, the trivial – the boulevard farces and detective stories: he tackles new plays, and some exciting revivals, such as de la Mare's *The Return* and Boucicault's *The Shaughraun*. I remember with particular pleasure Christopher Wilkinson's claustrophobic play, *Strip Jack Naked*, which transferred to the Royal Court in London, and Wilfred Harrison as Azdek in *The Caucasian Chalk Circle*.

References: 12, 25, 28, 29, 38, 45, 46, 59, 69, 85, 104, 105, 120, 129, 132, 136, 140, 145

St Andrews, *Byre Theatre*

Byre Theatre, Abbey Street, St Andrews. B/O: St Andrews 2388
A newly built, small repertory theatre, completed in 1970. The auditorium seats 128: and the stage (width, 35 feet; depth, 20 feet) is open-end. The old Byre Theatre was, as the name suggests, simply a converted cattleshed. In the thirties, it was used by an amateur company, the St Andrews Play Club, which leased the theatre from the Town Council. From April to September, the amateur company employed a small resident nucleus of a professional acting team, 4 members; and the seaons which they presented on the tiny original stage (P/A opening, 14 feet; height, 8 feet 8 inches; depth, 12 feet) aroused considerable local interest and support. The old theatre only held 74 people; and so performances were arranged twice nightly. There is a small subsidy from the Scottish Arts Council, £1250, and from the local council. The policy is for a limited form of repertoire: plays during the professional summer season run on alternate weeks.

The Byre Theatre is an astonishing example of the rule that good productions can, with ingenuity, be staged anywhere. The old theatre was tiny, cramped, and barely capable of holding five actors on the stage. Nevertheless, I saw an excellent production of *The Boston Story* there, and have heard good reports of the (1969) *Who's Afraid of Virginia Woolf?* The new theatre will retain the intimacy of the old one, but add greatly to the comfort of the audience and to the ease of staging productions. References: 73, 132, 158

Stoke-on-Trent, *Victoria Theatre*
Victoria Theatre, Hartshill Road, Stoke. B/O: 0782 65962
A cinema, converted in 1962 into an 'in-the-round' theatre. The auditorium seats 345: and the acting area is 26 feet by 22 feet. The lighting board has recently been modernized, together with the sound equipment. Stephen Joseph, who pioneered theatre-in-the-round in this country, chose this theatre as the first permanent home for his touring company. Peter Cheeseman, currently artistic director, was a member of this company, and put in charge of this project, which has flourished over the years. Now this company is without question the leading 'in-the-round' rep in the country and has an international reputation. There is a seasonally permanent acting team of about 14 members, who are encouraged to work together closely as a group: the acting skills required range from musicianship to singing, mime and improvisation. The grants include £18,000 from the Arts Council and £11,515 from the local authorities. In addition to pioneering the 'in-the-round' acting techniques, the Company has also produced some of the finest local documentaries, written by (among others) Peter Terson: *The Knotty*, a local documentary, represented British repertory theatre at the Florence Festival (1969). The ticket prices range from 5s to 7s 6d; and the policy is for repertoire all the year round.

Quite apart from the more obvious achievements of the Victoria Company – the local documentaries, the development of arena staging – the Company also scotched the opinion (very prevalent in the late fifties and early sixties) that expensive new theatres were required before repertory theatre could flourish. Peter Cheeseman emphasized the *forum* nature of theatre, a community meeting-place where ideas of common interest are discussed. From the start, writers have worked with the Company: and unlikely local topics have been used for the plays – the history of the North Staffordshire Railway (*The Knotty*), the federation of the six pottery towns (*Six into One*) and, most recently, *The 1861 Whitby Lifeboat Disaster* by Peter Terson. The productions have a rhythm to them, which profoundly differs from P/A technique: the scenes are short, punctuated by songs and different groupings; the atmosphere is not exactly *linear* – where somebody says or does something which provides the mainspring of an event or a story: rather the play proceeds by changing intensities. Every character – speaking or not –

contributes to each scene a new outlook, a different approach. Hence, the clear-cut stories which one finds in most stock rep plays are not only rare in the Stoke productions – they are a positive handicap. The Company can manage to build up an atmosphere of a place or a situation, from which many stories can develop, but which in fact transcends a purely linear plot. Hence, the plays are argumentative, evocative, nostalgic, informative – but rarely interesting on a solely narrative level. If this sounds vague and too abstract, perhaps even off-putting, I can only urge you to see the company which has given me so much pleasure for yourselves and judge.

References: 13, 28, 29, 40, 51, 60, 69, 91, 92, 99, 102, 110, 116, 129, 132, 141, 142, 143, 144, 157, 158

Stratford, *Royal Shakespeare Theatre Company*

Royal Shakespeare Theatre, Stratford-upon-Avon. B/O: 0789 2271
The Royal Shakespeare Company is, without doubt, one of the finest companies in the world. It is regarded by the Arts Council as one of the two national companies, and receives £200,000 from the Arts Council to support three major projects – the theatres at Stratford and in London, and the touring Theatre-Go-Round. It is therefore a company whose scope, activities and resources lie somewhat outside the main subject of this book. It is scarcely 'outside London' since many productions transfer from Stratford to the Aldwych: and it is certainly not an ordinary rep. Nor can one possibly convey in a few hundred words the value of the RSC to British Theatre.

The RSC at Stratford concentrates on Shakespearian, Elizabethan and Jacobean productions, whereas the company at the Aldwych also tackles some contemporary plays. The theatre at Stratford was founded in 1879, and largely rebuilt during the early thirties. The site overlooks the Avon, and it is surrounded by a park. The auditorium seats 1300, with a circle; and there is room for 400 people standing. The stage (P/A opening, 29 feet 6 inches; depth, 46 feet) has fine facilities, including a trucking system with winches for moving large pieces of scenery quickly into place, two large lifts and a computerized lighting board which, for perfect timing, can be if necessary manually overridden. There is also good flying, but in recent years the policy of the RSC has been to maintain a standard coloured box set – a dark, neutral background during 1967/8, a slightly lighter background during 1968/9 – for all the productions but to vary the impact with large object-scenery – such as the statue of Venus in Middleton's *Women Beware Women*. This neutral background has the double purpose of allowing the actors to appear almost highlit against the bare walls, and yet enables spectacular visual effects to be achieved – as in Peter Brook's production of *A Midsummer Night's Dream*. It also assists the policy of repertoire, for set changes do not require dismantling the walls of the visible stage. The Company includes a seasonally permanent acting team of 50, with many members under long-term contract; and there are seven directors, including John Barton, Trevor Nunn, Peter Hall and Peter Brook. The Theatre-Go-Round unit has a portable stage, and a separate company which stems from the main acting group. The season runs from April to December; and the ticket prices range from 6s (standing) to 36s. The Arts Council Theatre Enquiry Report revealed that the RSC was the only theatre in the country to have an *average* attendance-figure which exceeds its seating capacity. The average attendance-figure is 1349, which means that about fifty people stood at every performance, including matinées.

For me, the most astonishing and welcome feature of the RSC has been its capacity to evade an establishment style: the productions are rarely heavy with authority, and the artistic directors (Peter Hall, Trevor Nunn) are young men. In each season, one can feel the pressure of new outlooks, of ideas thought out carefully and carried through with sufficient time and meticulousness. And sometimes, to balance the occasional disasters, there are productions which, quite simply, change one's concept of a play or of theatre. One such production was (for me) John Barton's *Troilus and Cressida*: another, was his version of the History Plays: another still – Peter Brook's *A Midsummer Night's Dream*. Against the standards of these productions, all other contemporary Shakespeare productions have to be placed; and there is no other company in the country which can survive this comparison, which could include these masterpieces without finding that the rest of the repertoire was outshone. In the programmes of the RSC, these great evenings sit comfortably, not perhaps with equals but with intelligent competitors.

References: 19, 24, 28, 54, 56, 57, 59, 88, 91, 94, 98, 116, 129, 138, 155, 158

Watford, *Watford Civic Theatre*

Palace Theatre, Clarendon Road, Watford. B/O: 92 25671

A converted touring-theatre. The auditorium, with gallery, seats 640: the stage (P/A opening, 26 feet; height, 18 feet; depth, 20 feet) has adequate flying and a little wing space. There is no counterweight system. An apron stage can be erected over the orchestra pit. The grants include £11,000 from the Arts Council and £17,000 from the local council. The theatre runs an extensive theatre-in-education programme, both visiting schools and encouraging children into the theatre for improvisation sessions. There is no permanent company: plays are cast from London. The policy is for fortnightly rep, and the season runs from August to the beginning of June. The ticket prices range from 7s 6d to 9s 6d. The attendance-figures during the 1968/9 season were 65 per cent capacity.

This is an attractive theatre, which seems smaller than it is because the

dress circle seats 174 and the gallery (normally closed) 150. It is therefore suitable for intimate productions: no seat is far from the stage. Under the management of Giles Havergal, the Palace Theatre acquired a very enviable reputation for enterprise and ambitious programmes. Harold Pinter directed and acted in *The Homecoming* here, and Maureen Duffy's play, *The Silk Room*, was premièred. The subsidies were immediately challenged when the Council changed hands, from Labour to Tory, in 1968; and, after much instability, Giles Havergal left. For several months, the Company battled on with low-cast, 'subsistence' productions – *Relatively Speaking*: and, gradually, the situation eased in the Company's favour. Joe Orton's *What the Butler Saw* was given an amusing and slick production in February 1970.
References: 49, 50, 58, 60, 120, 129, 152

Wolverhampton, *1969 Repertory Theatre Company*
Grand Theatre, Wolverhampton. B/O: Wolverhampton 25244/5
A Victorian touring-theatre. The auditorium, which is a most attractive one, seats 1410 in three tiers. The stage (P/A opening, 34 feet 6 inches; depth, 40 feet) has good flying, though with no counterweight system. There are no workshops, and the conditions backstage are rather depressing. The theatre is managed by the New Theatre Trust; and in view of the heavy losses, which the theatre has sustained in recent years, the Arts Council Theatre Enquiry Report has suggested that this theatre should revert from repertory back to touring – to become part of the proposed touring-grid.

The New Theatre Trust used to engage outside repertory companies to run the summer repertory season. The policy of the 1969 Repertory Company was for weekly rep and small-cast, low-budget, popular plays. I saw one production, *Come Laughing Home*, by Waterhouse and Hall, and felt that the pressures of weekly rep were rather too much for the Company. Furthermore, the theatre was obviously too large for the play. A new Wolverhampton Theatre Company was formed in May 1970, with Humphrey Stanbury, formerly general manager at the Birmingham Rep, and a highly experienced director, in charge.
References: 29, 42, 61, 85, 99, 103, 105, 155

Windsor, *Capoco Ltd*
Theatre Royal, Thames Street, Windsor. B/O: 95 61107
The Theatre Royal is a privately owned theatre, at present leased to the Windsor Theatre Company, a non-profit-distributing company of which John Counsell is managing director. The auditorium seats 656, with a circle. There are no subsidies, and no resident company. John Counsell prefers to cast from London. The theatre has a beautiful setting, opposite Windsor Castle; and the auditorium has been decorated in whites and

blues. The attendance figures over the years have been remarkably high: about 80 per cent.

The programmes at the Theatre Royal have included many new plays, but modern perhaps in date rather than outlook. The Theatre Royal is one of the few places nowadays where an old retainer can give away half the plot on the telephone as the curtain rises and where a heroine can restrain her lusts by fingering a martini glass. Judith Guthrie's play, *Queen Bee*, which was premièred at Windsor, concerned a dowager duchess, deserted by her former admirers but still supported loyally by her faithful butler. Her wayward son returns drunk and hard-up from India, having gambled away the family fortunes and wants to persuade her to sell her family jewels . . . and so on. John Counsell states that he wishes to find the successors to the 'mainstream' dramatists – Priestley, Rattigan and Fry. The only play which I have seen premièred at his theatre and living up to this ideal was Kenneth Jupp's *The Photographer*. *Grab Me a Gondola*, a musical about film festivals, transferred successfully to London in the fifties.

References: 9, 12, 13, 15, 30, 61, 67, 68, 107, 156

Worcester, *Swan Theatre Company/Worcester Rep Company*
Swan Theatre, The Moors, Worcester. B/O: Worcester 27463
A new repertory theatre, completed in 1965 for a total cost of £65,000. The auditorium seats 353: and the stage (P/A opening (variable) between 24 feet and 36 feet; depth 24 feet 6 inches) has reasonably good facilities, though no flying space. The use of the theatre is divided between the amateur Swan Theatre Company and the professional rep company. There are grants of £6000 from the Arts Council and £2000 from the local council. The actors are engaged for short seasons, about 6 to 8 weeks. The policy is fortnightly rep; and in the first few seasons the audience attendance-figures have been fair: 55 per cent capacity. The ticket prices range from 5s to 8s.

The Swan Theatre has a most attractive site: and the design of the theatre seems to provide the nucleus for a good Worcester arts centre. The programme policy of the Worcester Rep has included some ambitious revivals, *The Knight of the Burning Pestle* (November 1969) and the British première of Albee's *The Ballad of the Sad Café*. The present amateur/professional association is a happy one, although they are using the same theatre: the distinction between the two companies is carefully maintained, and there are signs that some of the professional standards have infiltrated the amateur productions.

References: 132, 133

Worthing, *Connaught Theatre*

Connaught Theatre, Union Place, Worthing. B/O: 0903 35333

A converted cinema. The auditorium seats 710: the stage (P/A width, 30 feet; depth, 20 feet) has good flying for 14-foot flats, but limited wing space. There are workshops and storage facilities next door – in a disused theatre. The building first started to be used for repertory theatre in 1933; but during the war the Rank Organization took over the theatre as a charm school. The present rep company was formed in 1966. The acting team has a seasonally permanent nucleus of about 6: guest stars are introduced for particular productions. The grants include £15,000 from the Arts Council and £8000 from Worthing Corporation. There is a very active theatre-in-education programme, touring the schools. The policy is for fortnightly rep throughout the year. The average audience-figures for the past two seasons have been in the region of 42 per cent capacity. The ticket prices range from 5s to 10s.

Christopher Denys, currently artistic director, has followed a policy of encouraging young audiences, not only through the theatre-in-education programme, but also through a play selection which includes new plays, and comparatively 'controversial' modern works, such as *Who's Afraid of Virginia Woolf?* The Connaught Theatre, therefore, differs from the other seaside reps on the south coast, where the play selection policy is distinctly conservative. Nevertheless, his programmes also include farces like *Thark* for the tourists and (presumably) for the more elderly members of his public. *Thark* was slickly produced: and in 1969 there was also an interesting first performance of *Benbow Was His Name* by Caryl Brahms and Ned Sherrin.

References: 43, 107, 109, 116, 117, 120, 129, 132

York, *Theatre Royal*

York Theatre Royal, St Leonard's Place, York. B/O: 0904-23568

Parts of the Theatre Royal date back to 1765, when it was built: but extensive rebuilding programmes during the nineteenth century and in 1967 have effectively confined relics of the original building to a (non-public) area backstage. The 1967 modernization programme completely redecorated the auditorium which now seats 927, added a new restaurant and foyer wing and improved the general facilities backstage. There is an extensive theatre-in-education programme. The Arts Council grant is for £20,000 and the local council grant is for £1000. The policy is in general for three-weekly rep, although sometimes this alternates with fortnightly and even weekly runs. There is an offshoot company at Scarborough during the summer season. The ticket prices range from 7s 6d to 30s.

The interesting feature about the programmes of the Theatre Royal is that there seems to be little which can be predicted. Donald Bodley, the artistic director, mentioned to me that with his size of theatre the sub-

sidies were quickly swallowed up in overheads. Hence, it was hard –
indeed impossible – to keep a good acting team together. Two poorly
attended productions could spoil all the plans. Hence, in the programmes
of the theatre are some obvious money-raising farces, coupled with an
occasional revival or (for the 1969 York Festival) a first performance of a
forgotten play by Pirandello, *When One Is Somebody*. I was impressed by
the good visual production by Donald Bodley, enjoyed Rupert Davies's
fatherly performance as the Maestro but felt that a certain teamwork was
lacking in the timing during the first act.

References: 58, 60, 61, 73, 80, 120, 129, 132

Index of Persons